BACKYA
BARBECUES

Taste *of* **Home** BOOKS

READER'S DIGEST —
RDA ENTHUSIAST BRANDS, LLC

Taste of Home · Reader's Digest

A TASTE OF HOME/READER'S DIGEST BOOK

©2014 RDA Enthusiast Brands, LLC, 5400 S. 60th St., Greendale WI 53129. All rights reserved.
Taste of Home and Reader's Digest are registered trademarks of The Reader's Digest Association, Inc.

EDITORIAL

Editor-in-Chief: Catherine Cassidy
Creative Director: Howard Greenberg
Editorial Operations Director: Kerri Balliet

Managing Editor, Print and Digital Books: Mark Hagen
Associate Creative Director: Edwin Robles Jr.

Editor: Janet Briggs
Associate Editor: Molly Jasinski
Art Directors: Raeann Sundholm, Maggie Conners
Contributing Layout Designer: Catherine Fletcher
Editorial Production Manager: Dena Ahlers
Copy Chief: Deb Warlaumont Mulvey
Copy Editor: Mary C. Hanson
Content Operations Manager: Colleen King
Content Operations Assistant: Shannon Stroud
Executive Assistant: Marie Brannon

Chief Food Editor: Karen Berner
Food Editors: James Schend; Peggy Woodward, RD
Associate Food Editor: Krista Lanphier
Recipe Editors: Mary King; Annie Rundle; Jenni Sharp, RD; Irene Yeh

Test Kitchen and Food Styling Manager: Sarah Thompson
Test Cooks: Nicholas Iverson (lead), Matthew Hass, Lauren Knoelke
Food Stylists: Kathryn Conrad (senior), Leah Rekau, Shannon Roum
Prep Cooks: Megumi Garcia, Melissa Hansen, Nicole Spohrleder, Bethany Van Jacobson

Photography Director: Stephanie Marchese
Photographers: Dan Roberts, Jim Wieland
Photographer/Set Stylist: Grace Natoli Sheldon
Set Stylists: Stacey Genaw, Melissa Haberman, Dee Dee Jacq

Business Analyst: Kristy Martin
Billing Specialist: Mary Ann Koebernik

BUSINESS

General Manager, Taste of Home Cooking Schools: Erin Puariea

Vice President, Brand Marketing: Jennifer Smith
Vice President, Circulation and Continuity Marketing: Dave Fiegel

READER'S DIGEST NORTH AMERICA

Vice President, Business Development and Marketing: Alain Begun
President, Books and Home Entertainment: Harold Clarke
General Manager, Canada: Philippe Cloutier
Vice President, Operations: Mitch Cooper
Vice President, Chief Marketing Officer: Leslie Doty
Chief Operating Officer: Howard Halligan
Vice President, Chief Sales Officer: Mark Josephson
Vice President, Digital Sales: Steve Sottile
Vice President, Chief Content Officer: Liz Vaccariello
Vice President, Global Financial Planning and Analysis: Devin White

THE READER'S DIGEST ASSOCIATION, INC.

President and Chief Executive Officer: Robert E. Guth

For other **Taste of Home books** and products, visit us at **tasteofhome.com.**

For more **Reader's Digest** products and information, visit **rd.com** (in the United States) or **rd.ca** (in Canada).

International Standard Book Number: 978-1-61765-277-6
Library of Congress Control Number: 2013919975

Cover Photographer: Grace Natoli Sheldon
Set Stylist: Stacey Genaw
Food Stylist: Leah Rekau

Pictured on front cover: Grilled Vegetable Platter, page 13, and Caribbean Grilled Ribeyes, page 13
Pictured on back cover: Corn with Cilantro Butter, page 51, Scrum-Delicious Burgers, page 136, Honey Chipotle Ribs, page 184, and Sensational Slush, page 233

PRINTED IN CHINA.
1 3 5 7 9 10 8 6 4 2

IT'S TIME TO BARBECUE...

FIRE UP THE GRILL FOR A
Sizzling Good Time!

When the temperature rises and the days get longer, there's just one thing to do—**bring out the grill!** Whether charbroiling a quick weeknight dinner, hosting a friendly cookout or tailgating at the big game, *Taste of Home Backyard Barbecues* is your one-stop shop for fantastic summertime fare.

The **405** dishes found here offer everything you need for a great barbecue! You'll find hundreds of recipes for grilled steaks, juicy burgers, easy chicken, buttery seafood, and hot dogs and brats loaded with flavor. There are also appetizers, side dishes and desserts that come together on the grill.

With *Backyard Barbecues,* however, you'll discover even more! Dig into garden-fresh salads that round out meals, as well as no-fuss side dishes ideal for family reunions and block parties. In addition, you'll find cookies, bars and desserts that celebrate summer's best, and icy beverages just **perfect for warm-weather parties.**

Prep and cook times are listed with each item, making meal planning a snap. Best of all, these recipes come from home cooks who know how to **host a great barbecue!** So what are you waiting for? Invite a few friends, call everyone to the table and fire up that grill for a sizzling supper not to be missed! With *Taste of Home Backyard Barbecues* at your fingertips, a memorable cookout can be on the menu in no time.

TASTY TIPS FOR ALFRESCO SUCCESS

FAST FIX

- **Short on time?** Look for the Fast Fix icons (see above) scattered throughout the cookbook. These indicate recipes that are table-ready in 30 minutes or less!

- **If you're grilling at a park,** be sure to look for signs when disposing charcoal; many places have designated spots for it. Charcoal should be cool or cold, not hot, when discarding. Pour water over the coals if they're not cool enough.

- **When grilling shrimp,** watch for the shrimp to turn pink. Once the shrimp change from translucent to pink, they're ready to eat. Grilled fish is ready when it flakes easily with a fork.

- **Heading to the beach?** Fill several aluminum pans with water a day before and freeze them. These homemade Ice blocks are perfect for coolers because they melt more slowly than ice cubes, keeping food colder for longer.

- **When hosting a large group,** make things easy on yourself by using paper plates and disposable flatware. Have a trash bin handy so that guests can toss their plates and whatnot on their own.

- **Always wash your hands** after touching uncooked meat, along with any other utensils and dishes that came in contact with the raw food.

- **Check the internal temperature** of meats with a meat thermometer before removing items from the grill to eat. Check the temperature shortly before the end of the recipe's recommended cooking time.

- **Soaking wooden skewers** before threading on the ingredients will prevent the wood from splintering and burning on the grill. Soak the skewers for at least 15 minutes before placing them over the flames.

- **Make note of the time** you set food out. Cold foods and dishes featuring dairy products, such as potato salads, should only be out for 2 hours. If it's a particularly warm day (90° or above), only let these items sit out for an hour.

- **Hosting a nighttime cookout?** Set out candles early on so that you can quickly light them right before guests arrive. Always make sure the buffet and bar areas are adequately lit.

Linda's Best Marinated Chicken, page 12;
Basil Dill Coleslaw, page 12; Grilled Vegetable
Platter, page 13; Refreshing Beer Margaritas, page 12

Summer Corn
Salad, page 25

IT'S TIME TO BARBECUE...

IN THE
Backyard!

Whipping up a **sizzling weeknight dinner**? Planning a casual weekend get-together? Turn here for fast **charbroiled sensations**, garden-fresh dishes and sweet desserts! Enjoying your backyard has never been easier...or more delicious!

Grilled Sausages with Peppers

Herby Potatoes with Sour Cream

Colorful potatoes, a fun farmers market find, are flecked with home-grown herbs and have a peppery bite tamed by cool sour cream. Red potatoes will work in this recipe you won't be able to stop eating!

—**EMILY FALKE** SANTA BARBARA, CA

PREP: 15 MIN. • **BAKE:** 35 MIN.
MAKES: 4 SERVINGS

- 2 tablespoons butter, melted
- 2 tablespoons olive oil
- 2 tablespoons minced fresh basil
- 2 tablespoons minced fresh parsley
- 1 tablespoon minced fresh rosemary
- 1 tablespoon minced fresh thyme
- 1 teaspoon paprika
- ½ teaspoon kosher salt
- ¼ teaspoon cayenne pepper
- 1½ pounds small red, purple and yellow potatoes, halved
- ¾ cup sour cream
- 2 tablespoons minced fresh chives

1. In a large bowl, combine the first nine ingredients. Add potatoes; toss to coat. Transfer to a greased 15-in. x 10-in. x 1-in. baking pan. Bake at 375° for 35-40 minutes or until tender, stirring occasionally.
2. In a small bowl, combine the sour cream and chives; serve with potatoes.

FAST FIX ▶ Grilled Sausages with Peppers

Tuck something new and different in a bun at your next outdoor gathering. These easy sausages are fast and tasty. They're great with a side of homemade fried potatoes for a quick meal.

—**STEVEN SCHEND** GRAND RAPIDS, MI

START TO FINISH: 25 MIN.
MAKES: 2 SERVINGS

- 2 teaspoons olive oil
- 1 small green pepper, julienned
- 1 small onion, thinly sliced
- 1 tablespoon brown sugar
- 1 tablespoon red wine vinegar
- 1 garlic clove, minced
  Dash salt
  Dash pepper
- 2 Italian sausage links (4 ounces each)
- 2 brat buns
  Spicy brown mustard, optional

1. In a skillet, heat oil over medium-high heat. Add the green pepper and onion; cook and stir until softened. Stir in the brown sugar, vinegar, garlic, salt and pepper. Reduce heat to medium-low; cook, stirring occasionally, 12-15 minutes or until onion is golden brown.
2. Meanwhile, grill sausages, covered, over medium heat 12-15 minutes or until a thermometer reads 160°, turning occasionally. Serve in buns with pepper mixture; if desired, top with mustard.

Herby Potatoes with Sour Cream

Beer Can Chicken

This is a stand-up chicken that you'll be proud to serve at any family gathering. Treated to a savory rub, then roasted over a beer can for added moisture, it's so tasty.

—SHIRLEY WARREN THIENSVILLE, WI

PREP: 20 MIN. • **GRILL:** 1¼ HOURS + STANDING • **MAKES:** 4 SERVINGS

- 4 **teaspoons chicken seasoning**
- 2 **teaspoons sugar**
- 2 **teaspoons chili powder**
- 1½ **teaspoons paprika**
- 1¼ **teaspoons dried basil**
- ¼ **teaspoon pepper**
- 1 **broiler/fryer chicken (3 to 4 pounds)**
- 1 **tablespoon canola oil**
- 2 **lemon slices**
- 1 **can (12 ounces) beer or nonalcoholic beer**

1. In a small bowl, combine the first six ingredients. Gently loosen skin from the chicken. Brush chicken with oil. Sprinkle 1 teaspoon of spice mixture into cavity. Rub the remaining spice mixture over and under the skin. Place lemon slices in neck cavity. Tuck wing tips behind the back.

2. Prepare grill for indirect heat, using a drip pan. Pour out half of the beer, reserving for another use. Poke additional holes in top of the can with a can opener. Holding the chicken with legs pointed down, lower chicken over the can so it fills the body cavity.

3. Place chicken over drip pan; grill, covered, over indirect medium heat for 1¼ to 1½ hours or until a thermometer inserted in thigh reads 180°. Remove chicken from grill; cover and let stand for 10 minutes. Remove beer can.

NOTE *This recipe was tested with McCormick's Montreal Chicken Seasoning. Look for it in the spice aisle.*

Beer Can
Chicken

Appetizer Pizzas

Appetizer Pizzas

To keep a summer kitchen cool, we suggest preparing pizzas on the grill! A variety of ingredients tops these flour tortillas for three terrific tastes.
—TASTE OF HOME TEST KITCHEN

PREP: 30 MIN. • **GRILL:** 10 MIN.
MAKES: 9 APPETIZER PIZZAS

- 9 flour tortillas (6 inches)
- 3 tablespoons olive oil

TRADITIONAL PIZZAS
- ⅓ cup chopped pepperoni
- ¾ cup shredded Colby-Monterey Jack cheese
- 1 jar (14 ounces) pizza sauce

MEDITERRANEAN PIZZAS
- ½ cup chopped seeded tomato
- ⅓ cup sliced ripe olives
- ¾ cup crumbled feta cheese
- ¼ cup thinly sliced green onions
- 1 carton (7 ounces) hummus

MARGHERITA PIZZAS
- 9 thin slices tomato
- 1 package (8 ounces) small fresh mozzarella cheese balls, sliced
- 1 tablespoon minced fresh basil
- 1 cup prepared pesto

Brush one side of each tortilla with oil. Place oiled side down on grill rack. Grill, uncovered, over medium heat for 2-3 minutes or until puffed. Brush tortillas with oil; turn and top with pizza toppings.

FOR TRADITIONAL PIZZAS *Top three grilled tortillas with pepperoni and cheese. Cover and grill for 2-3 minutes or until cheese is melted. Cut into wedges; serve with pizza sauce.*

FOR MEDITERRANEAN PIZZAS *Top three grilled tortillas with tomato, olives, feta cheese and onions. Cover and grill for 2-3 minutes or until cheese is heated through. Cut into wedges; serve with hummus.*

FOR MARGHERITA PIZZAS *Top three grilled tortillas with tomato slices, mozzarella cheese and basil. Cover and grill for 2-3 minutes or until cheese is melted. Cut into wedges; serve with pesto.*

FAST FIX ▸ Rosemary-Lemon Grilled Chicken

Here's a simple dish with big bold lemon and rosemary flavors that's made with very few ingredients. It's great by itself but can also be sliced on top of salad greens as another creative dinner option.
—DEBBIE CARTER KINGSBURG, CA

START TO FINISH: 25 MIN.
MAKES: 4 SERVINGS

- 1 medium lemon
- ⅓ cup butter, cubed
- 4 teaspoons minced fresh rosemary or 1 teaspoon dried rosemary, crushed
- 2 garlic cloves, minced
- ¼ teaspoon salt
- ¼ teaspoon pepper
- 4 boneless skinless chicken breast halves (6 ounces each)

1. Finely grate peel from lemon and juice lemon. In a microwave, melt butter. Stir in lemon juice and peel, rosemary, garlic, salt and pepper.
2. Grill chicken, covered, over medium heat or broil 4 in. from the heat for 5-7 minutes on each side or until a thermometer reads 165°, basting frequently with butter mixture during the last 5 minutes of cooking.

Rosemary-Lemon Grilled Chicken

IN THE BACKYARD!

Refreshing Beer Margaritas

Linda's Best Marinated Chicken

I have been using this grilled chicken recipe for 40-plus years! It is so juicy and delicious, it will melt in your mouth.

—**LINDA PACE** LEES SUMMIT, MO

PREP: 15 MIN. + MARINATING
GRILL: 40 MIN. • **MAKES:** 4 SERVINGS

- 1¼ cups olive oil
- ½ cup red wine vinegar
- ⅓ cup lemon juice
- ¼ cup reduced-sodium soy sauce
- ¼ cup Worcestershire sauce
- 2 tablespoons ground mustard
- 1 tablespoon pepper
- 3 garlic cloves, minced
- 1 broiler/fryer chicken (3 to 4 pounds), cut up

1. Place the first eight ingredients in a blender; cover and process until blended. Pour 2 cups marinade into a large resealable plastic bag. Add the chicken; seal bag and turn to coat. Refrigerate 4 hours or overnight. Cover and refrigerate remaining marinade.
2. Drain chicken, discarding marinade in bag. Grill chicken, covered, over medium heat 40-45 minutes or until juices run clear, turning occasionally and basting with reserved marinade during the last 15 minutes.

FAST FIX ▶ Basil Dill Coleslaw

When I married into an Italian family, my love affair with basil began. The aromatic fragrance and flavor of this herb is wonderful, and I use it in everything. Basil and dill add a unique touch to this slaw.

—**JUNE CAPPETTO** SEATTLE, WA

START TO FINISH: 10 MIN.
MAKES: 6 SERVINGS

- 6 cups shredded cabbage or coleslaw mix
- 3 to 4 tablespoons chopped fresh basil or 1 tablespoon dried basil
- 3 tablespoons snipped fresh dill or 1 tablespoon dill weed

DRESSING
- ½ cup mayonnaise
- 3 tablespoons sugar
- 2 tablespoons cider vinegar
- 2 tablespoons half-and-half cream
- 1 teaspoon coarsely ground pepper

In a large bowl, combine the cabbage, basil and dill. In a small bowl, whisk dressing ingredients until blended. Drizzle over the cabbage mixture; toss to coat. Refrigerate until serving.

FAST FIX ▶ Refreshing Beer Margaritas

It's always a surprise when people say they didn't know this drink existed. It's a great summertime cocktail and so easy to double or triple the recipe.

—**ARIANNE BARNETT** KANSAS CITY, MO

START TO FINISH: 5 MIN.
MAKES: 6 SERVINGS

- Lime slices and kosher salt, optional
- 2 bottles (12 ounces each) beer
- 1 can (12 ounces) frozen limeade concentrate, thawed
- ¾ cup tequila
- ¼ cup sweet and sour mix
- Ice cubes

GARNISH
- Lime slices

1. If desired, use lime slices to moisten the rims of six margarita or cocktail glasses. Sprinkle salt on a plate; hold each glass upside down and dip rims into salt. Discard any remaining salt on the plate.
2. In a pitcher, combine the beer, concentrate, tequila and sweet and sour mix. Serve in prepared glasses over ice. Garnish with lime slices.

Basil Dill Coleslaw

Linda's Best Marinated Chicken

2. Transfer vegetables to a grilling grid; place grid on grill rack. Grill vegetables, covered, over medium heat 8-12 minutes or until crisp-tender, turning occasionally.

3. Place the vegetables on a large serving plate. Drizzle with remaining marinade.

Caribbean Grilled Ribeyes

If you like hot and spicy, you'll really enjoy this mind-blowing steak that I created for my father-in-law. He loved it, and so did everyone else. You can serve it for casual suppers in the backyard or more elaborate parties on the weekend.

—DE'LAWRENCE REED DURHAM, NC

PREP: 10 MIN. + MARINATING
GRILL: 10 MIN. • **MAKES:** 4 SERVINGS

- ½ cup Dr Pepper
- 3 tablespoons honey
- ¼ cup Caribbean jerk seasoning
- 1½ teaspoons chopped seeded habanero pepper
- ½ teaspoon salt
- ½ teaspoon pepper
- 4 beef ribeye steaks (¾ pound each)

1. Place the first six ingredients in a blender; cover and process until blended. Pour into a large resealable plastic bag. Add the steaks; seal bag and turn to coat. Refrigerate for at least 2 hours.

2. Drain and discard marinade. Grill steaks, covered, over medium heat or broil 3-4 in. from heat for 4-6 minutes on each side or until meat reaches desired doneness (for medium-rare, a thermometer should read 145°; for medium, 160°; for well-done, 170°).

NOTE *Wear disposable gloves when cutting hot peppers; the oils can burn skin. Avoid touching your face.*

Grilled Vegetable Platter

Caribbean Grilled Ribeyes

Grilled Vegetable Platter

The best of summer in one dish! These veggies are meant for sharing. Grilling brings out their natural sweetness, and the easy marinade really kicks up the flavor.

—HEIDI HALL NORTH ST. PAUL, MN

PREP: 20 MIN. + MARINATING
GRILL: 10 MIN. • **MAKES:** 6 SERVINGS

- ¼ cup olive oil
- 2 tablespoons honey
- 4 teaspoons balsamic vinegar
- 1 teaspoon dried oregano
- ½ teaspoon garlic powder
- ⅛ teaspoon pepper
  Dash salt

- 1 pound fresh asparagus, trimmed
- 3 small carrots, cut in half lengthwise
- 1 large sweet red pepper, cut into 1-inch strips
- 1 medium yellow summer squash, cut into ½-inch slices
- 1 medium red onion, cut into wedges

1. In a small bowl, whisk the first seven ingredients. Place 3 tablespoons marinade in a large resealable plastic bag. Add vegetables; seal bag and turn to coat. Marinate 1½ hours at room temperature.

Blue-Cheese Flat Iron Steak

Blue-Cheese Flat Iron Steak

If you have yet to enjoy the rich, creamy pairing of blue cheese with your favorite steak, stop reading and get cooking!
—**AMANDA MARTIN** MONSON, MA

PREP: 15 MIN. + MARINATING
GRILL: 10 MIN. • **MAKES:** 4 SERVINGS

- ¼ cup olive oil
- 2 tablespoons red wine vinegar
- 2 garlic cloves, minced
- 1 teaspoon dried oregano
- 1 teaspoon dried rosemary, crushed
- 1 teaspoon pepper
- ¼ teaspoon salt
- 1¼ pounds beef flat iron steaks or top sirloin steak (1 inch thick)

BLUE CHEESE BUTTER

- ¼ cup crumbled blue cheese
- 3 tablespoons butter, softened
- 1 tablespoon minced fresh chives
- ⅛ teaspoon pepper

1. In a large resealable plastic bag, combine the first seven ingredients. Add beef; seal bag and turn to coat. Refrigerate 30 minutes.
2. In a small bowl, mix blue cheese, butter, chives and pepper; set aside. Drain beef, discarding marinade.
3. Grill steaks, covered, over medium heat or broil 4 in. from the heat for 5-7 minutes on each side or until meat reaches desired doneness (for medium-rare, a thermometer should read 145°; medium, 160°; well-done, 170°). Serve with blue cheese butter.

FAST FIX Grilled Cajun Green Beans

This is a perfect way to use up your garden's green beans. The Cajun flavor makes it different from your regular green bean recipes.
—**SHANNON LEWIS** ANDOVER, MN

START TO FINISH: 30 MIN.
MAKES: 4 SERVINGS

- 1 pound fresh green beans, trimmed
- ½ teaspoon Cajun seasoning
- 1 tablespoon butter

1. Place green beans on a double thickness of heavy-duty foil (about 18 in. square). Sprinkle with Cajun seasoning and dot with butter. Fold foil around beans and seal tightly.
2. Grill, covered, over medium heat for 10 minutes. Turn packet over; grill 8-12 minutes longer or until the beans are tender. Carefully open foil packet to allow steam to escape.

Blueberry
Romaine Salad

I love to bring this delicious salad to school gatherings. The homemade dressing couldn't be simpler, so I whip it up in advance and give it a quick toss with the other ingredients when I get to an event.
—**KRIS BRISTOL** CHARLOTTE, MI

**Blueberry
Romaine Salad**

START TO FINISH: 15 MIN.
MAKES: 8 SERVINGS

- ⅓ **cup white vinegar**
- ¼ **cup sugar**
- 1 **tablespoon chopped red onion**
- 2 **teaspoons poppy seeds**
- 1 **teaspoon ground mustard**
- ½ **teaspoon salt**
- ¼ **teaspoon pepper**
  Dash Worcestershire sauce
- 1 **cup canola oil**

SALAD

- 1 **package (10 ounces) hearts of romaine salad mix**
- 1 **cup unsalted cashews**
- 1 **cup (4 ounces) shredded Swiss cheese**
- 1 **cup fresh blueberries**

In a small bowl, whisk the first eight ingredients. Gradually whisk in oil. In a large bowl, combine salad ingredients. To serve, pour dressing over salad; toss to coat.

**Beef and Blue Cheese
Penne with Pesto**

Beef and Blue Cheese Penne with Pesto

Steak and blue cheese over pasta is a dream for hearty eaters, and this healthy option packs in 9 grams of fiber per serving. Best of all, it takes just 30 minutes to prepare.

—FRANCES PIETSCH
FLOWER MOUND, TX

START TO FINISH: 30 MIN.
MAKES: 4 SERVINGS

- 2 cups uncooked whole wheat penne pasta
- 2 beef tenderloin steaks (6 ounces each)
- ¼ teaspoon salt
- ¼ teaspoon pepper
- 6 cups fresh baby spinach, chopped
- 2 cups grape tomatoes, halved
- 5 tablespoons prepared pesto
- ¼ cup chopped walnuts
- ¼ cup crumbled Gorgonzola cheese

1. Cook the pasta according to package directions.
2. Meanwhile, sprinkle steaks with salt and pepper. Grill steak, covered, over medium heat for 5-7 minutes on each side or until the meat reaches desired doneness (for medium-rare, a thermometer should read 145° medium, 160° well-done, 170°).

Drain pasta and transfer to a large bowl. Add the spinach, tomatoes, pesto and walnuts; toss to coat. Thinly slice steaks. Divide pasta mixture among four serving plates. Top with beef; sprinkle with cheese.

FAST FIX Campfire Cobbler

At your next campfire, try serving this wonderful dish for dessert. It is so quick and simple.

—TASTE OF HOME TEST KITCHEN

START TO FINISH: 30 MIN.
MAKES: 6 SERVINGS

- 1¼ cups biscuit/baking mix
- 1 envelope instant maple and brown sugar oatmeal
- ¼ cup cold butter, cubed
- ⅓ cup milk
- 2 cans (21 ounces each) blueberry pie filling
- ¾ cup unsweetened apple juice
  Vanilla ice cream, optional

1. Prepare grill or campfire for low heat, using 12-16 charcoal briquettes or large wood chips.
2. In a large resealable plastic bag, combine biscuit mix and oatmeal. Add butter; squeeze bag until mixture resembles coarse crumbs. Gradually add milk; knead to form a soft dough. Spread into a greased ovenproof Dutch oven. Combine pie filling and apple juice; pour over dough.
3. Cover Dutch oven. When briquettes or wood chips are covered with white ash, place Dutch oven directly on top of 6-8 of them. Using long-handled tongs, place 6-8 briquettes on pan cover. Cook for 15 minutes or until filling is bubbly.
4. To check for doneness, use the tongs to carefully lift cover. If necessary, cook 5 minutes longer. Serve with ice cream if desired.

Campfire Cobbler

**Grilled Chicken with
Black Bean Salsa**

Grilled Chicken with Black Bean Salsa

Black bean salsa with mango gives this dish a Mexican taste without too much heat. I like to slice the chicken and serve it over a long grain-and-wild rice mix.
—TERRI CLOUSE
CONNOQUENESSING, PA

PREP: 15 MIN. + MARINATING
GRILL: 10 MIN. • **MAKES:** 5 SERVINGS

- 1 cup lime juice
- 2 tablespoons olive oil
- 2 teaspoons ground cumin
- 1 teaspoon salt
- 1 teaspoon dried oregano
- ½ teaspoon pepper
- 5 boneless skinless chicken breast halves (4 ounces each)

BLACK BEAN SALSA
- 1 can (15 ounces) black beans, rinsed and drained
- 1 mango, peeled and cubed
- ¼ cup minced fresh cilantro
- 3 tablespoons lime juice
- 1 tablespoon olive oil
- 2 teaspoons brown sugar
- 1 teaspoon minced jalapeno pepper

1. In a small bowl, whisk the first six ingredients. Pour ⅔ cup marinade into a large resealable plastic bag. Add the chicken; seal bag and turn to coat. Refrigerate 1-2 hours. Reserve the remaining marinade for basting. In a small bowl, combine salsa ingredients; toss to combine.
2. Drain chicken, discarding the marinade. Grill chicken, covered, over medium heat or broil 4 in. from heat for 5-6 minutes on each side or until a thermometer reads 165°, basting occasionally with the reserved marinade during the last 4 minutes. Serve with salsa.
NOTE *Wear disposable gloves when cutting hot peppers; the oils can burn skin. Avoid touching your face.*

Farmer's Market Corn Salad

4. Place pork over drip pan and grill, covered, over indirect medium heat for 10-13 minutes on each side or until a thermometer reads 160°, brushing with glaze during the last 10 minutes.

5. Let stand for 5 minutes before slicing. Serve with any remaining glaze.

Farmer's Market Corn Salad

I love fresh corn, especially when it's grilled, so I am always looking for new ways to serve it. This salad takes the corn right off the cob and pairs it with fresh basil.

—CINDIE HARAS JUPITER, FL

PREP: 25 MIN. • **COOK:** 10 MIN.
MAKES: 6 SERVINGS

- 6 **medium ears sweet corn**
- 3 **tablespoons butter, melted**
- ½ **cup chopped cucumber**
- ½ **cup fresh or frozen shelled edamame, thawed**
- ½ **cup julienned radishes**
- ¼ **cup fresh basil leaves, thinly sliced**

DRESSING
- ¼ **cup olive oil**
- 3 **tablespoons sherry vinegar**
- 1 **tablespoon white balsamic vinegar**
- ½ **teaspoon salt**
  Dash pepper

1. Brush corn with butter. Grill the corn, covered, over medium heat for 10-12 minutes or until lightly browned, turning and basting occasionally.

2. Cut corn from cobs; transfer to a large bowl. Add cucumber, edamame, radishes and basil.

3. In a small bowl, whisk the dressing ingredients. Pour over vegetables; toss to coat.

Ginger-Orange Pork Tenderloins

This fork-tender pork has a citrus, smoky flavor that my whole family loves. The combination of ingredients is unbeatable!

—ELAINE SWEET DALLAS, TX

PREP: 20 MIN. + MARINATING
GRILL: 20 MIN. • **MAKES:** 6-8 SERVINGS

- ½ **cup thawed orange juice concentrate**
- 2 **tablespoons sherry or chicken broth**
- 2 **tablespoons soy sauce**
- 1 **tablespoon sesame oil**
- 2 **tablespoons minced fresh thyme**
- 1 **tablespoon minced fresh gingerroot**
- 3 **garlic cloves, minced**
- 1 **teaspoon pepper**
- 2 **pork tenderloins (1 pound each)**

GLAZE
- ¼ **cup thawed orange juice concentrate**
- 2 **tablespoons brown sugar**
- 2 **tablespoons cider vinegar**
- 2 **tablespoons molasses**
- 2 **teaspoons minced fresh gingerroot**
- ½ **teaspoon salt**
- ½ **teaspoon pepper**

1. In a blender or food processor, combine the first eight ingredients; cover and process until smooth. Pour into a large resealable plastic bag; add the pork. Seal bag and turn to coat. Refrigerate for 8 hours or overnight.

2. In a small saucepan, combine the glaze ingredients. Cook and stir over medium heat until glaze is thickened; set aside.

3. Drain pork and discard marinade. Moisten a paper towel with cooking oil; using long-handled tongs, rub on grill rack to coat lightly. Prepare grill for indirect heat using a drip pan.

Grilled Whiskey Chops

FAST FIX Grilled Whiskey Chops

Here's a fast favorite for summertime. The molasses butter nicely contrasts with the whiskey-and-peppercorn chops.
—**KELLY HODSON** ANDERSON, IN

START TO FINISH: 25 MIN.
MAKES: 4 SERVINGS

- ¼ cup butter, softened
- 1 tablespoon molasses
- ½ teaspoon ground cinnamon
- ½ teaspoon lemon juice
- 3 tablespoons coarsely ground pepper
- ⅓ cup whiskey
- ½ teaspoon salt
- 4 bone-in pork loin chops (¾ inch thick)

1. In a small bowl, mix the butter, molasses, cinnamon and lemon juice; refrigerate until serving.
2. Place pepper in a shallow bowl. In a separate shallow bowl, mix whiskey and salt. Dip chops in whiskey mixture, then in pepper.
3. Moisten a paper towel with cooking oil; using long-handled tongs, rub on grill rack to coat lightly. Grill chops, covered, over medium heat or broil 4 in. from heat 4-5 minutes on each side or until a thermometer reads 145°. Let stand 5 minutes. Serve with the molasses butter.

Grilled Potatoes & Peppers

My husband grills these veggies for summer parties. They're perfect for casual get-togethers in our backyard!
—**SUSAN NORDIN** WARREN, PA

PREP: 20 MIN. • **GRILL:** 40 MIN.
MAKES: 10 SERVINGS

Grilled Potatoes & Peppers

- 8 medium red potatoes, cut into wedges
- 2 medium green peppers, sliced
- 1 medium onion, cut into thin wedges
- 2 tablespoons olive oil
- 5 garlic cloves, thinly sliced
- 1 teaspoon paprika
- 1 teaspoon Montreal steak seasoning
- 1 teaspoon Italian seasoning
- ¼ teaspoon salt
- ¼ teaspoon pepper

1. In a large bowl, combine all the ingredients. Divide between two pieces of heavy-duty foil (about 18 in. square). Fold foil around potato mixture and crimp edges to seal.
2. Grill, covered, over medium heat 40-45 minutes or until potatoes are tender. Open foil carefully to allow steam to escape.

**Maple-Bacon
Doughnut Bites**

Grilled Peach-Berry Crisps

As dinner is winding down, put these individual fruit crisps on the grill. They're a fast and easy weeknight treat, particularly if your main dish was barbecued, too! A scoop of vanilla ice cream can be the crowning touch.
—**TASTE OF HOME TEST KITCHEN**

PREP: 20 MIN. • **GRILL:** 15 MIN.
MAKES: 4 SERVINGS

- 3 **cups chopped peeled fresh peaches**
- 1½ **cups fresh raspberries**
- 3 **tablespoons sugar**
- 3 **tablespoons plus ¼ cup all-purpose flour, divided**
- ¼ **teaspoon ground cinnamon**
- ½ **cup quick-cooking oats**
- 2 **tablespoons brown sugar**
- 2 **tablespoons cold butter**
  Vanilla ice cream, optional

1. In a large bowl, combine peaches, raspberries, sugar, 3 tablespoons flour and cinnamon. Divide mixture evenly among four 4½-in. disposable foil tart pans coated with cooking spray, and set aside.
2. In a bowl, combine the oats, brown sugar and remaining flour; cut in butter until crumbly. Sprinkle over filling.
3. Prepare grill for indirect heat. Grill crisps, covered, over indirect medium heat for 15-20 minutes or until the filling is bubbly. Serve warm with ice cream if desired.

Maple-Bacon Doughnut Bites

While these delicious bite-size treats are ready in minutes, they'll disappear in a flash! They're perfect after a grilled dinner or as a fun appetizer at casual parties.
—**CHELSEA TURNER** LAKE ELSINORE, CA

PREP: 20 MIN. • **COOK:** 5 MIN./BATCH
MAKES: ABOUT 2 DOZEN

- 1½ **cups all-purpose flour**
- ½ **cup sugar**
- 2 **teaspoons baking powder**
- ½ **teaspoon salt**
- 1 **egg**
- ½ **cup 2% milk**
- 1 **tablespoon butter, melted**
  Oil for deep-fat frying

GLAZE

- 1 **cup confectioners' sugar**
- 3 **tablespoons maple syrup**
- 1 **tablespoon 2% milk**
- 1 **teaspoon vanilla extract**
- 7 **maple-flavored bacon strips, cooked and crumbled**

1. In a large bowl, whisk flour, sugar, baking powder and salt. In another bowl, whisk egg, milk and melted butter until blended. Add to flour mixture; stir just until moistened.
2. Heat oil to 350° in an electric skillet or deep fryer. Drop tablespoonfuls of batter, a few at a time, into hot oil. Fry 3-4 minutes or until golden brown, turning often. Drain on paper towels.
3. In a small bowl, mix confectioners' sugar, maple syrup, milk and vanilla until smooth. Dip warm doughnuts into glaze; sprinkle tops with bacon.

FAST FIX ▸ Santa Fe Strip Steaks

We love Southwestern flavor, and this recipe certainly provides it!

—JOAN HALLFORD

NORTH RICHLAND HILLS, TX

START TO FINISH: 25 MIN.
MAKES: 4 SERVINGS

- ½ cup chopped onion
- 1 tablespoon olive oil
- 2 cans (4 ounces each) chopped green chilies
- ½ cup fresh cilantro leaves
- 1 jalapeno pepper, seeded
- 2 teaspoons red currant jelly
- 1 teaspoon chicken bouillon granules
- 1 teaspoon Worcestershire sauce
- 1 garlic clove, peeled
- ½ teaspoon seasoned salt
- ¼ teaspoon dried oregano
- 4 boneless beef top loin steaks (1 inch thick and 8 ounces each) Salt and pepper to taste
- ½ cup shredded Monterey Jack cheese, optional

1. In a small saucepan, cook onion in oil over medium-high heat until tender. Place in a blender. Add green chilies, cilantro, jalapeno, jelly, bouillon, Worcestershire sauce, garlic, seasoned salt and oregano; cover and puree.

2. Return mixture to pan; cook over medium heat until heated, stirring occasionally. Set aside; keep warm.

3. Sprinkle steaks with salt and pepper. Grill, covered, over medium heat for 5-8 minutes on each side or until meat reaches desired doneness (for medium-rare, a thermometer should read 145°; medium, 160°; well-done, 170°). Sprinkle steaks with cheese if desired; serve with green chili sauce.

NOTE *When cutting hot peppers, disposable gloves are recommended. Avoid touching your face.*

Santa Fe Strip Steaks

top tip · A Steak by Many Names

Top loin steak goes by many names. It may be labeled as strip steak, Kansas City steak, New York strip steak, ambassador steak or boneless club steak in your region.

Pork Burgers with Sassy Barbecue Sauce

Pork Burgers with Sassy Barbecue Sauce

When it comes to backyard meals, burgers can't be beat! My thick, juicy patties appeal to everyone—even your spicy-phobic friends will like them. The sauce tastes wonderful on chops or ribs as well.

—**ALISA FUNK** KANSAS CITY, MO

PREP: 25 MIN. • **GRILL:** 15 MIN.
MAKES: 6 SERVINGS

- 1¼ cups fresh or frozen pitted dark sweet cherries, thawed
- ½ cup ketchup
- ½ cup cherry preserves
- 1 tablespoon Worcestershire sauce
- 1 tablespoon honey
- 1¼ teaspoons cayenne pepper
- ¾ teaspoon fennel seed, crushed
- 12 center-cut bacon strips
- ⅓ cup chopped onion
- 1 garlic clove, minced
- 2¼ pounds ground pork
- 2 teaspoons coarsely ground pepper
- 1½ teaspoons salt
- 6 ounces Havarti cheese, sliced
- 6 hamburger buns, split and toasted
- 3 cups fresh arugula

1. Place the first seven ingredients in a food processor; cover and process until blended. Set aside. In a large skillet, cook bacon over medium heat until crisp. Remove to paper towels; drain, reserving 1 tablespoon drippings.
2. Saute the onion in drippings until tender. Add the garlic; cook 1 minute longer. Add the cherry mixture; bring to a boil. Reduce the heat; simmer, uncovered, for 5-7 minutes or until slightly thickened.
3. Meanwhile, in a large bowl, combine the pork, pepper and salt. Shape into six patties.
4. Moisten a paper towel with cooking oil; using long-handled tongs, rub on grill rack to coat lightly. Grill burgers, covered, over medium heat or broil 4 in. from the heat for 6-8 minutes on each side or until a thermometer reads 160° and juices run clear.
5. Top with cheese; cover and grill 1-2 minutes longer or until cheese is melted. Serve on buns with arugula, bacon and sauce mixture.

Summer Corn Salad

Summer Corn Salad

Here's a beautiful salad that truly captures the summer season. It's chock-full of fresh veggies, and the feta gives it a rich flavor.

—**PRISCILLA YEE** CONCORD, CA

PREP: 20 MIN. + STANDING
MAKES: 4 SERVINGS

- 5 teaspoons olive oil, divided
- 1 tablespoon lime juice
- ¼ teaspoon salt
- ¼ teaspoon hot pepper sauce
- 1½ cups fresh or frozen corn, thawed
- 1½ cups cherry tomatoes, halved
- ½ cup finely chopped cucumber
- ¼ cup finely chopped red onion
- 2 tablespoons minced fresh basil or 2 teaspoons dried basil
- ¼ cup crumbled feta cheese

1. In a small bowl, whisk 4 teaspoons oil, lime juice, salt and pepper sauce; set aside.
2. In a large skillet, cook and stir corn in remaining oil over medium-high heat until tender. Transfer to a salad bowl; cool slightly. Add the tomatoes, cucumber, onion and basil. Drizzle with dressing and toss to coat.
3. Let stand for 10 minutes before serving or refrigerate until chilled. Sprinkle with the feta cheese just before serving.

Chilled Tomato Salad

I use homegrown veggies to make this special salad. It's always popular.
—**CATHLEEN BUSHMAN** GENEVA, IL

PREP: 20 MIN. + CHILLING
MAKES: 8 SERVINGS

- 3 **large tomatoes, peeled and sliced**
- 2 **medium cucumbers, sliced**
- 2 **medium sweet red peppers, sliced into rings**
- 2 **medium green peppers, sliced into rings**

DRESSING

- ¼ **cup canola oil**
- ¼ **cup minced fresh parsley**
- 2 **tablespoons white vinegar**
- 2 **teaspoons prepared mustard**
- 1 **teaspoon sugar**
- 1 **garlic clove, minced**
- ¼ **teaspoon pepper**

In a large serving bowl, combine the tomatoes, cucumbers and peppers. In a jar with a tight-fitting lid, combine the dressing ingredients; shake well. Pour over vegetables; toss gently to coat. Cover and refrigerate for at least 3 hours. Serve with a slotted spoon.

Mini Pear Crisps

While everyone is enjoying dinner, I slip these delicious crisps on the grill to cook.
—**JONI HILTON** ROCKLIN, CA

PREP: 25 MIN. • **GRILL:** 20 MIN.
MAKES: 8 SERVINGS

- 1 **cup quick-cooking oats**
- 1 **cup packed brown sugar**
- ⅓ **cup all-purpose flour**
- 1 **teaspoon ground cinnamon**
- ½ **teaspoon ground nutmeg**
- ½ **cup cold butter**
- ½ **cup chopped pecans**
- ½ **cup raisins**
- 8 **medium pears, peeled and sliced**
  Vanilla ice cream, optional

1. In a large bowl, combine the first five ingredients. Cut in butter until crumbly. Stir in pecans and raisins.

2. Divide the pears among eight greased 4½-in. disposable foil tart pans. Sprinkle with oat mixture.
3. Prepare grill for indirect heat. Grill crisps, covered, over indirect medium heat for 15-20 minutes or until pears are tender. Serve warm with ice cream if desired.

Grilled Corn with Chive Butter

When our son was young, corn was the only vegetable he'd eat. My husband and I soon got bored with the simple salt and butter topping, so I stirred in some lemon juice and chives. Wonderful!
—**SUE KIRSCH** EDEN PRAIRIE, MN

PREP: 10 MIN. + SOAKING • **GRILL:** 25 MIN.
MAKES: 6 SERVINGS

- 6 **medium ears sweet corn in husks**
- ½ **cup butter, melted**
- 2 **tablespoons minced chives**
- 1 **tablespoon sugar**
- 1½ **teaspoons lemon juice**
  Salt and pepper

1. Soak the corn in cold water for 1 hour. In a small bowl, combine the butter, chives, sugar, lemon juice, salt and pepper. Carefully peel back corn husks to within 1 in. of bottom; remove silk. Brush with the butter mixture. Rewrap corn in husks and secure with kitchen string.
2. Grill the corn, uncovered, over medium heat for 25-30 minutes, turning occasionally.

Grilled Corn with Chive Butter

Sun-Dried Tomato
Turkey Burgers

Herb Beef Burgers

These moist, tender burgers are great at any summer meal. You can prepare the patties ahead of time and keep them covered in the fridge until ready to grill.

—**PAT HABIGER** SPEARVILLE, KS

PREP: 30 MIN. • **GRILL:** 10 MIN.
MAKES: 4 SERVINGS

- 1 **medium tomato, seeded and chopped**
- ⅓ **cup canned chopped green chilies**
- ¼ **cup chopped ripe olives**
- ¼ **cup chopped onion**
- 2 **garlic cloves, minced**
- 2 **teaspoons chili powder**
- 2 **teaspoons Dijon mustard**
- 1 **teaspoon each minced fresh oregano, thyme, basil and parsley**
- ½ **to 1 teaspoon minced fresh dill**
- ½ **to 1 teaspoon grated lemon peel**
- 1 **pound ground beef**
- 4 **hamburger buns, split**
  Sliced tomato, lettuce leaves and sliced onion, optional

1. In a large bowl, combine the tomato, chilies, olives, onion, garlic, chili powder, mustard, herbs and lemon peel. Crumble beef over mixture and mix well. Shape into four patties.

2. Grill, covered, over medium heat for 5-7 minutes on each side or until no longer pink. Serve on buns with tomato, lettuce and onion if desired.

FAST FIX ▶ Sun-Dried
Tomato Turkey Burgers

This recipe always brings back memories of my mom's homemade sun-dried tomatoes. I've prepared it with ground beef and ground turkey. Either way, it's fast to fix and tastes great!

—**SAMMY STAAB** PENSACOLA, FL

START TO FINISH: 25 MIN.
MAKES: 6 SERVINGS

- 1 **large red onion**
- 1 **cup (4 ounces) crumbled feta cheese, divided**
- ⅔ **cup chopped oil-packed sun-dried tomatoes**
- ¼ **teaspoon salt**
- ¼ **teaspoon pepper**
- 2 **pounds lean ground turkey**
- 6 **ciabatta rolls, split**

1. Cut onion in half. Finely chop one half and thinly slice the remaining half. In a large bowl, combine ½ cup feta, sun-dried tomatoes, chopped onion, salt and pepper. Crumble the turkey over mixture and mix well. Shape into six patties.

2. Grill burgers, covered, over medium heat or broil 4 in. from the heat for 5-7 minutes on each side or until a thermometer reads 165° and the juices run clear.

3. Meanwhile, saute sliced onion in a small nonstick skillet coated with cooking spray until tender. Top burgers with remaining feta; cover and grill 1-2 minutes longer or until cheese is melted. Serve on buns with onion.

No Stick!

Cleaning the food grate with a stiff wire brush after cooking—and while the coals are still hot—will help prevent food from sticking next time you fire up the grill.

Grilled Mushrooms

FAST FIX ## Grilled Mushrooms

Mushrooms cooked over hot coals taste good, but this makes them taste fantastic!

—**MELANIE KNOLL** MARSHALLTOWN, IA

START TO FINISH: 15 MIN.
MAKES: 4 SERVINGS

- ½ **pound whole fresh medium mushrooms**
- ¼ **cup butter, melted**
- ½ **teaspoon dill weed**
- ½ **teaspoon garlic salt**

Thread mushrooms on skewers. Mix butter, dill and garlic salt; brush over mushrooms. Moisten a paper towel with cooking oil; using long-handled tongs, rub on grill rack to coat lightly. Grill over hot heat for 10-15 minutes, basting and turning every 5 minutes.

Campfire Fried Fish

You'll be cooking up the catch of the day in no time with this tasty recipe.

—**TASTE OF HOME TEST KITCHEN**

PREP: 15 MIN. • **COOK:** 10 MIN./BATCH
MAKES: 6 SERVINGS

- 2 **eggs**
- ¾ **cup all-purpose flour**
- ½ **cup cornmeal**
- 1 **teaspoon salt**
- 1 **teaspoon paprika**
- 3 **pounds walleye, bluegill or perch fillets**
  Canola oil

1. In a bowl, whisk eggs. In a large resealable plastic bag, mix flour, cornmeal, salt and paprika. Dip fillets in eggs, then shake in flour mixture.

2. Add ¼ in. of oil to a large cast-iron skillet; place skillet on grill rack over medium-hot heat. Fry fillets in oil in batches for 3-4 minutes on each side or until fish flakes easily with a fork.

FAST FIX ▶ Chili-Cheese Burgers

Instead of putting cheese on the top of burgers, I like to shred and mix it into the meat when shaping the patties. This way, you're sure to get a little cheesy goodness in every mouthwatering bite.

—**DEB WILLIAMS** PEORIA, AZ

START TO FINISH: 25 MIN.
MAKES: 4 SERVINGS

- ½ **cup shredded cheddar cheese**
- 6 **tablespoons chili sauce, divided**
- 1 **tablespoon chili powder**
- 1 **pound ground beef**
- 4 **hamburger buns, split**
  Lettuce leaves, tomato slices and mayonnaise, optional

1. In a large bowl, combine cheese, 2 tablespoons chili sauce and chili powder. Add the beef; mix lightly but thoroughly. Shape into four ½-in.-thick patties.
2. Grill burgers, covered, over medium heat or broil 4 in. from heat 4-5 minutes on each side or until a thermometer reads 160°. Serve on buns with the remaining chili sauce and, if desired, lettuce, tomato and mayonnaise.

FAST FIX ▶ Grilled Romaine Salad

For a great tasting salad, try this recipe on the grill! Add any dressing of your choice to complete it.

—**TASTE OF HOME TEST KITCHEN**

START TO FINISH: 20 MIN.
MAKES: 12 SERVINGS

- ⅓ **cup plus 3 tablespoons olive oil, divided**
- 2 **tablespoons white wine vinegar**
- 1 **tablespoon dill weed**
- ½ **teaspoon garlic powder**
- ⅛ **teaspoon crushed red pepper flakes**
- ⅛ **teaspoon salt**
- 6 **green onions**
- 4 **plum tomatoes, halved**
- 1 **large cucumber, peeled and halved lengthwise**
- 2 **romaine hearts**

1. In a small bowl, whisk ⅓ cup oil, vinegar and seasonings. Set aside.
2. Brush the onions, tomatoes, cucumber and romaine with remaining oil. Grill the onions, tomatoes and cucumber, uncovered, over medium heat for 4-5 minutes on each side or until onions are crisp-tender. Grill romaine for 30 seconds on each side or until heated through.
3. Chop the vegetables; place in a large bowl. Whisk dressing and pour over salad; toss to coat. Serve immediately.

Chili-Cheese Burgers

Chipotle-Honey Grilled T-Bones

If you like to kick flavors up, this is the steak for you (or your man). My husband has even made this in a Dutch oven, and the meat just sizzles.

—DONNA GOUTERMONT JUNEAU, AK

PREP: 20 MIN. + MARINATING
GRILL: 10 MIN. • **MAKES:** 4 SERVINGS

- ½ cup minced fresh cilantro
- ½ cup lime juice
- ½ cup honey
- 2 tablespoons adobo sauce
- 3 garlic cloves, minced
- 1 tablespoon chopped chipotle pepper in adobo sauce
- 1 teaspoon salt
- 1 teaspoon ground cumin
- ½ teaspoon ground allspice
- ½ teaspoon pepper
- ¼ teaspoon Dijon mustard
- 4 beef T-bone steaks (12 ounces each)

1. In a small bowl, combine the first 11 ingredients. Pour ½ cup marinade into a large resealable plastic bag. Add the steaks; seal bag and turn to coat. Refrigerate for up to 1 hour. Cover and refrigerate remaining marinade.

2. Drain and discard marinade from steak. Grill steaks, covered, over medium heat or broil 4 in. from the heat for 5-6 minutes on each side or until meat reaches desired doneness (for medium-rare, a thermometer should read 145°; medium, 160°; well-done, 170°), basting occasionally with ½ cup reserved marinade. Serve with remaining marinade.

Chipotle-Honey Grilled T-Bones

Baja Bean Salad

My mayo-free Baja Bean Salad uses bright, fresh flavors of lime, jalapeno and cilantro to really bring this colorful bean-medley salad to life!

—JEANNE HOLT MENDOTA HEIGHTS, MN

PREP: 30 MIN. + CHILLING
MAKES: 12 SERVINGS (¾ CUP EACH)

- 1 pound cut fresh green beans
- 1 can (15 ounces) black beans, rinsed and drained
- 1 can (15 ounces) garbanzo beans or chickpeas, rinsed and drained
- 1 can (14½ ounces) cut wax beans, drained
- 1 cup julienned peeled jicama
- 1 medium sweet red pepper, finely chopped
- 4 green onions, thinly sliced
- 2 tablespoons finely chopped seeded jalapeno pepper
- ⅓ cup sugar
- ⅓ cup cider vinegar
- ¼ cup canola oil
- 2 tablespoons lime juice
- 2 tablespoons minced fresh cilantro
- ½ teaspoon salt
- ¼ teaspoon pepper

1. In a saucepan, bring 5 cups water to a boil. Add green beans; cover and cook for 4-6 minutes or until crisp-tender. Drain and immediately place beans in ice water. Drain and pat dry.

2. In a large bowl, combine the black beans, garbanzo beans, wax beans, jicama, red pepper, onions, jalapeno and green beans.

3. In a bowl, whisk the sugar, vinegar, oil, lime juice, cilantro, salt and pepper. Pour over salad; toss to coat. Cover and refrigerate for at least 1 hour before serving. Serve with a slotted spoon.

NOTE *Wear disposable gloves when cutting hot peppers; the oils can burn skin. Avoid touching your face.*

Greek-Style Chicken Burgers

Greek-Style Chicken Burgers

The original recipe for these burgers called for lamb or beef, but I decided to try ground chicken to decrease the fat. The sauce easily doubles as a great dip for veggies and toasted pita chips.
—**JUDY PUSKAS** WALLACEBURG, ON

PREP: 25 MIN. + CHILLING • **GRILL:** 10 MIN.
MAKES: 4 SERVINGS

SAUCE
- ⅓ cup fat-free plain Greek yogurt
- ¼ cup chopped peeled cucumber
- ¼ cup crumbled reduced-fat feta cheese
- 1½ teaspoons snipped fresh dill
- 1½ teaspoons lemon juice
- 1 small garlic clove, minced

BURGERS
- 1 medium onion, finely chopped
- ¼ cup dry bread crumbs
- 1 tablespoon dried oregano
- 1 tablespoon lemon juice
- 2 garlic cloves, minced
- ½ teaspoon salt
- ¼ teaspoon pepper
- 1 pound ground chicken
- 4 hamburger buns, split
- 4 lettuce leaves
- 4 tomato slices

1. In a small bowl, mix the sauce ingredients; refrigerate until serving.
2. In a large bowl, combine the first seven burger ingredients. Add chicken; mix lightly but thoroughly. Shape into four ½-in.-thick patties.
3. Moisten a paper towel with cooking oil; using long-handled tongs, rub on grill rack to coat lightly. Grill burgers, covered, over medium heat or broil 4 in. from heat 5-7 minutes on each side or until a thermometer reads 165°. Serve on buns with the lettuce, tomato and the sauce.

FAST FIX Grilled Corn Relish

Here's an instant upgrade for hot dogs—my colorful relish. It's also a great way to get kids to eat their veggies.
—**ELLEN RILEY** BIRMINGHAM, AL

START TO FINISH: 25 MIN.
MAKES: 2 CUPS

- 1 large sweet red pepper
- 2 medium ears sweet corn, husks removed
- 5 tablespoons honey Dijon vinaigrette, divided
- 2 green onions, thinly sliced
- ½ teaspoon coarsely ground pepper
- ¼ teaspoon salt

1. Cut red pepper lengthwise in half; remove seeds. Grill the red pepper and corn, covered, over medium heat for 10-15 minutes or until tender; turn and baste occasionally with 3 tablespoons of the vinaigrette.
2. Remove corn from cobs and chop red pepper; transfer to a small bowl. Add green onions, pepper, salt and remaining vinaigrette; toss to combine.

Grilled Corn Relish

IN THE BACKYARD!

Skillet Jalapeno Corn Bread, page 33,
Lemon-Ginger Barbecued Ribs, page 34,
Three-Bean Bake, page 33,
Cilantro-Lime Sweet Corn, page 33

Three-Bean Bake

I've come across many recipes for baked beans throughout the years, but none had the right amount of "kick." So I created this dish by combining several different ideas.
—ROMI PLATH SWEETSER, IN

PREP: 20 MIN. • **BAKE:** 50 MIN.
MAKES: 8 SERVINGS

- 6 bacon strips, cut into 1-inch pieces
- ½ cup chopped onion
- 3 garlic cloves, minced
- 1 can (28 ounces) baked beans
- 1 can (16 ounces) kidney beans, rinsed and drained
- 1 can (16 ounces) butter beans, rinsed and drained
- ⅓ cup packed brown sugar
- ¼ cup ketchup
- 2 tablespoons Dijon mustard
- ½ teaspoon chili powder
- ½ teaspoon pepper

1. In a skillet, partially cook the bacon. Remove with a slotted spoon to paper towels. Drain, reserving 1 tablespoon drippings. In the drippings, saute onion and garlic until tender. In a large bowl, combine the beans, onion mixture and bacon. Stir in the brown sugar, ketchup, mustard, chili powder and pepper.
2. Transfer to a greased 2-qt. baking dish. Bake, uncovered, at 350° for 50-60 minutes or until bubbly.

Skillet Jalapeno Corn Bread

You can bake this moist corn bread in an ovenproof skillet to accompany almost any barbecued main course. The jalapeno pepper adds an extra bit of zip.
—TASTE OF HOME TEST KITCHEN

PREP: 15 MIN. • **BAKE:** 20 MIN.
MAKES: 8-10 SERVINGS

- 6 bacon strips
- 1 cup all-purpose flour
- 1 cup yellow cornmeal
- ¼ cup sugar
- 3 teaspoons baking powder
- ½ teaspoon salt
- 2 eggs
- 1 cup buttermilk
- ½ cup canola oil
- ¾ cup shredded cheddar cheese
- 2 tablespoons chopped seeded jalapeno pepper

1. In a 10-in. ovenproof skillet, cook bacon over medium heat until crisp. Remove with a slotted spoon to paper towels. Drain, reserving 1 tablespoon drippings in skillet; set aside.
2. In a large bowl, combine the flour, cornmeal, sugar, baking powder and salt. In another bowl, combine the eggs, buttermilk and oil; stir into dry ingredients just until moistened. Fold in the cheese, jalapeno and bacon.
3. Pour into the skillet. Bake at 425° for 20-25 minutes or until golden brown. Cut into wedges; serve warm.

NOTE *Wear disposable gloves when cutting hot peppers; the oils can burn skin. Avoid touching your face.*

Cilantro-Lime Sweet Corn

It's a snap to lend definite Southwestern flair to corn on the cob with just a little cilantro and lime juice.
—TASTE OF HOME TEST KITCHEN

PREP: 35 MIN. + SOAKING • **GRILL:** 25 MIN.
MAKES: 8 SERVINGS

- 8 medium ears sweet corn in husks
- ⅓ cup plus ¼ cup butter, softened, divided
- 2 to 3 tablespoons minced fresh cilantro
- 1½ teaspoons grated lime peel
- 1 teaspoon salt
- 1 teaspoon plus 2 tablespoons lime juice, divided
- ½ teaspoon garlic powder

1. Soak the corn in cold water for 1 hour. Meanwhile, in a small bowl, combine ⅓ cup butter, cilantro, lime peel, salt, 1 teaspoon lime juice and garlic powder; set aside.
2. Carefully peel back husks from corn to within 1 in. of bottom; remove silk. Spread each ear of corn with butter mixture. Rewrap corn husks and secure with kitchen string.
3. Moisten a paper towel with cooking oil; using long-handled tongs, rub on grill rack to coat. Grill corn, covered, over medium heat for 25-30 minutes or until tender, turning occasionally.
4. Melt remaining butter; stir in the remaining juice. Cut string; peel back husks. Brush corn with lime butter.

Last-Minute Lifesaver

When my family is in a rush, I put corn cobs (husks and all) in the microwave for 2½ minutes per cob. The husks seal in the freshness and steam the corn. Then, your only cleanup is tossing the husks and cobs after dinner. **—KATHY R.** SHELBY, MI

FAST FIX ## Kielbasa Fruit Kabobs

My sausage kabobs feature sweet and savory flavors in one main entree. You can change up the fruits depending on whatever is in season.

—**MARY RELYEA** CANASTOTA, NY

START TO FINISH: 30 MIN.
MAKES: 4 SERVINGS

- 3 tablespoons orange marmalade
- 1 teaspoon Chinese five-spice powder
- 1 pound smoked kielbasa or Polish sausage, cut into 1-inch pieces
- 3 large apricots, pitted and quartered
- 2 medium plums, pitted and quartered

1. In a small bowl, mix marmalade and five-spice powder. Alternately thread kielbasa, apricots and plums onto four metal or soaked wooden skewers.

2. Moisten a paper towel with cooking oil; using long-handled tongs, rub on grill rack to coat lightly. Grill kabobs, covered, over medium heat or broil 4-6 in. from heat 6-8 minutes or until heated through, turning and basting frequently with marmalade mixture during the last 3 minutes.

Lemon-Ginger Barbecued Ribs

Lemon-Ginger Barbecued Ribs

Although my husband does most of the cooking for us, the kitchen is all mine on weekends! I was inspired to make this recipe for a family member who's allergic to tomatoes.

—**MEG CASH** LADY LAKE, FL

PREP: 5 MIN. • **COOK:** 2 HOURS 10 MIN.
MAKES: 8 SERVINGS

- 8 pounds pork baby back ribs, cut into serving-size pieces
- ½ cup water
- ½ cup lemon juice
- ½ cup light corn syrup
- 4 garlic cloves, peeled
- 2 tablespoons ground ginger
- 1 tablespoon onion powder
- 1 tablespoon dried basil
- 1 tablespoon dried thyme
- 1 tablespoon pepper
- 1½ teaspoons salt
- 1½ teaspoons paprika
- ¾ cup canola oil

1. Place ribs in two shallow roasting pans; add water. Cover and bake at 325° for 2 hours.

2. For sauce, in a blender, combine the lemon juice, corn syrup, garlic and seasonings; cover and process until blended. While processing, gradually add oil in a steady stream.

3. Drain ribs. Moisten a paper towel with cooking oil; using long-handled tongs, rub on grill rack to coat lightly. Spoon some of the sauce over ribs.

4. Grill, uncovered, over medium-low heat or broil 4 in. from the heat for 8-10 minutes or until browned, turning occasionally and brushing with sauce. Serve remaining sauce with ribs.

Potato Salad with Bacon

My young nephew refuses to eat any potato salad but mine! Italian salad dressing, sour cream and bacon give it a one-of-a-kind flavor.

—**COLLETTE REYNOLDS** RALEIGH, NC

PREP: 45 MIN. + CHILLING
MAKES: 16 SERVINGS

- 3 pounds red potatoes (about 12 medium)
- 4 hard-cooked eggs
- ¾ cup sour cream
- ⅔ cup mayonnaise
- 1 teaspoon salt
- 1 teaspoon prepared mustard
- ½ teaspoon garlic powder
- ¼ teaspoon pepper
- 11 bacon strips, cooked and crumbled
- ½ cup chopped celery
- ¼ cup chopped green onions
- ¼ cup Italian salad dressing

1. Cut potatoes into ½-in. cubes; place in a large Dutch oven and cover with water. Bring to a boil. Reduce heat; cover and simmer for 10-15 minutes or until tender. Drain and cool to room temperature.
2. Cut eggs in half; chop egg whites and set aside. In a small bowl, mash the egg yolks. Stir in sour cream, mayonnaise, salt, mustard, garlic powder and pepper; set aside.
3. In a bowl, combine the potatoes, bacon, egg whites, celery, onions and Italian dressing. Fold in mayonnaise mixture. Cover and refrigerate for at least 2 hours before serving.

Potato Salad with Bacon

Pear-Apple Pie Bars

Pear-Apple Pie Bars

With two kinds of fruit, these summery bars have mass appeal. The lovely lattice top makes them nice for get-togethers.

—**TASTE OF HOME TEST KITCHEN**

PREP: 30 MIN. + CHILLING
BAKE: 40 MIN. + COOLING
MAKES: 2 DOZEN

- 4 cups all-purpose flour
- 1 teaspoon salt
- 1 teaspoon baking powder
- 1 cup shortening
- 4 egg yolks
- 9 tablespoons cold water
- 2 tablespoons lemon juice

FILLING

- 1½ cups sugar
- 3 tablespoons all-purpose flour
- 1 teaspoon ground cinnamon
  Dash ground nutmeg
- 4 cups finely chopped peeled apples
- 3 cups finely chopped peeled ripe pears
- 1 egg white, beaten

1. In a large bowl, combine the flour, salt and baking powder. Cut in the shortening until mixture resembles coarse crumbs. In a small bowl, whisk egg yolks, water and lemon juice; gradually add to flour mixture, tossing with a fork until dough forms a ball. Divide in half, making one portion slightly larger. Chill for 30 minutes.
2. Roll out larger portion of dough between two large sheets of waxed paper into a 17-in. x 12-in. rectangle. Transfer to an ungreased 15-in. x 10-in. x 1-in. baking pan. Press pastry onto the bottom and up the sides of pan; trim pastry even with top edges.
3. In a large bowl, combine the sugar, flour, cinnamon and nutmeg. Add apples and pears; toss to coat. Spoon over crust.
4. Roll out remaining pastry; make a lattice crust. Trim and seal edges. Brush lattice top with egg white.
5. Bake at 375° for 40-45 minutes or until crust is golden brown. Cool on a wire rack.

Curried Pork & Orange Kabobs

FAST FIX Curried Pork & Orange Kabobs

I love the sweet flavor of red, yellow and orange peppers and always go for them in the summer when they're inexpensive and plentiful. Plus, I just think they taste a whole lot better than green peppers.
—LIV VORS PETERBOROUGH, ON

START TO FINISH: 30 MIN.
MAKES: 4 SERVINGS

- ½ cup canola oil
- 2 tablespoons dried minced onion
- 1 garlic clove, minced
- 1 to 2 tablespoons curry powder
- ½ teaspoon each ground cumin, coriander and cinnamon
- 1½ pounds pork tenderloin
- 1 large sweet red pepper
- 1 large sweet yellow or orange pepper
- 1 small onion
- 1 large unpeeled navel orange

1. In a small bowl, mix oil, minced onion, garlic and spices; reserve half of mixture for basting kabobs while grilling. Cut pork, peppers, onion and unpeeled orange into 1-in. pieces. On four metal or soaked wooden skewers, alternately thread the pork, vegetables and orange; brush with the remaining curry mixture.

2. Grill the kabobs, covered, over medium heat 10-15 minutes or until vegetables and pork are tender, turning occasionally. Baste frequently with the reserved curry mixture during the last 4 minutes of cooking.

Horseradish-Dill Grilled Corn

Give corn on the cob some zing with this recipe. You'll be surprised how little it takes to add so much flavor to an ear of corn.

—TASTE OF HOME TEST KITCHEN

PREP: 30 MIN. + SOAKING • **GRILL:** 25 MIN.
MAKES: 5 SERVINGS

- 5 medium ears sweet corn in husks
- ⅓ cup butter, softened
- 1 tablespoon prepared horseradish
- ½ teaspoon salt
- ¼ teaspoon garlic powder
- ¼ teaspoon white pepper
- ¼ teaspoon snipped fresh dill
- 10 fresh dill sprigs

1. Soak corn in cold water for 1 hour. Meanwhile, in a small bowl, combine butter, horseradish, salt, garlic powder, pepper and snipped dill; set aside.

2. Carefully peel back husks from corn to within 1 in. of bottom; remove silk. Spread butter mixture over corn; place two sprigs of dill on opposite sides of each ear. Rewrap husks and secure with kitchen string.

3. Moisten a paper towel with cooking oil; using long-handled tongs, rub on grill rack to coat lightly. Grill corn, covered, over medium heat for 25-30 minutes or until tender, turning occasionally.

4. Cut string and peel back husks. Remove and discard dill sprigs before serving.

Grilled
Italian Burgers

FAST FIX ▶ Grilled Italian Burgers

While trying to think of a new way to fix hamburgers with the same old ground beef, I came up with this recipe. A good dose of Italian seasonings and mozzarella makes them unique. They're great with a side salad or fresh green beans.

—REBEKAH BEYER SABETHA, KS

START TO FINISH: 20 MIN.
MAKES: 4 SERVINGS

- 1 cup (4 ounces) shredded part-skim mozzarella cheese, divided
- 1 teaspoon Worcestershire sauce
- ¼ teaspoon Italian seasoning
- ⅛ teaspoon salt
- ⅛ teaspoon pepper
- 1 pound ground beef
  Marinara or spaghetti sauce, warmed

1. In a large bowl, combine ½ cup cheese and seasonings. Add beef; mix lightly but thoroughly. Shape into four ½-in.-thick patties.

2. Grill the burgers, covered, over medium heat or broil 4 in. from heat 4-5 minutes on each side or until a thermometer reads 160°. Sprinkle with the remaining cheese; grill, covered, 1-2 minutes longer or until cheese is melted. Serve with marinara sauce.

Dilly Vegetable
Medley

Dilly Vegetable Medley

I love to eat what I grow, and I have tried many combinations of the fresh vegetables from my garden. This one is really great! In fact, I never have leftovers. Ever.

—REBECCA BARJONAH CORALVILLE, IA

PREP: 25 MIN. • **GRILL:** 20 MIN.
MAKES: 13 SERVINGS

- ¼ cup olive oil
- 2 tablespoons minced fresh basil
- 2 teaspoons dill weed
- ½ teaspoon salt
- ½ teaspoon pepper
- 7 small yellow summer squash, cut into ½-inch slices
- 1 pound Yukon Gold potatoes, cut into ½-inch cubes
- 5 small carrots, cut into ½-inch slices

1. In a very large bowl, combine the first five ingredients. Add vegetables and toss to coat.
2. Place half of the vegetables on a double thickness of heavy-duty foil (about 18 in. square). Fold foil around vegetables and seal tightly. Repeat with remaining vegetables.
3. Grill, covered, over medium heat for 20-25 minutes or until potatoes are tender, turning once. Open foil carefully to allow steam to escape.

Creamy Jalapeno Popper Dip

Creamy Jalapeno Popper Dip

This recipe will remind you of a jalapeno popper without all the fuss. If my husband had his way, he would have me make this for him every weekend!

—DEBORAH PEIRCE VIRGINIA BEACH, VA

PREP: 15 MIN. • **BAKE:** 30 MIN.
MAKES: 2 CUPS

- 4 bacon strips, chopped
- 1 package (8 ounces) cream cheese, softened
- 2 cups (8 ounces) shredded cheddar cheese
- ½ cup sour cream
- ¼ cup 2% milk
- 3 jalapeno peppers, seeded and chopped
- 1 teaspoon white wine vinegar
- ⅓ cup panko (Japanese) bread crumbs
- 2 tablespoons butter
  Tortilla chips

1. Preheat oven to 350°. In a small skillet, cook bacon over medium heat until crisp, stirring occasionally. Remove with a slotted spoon; drain on paper towels. Discard drippings, reserving 1 tablespoon.
2. In a large bowl, mix cream cheese, cheddar cheese, sour cream, milk, jalapenos, vinegar, cooked bacon and reserved drippings. Transfer to a greased 8-in.-square baking dish. Sprinkle with the bread crumbs; dot with butter.
3. Bake 30-35 minutes or until bubbly and topping is golden brown. Serve with chips.
NOTE *Wear disposable gloves when cutting hot peppers; the oils can burn skin. Avoid touching your face.*

Chicken Fajitas

This is the best fajita recipe I've ever tried. It sounds complicated, but it really isn't. The servings are hearty, but the chicken is so good that my husband and I never have a problem finishing every bit of it!

—KATHLEEN SMITH PITTSBURGH, PA

PREP: 15 MIN. + MARINATING
COOK: 20 MIN. • **MAKES:** 2 SERVINGS

- ¼ cup lime juice
- 1 tablespoon reduced-sodium soy sauce
- 2 teaspoons canola oil
- 1 garlic clove, minced
- ½ teaspoon salt
- ½ teaspoon chili powder
- ½ teaspoon cayenne pepper
- ¼ teaspoon pepper
- ½ teaspoon liquid smoke, optional
- 2 boneless skinless chicken breast halves (4 ounces each)

FILLING

- 2 teaspoons canola oil
- 1 medium onion, julienned
- ½ small sweet red or green pepper, julienned
- 1 teaspoon reduced-sodium soy sauce
- ½ teaspoon lime juice
- 4 fat-free tortillas (6 inches), warmed
  Salsa and sour cream, optional

Chicken Fajitas

1. In a large resealable plastic bag, combine the first eight ingredients; if desired, add liquid smoke. Add the chicken; seal bag and turn to coat. Refrigerate at least 2 hours.

2. Drain the chicken, discarding marinade. Moisten a paper towel with cooking oil; using long-handled tongs, rub on grill rack to coat lightly. Grill chicken, covered, over medium heat or broil 4 in. from heat 4-6 minutes on each side or until a thermometer reads 165°.

3. In a large nonstick skillet, heat oil over medium-high heat. Add onion and red pepper; cook and stir for 5-7 minutes or until tender. Stir in the soy sauce and lime juice.

4. Cut chicken into thin slices; add to vegetables. Serve with tortillas and, if desired, salsa and sour cream.

FAST FIX

Kiwi-Strawberry Spinach Salad

Here's a pretty salad that's always a hit when I serve it! The recipe came from a cookbook, but I personalized it. It's funny how just a small change in ingredients can create a big taste difference.

—LAURA POUNDS ANDOVER, KS

START TO FINISH: 20 MIN.
MAKES: 12 SERVINGS (1 CUP EACH)

- ¼ cup canola oil
- ¼ cup raspberry vinegar
- ¼ teaspoon Worcestershire sauce
- ⅓ cup sugar
- ¼ teaspoon paprika
- 2 green onions, chopped
- 2 tablespoons sesame seeds, toasted
- 1 tablespoon poppy seeds
- 12 cups torn fresh spinach (about 9 ounces)
- 2 pints fresh strawberries, halved
- 4 kiwifruit, peeled and sliced

1. Place the first five ingredients in a blender; cover and process 30 seconds or until blended. Transfer to a bowl; stir in green onions, sesame seeds and poppy seeds.

2. In a large bowl, combine spinach, strawberries and kiwi. Drizzle with dressing; toss to coat.

FAST FIX Chocolate Dessert Wraps

When I needed a special dessert for a backyard barbecue, I came up with this chocolate-and-peanut butter treat. The wraps take just minutes on the grill and get a chewy consistency from the warm melty marshmallows.
—**LAURIE GWALTNEY** INDIANAPOLIS, IN

START TO FINISH: 20 MIN.
MAKES: 4 SERVINGS

- ½ **cup creamy peanut butter**
- 4 **flour tortillas (8 inches)**
- 1 **cup miniature marshmallows**
- ½ **cup miniature semisweet chocolate chips**
- **Vanilla ice cream**
- **Chocolate shavings, optional**

1. Spread 2 tablespoons of peanut butter on each tortilla. Sprinkle ¼ cup marshmallows and 2 tablespoons chocolate chips on half of each tortilla.
2. Roll up, beginning with the topping side. Wrap each tortilla in heavy-duty foil; seal tightly.
3. Grill, covered, over low heat for 5-10 minutes or until heated through.
4. Unwrap tortillas; place on dessert plates. Serve with ice cream. Garnish with chocolate shavings if desired.
NOTE *Crunchy peanut butter is not recommended for this recipe.*

Chocolate Dessert Wraps

Favorite Chili Cheeseburgers

FAST FIX Favorite Chili Cheeseburgers

I like to experiment when making burgers—and stuffing them with sharp cheddar cheese makes them absolutely delicious! For lighter fare, I sometimes make the patties with a combination of lean ground beef and ground turkey.
—**DEB WILLIAMS** PEORIA, AZ

START TO FINISH: 20 MIN.
MAKES: 4 SERVINGS

- 1 **pound ground beef**
- 2 **tablespoons chili sauce**
- 1 **tablespoon chili powder**
- ½ **cup shredded cheddar cheese**
- 4 **hamburger-size pretzel buns or hamburger buns, split**
- ½ **cup nacho cheese sauce, warmed**

1. In a large bowl, combine the beef, chili sauce and chili powder, mixing lightly but thoroughly. Shape into eight ¼-in.-thick patties. Place 2 tablespoons of cheese onto the center of each of four patties. Top with the remaining patties; press edges firmly to seal.
2. Grill the burgers, covered, over medium heat or broil 4 in. from heat for 4-6 minutes on each side or until a thermometer reads 160°. Serve on buns with nacho cheese sauce.

Bread & Butter Peppers

If your pepper plants are as prolific as mine, this recipe will come in handy. The crunchy mix of sliced peppers gives a kick to grilled burgers, salads, side dishes and deli sandwich toppings.
—**STARR MILAM** SHELDON, WI

PREP: 20 MIN. + STANDING
COOK: 5 MIN. + CHILLING
MAKES: 1 QUART

- 2½ cups seeded sliced banana peppers (about 7 peppers)
- 1 medium green pepper, julienned or 1 medium green tomato, halved and sliced
- 1 jalapeno pepper, seeded and sliced
- 1 small onion, sliced
- ¼ cup canning salt
- 12 to 15 ice cubes
- 2 cups sugar
- 1 cup white vinegar
- 1 tablespoon mustard seed
- ½ teaspoon celery seed

1. In a bowl, combine the peppers, onion and salt; top with ice. Let stand for 2 hours. Rinse and drain well.

2. In a large saucepan, combine the sugar, vinegar, mustard seed and celery seed. Bring to a boil; cook and stir just until sugar is dissolved. Pour over pepper mixture; cool. Cover tightly and refrigerate for at least 24 hours. Store in the refrigerator for up to 3 months.

NOTE *Wear disposable gloves when cutting hot peppers; the oils can burn skin. Avoid touching your face.*

Bread & Butter Peppers

top tip | Picking Peppers

Always purchase mild, sweet banana peppers with evenly colored skins free of blemishes.

Marshmallow Fruit Kabobs

Here's a way to slip more fruit into your family's diet! The sauce can be made ahead of time. Kids will have a great time helping to assemble the kabobs, too.
—CLAUDIA RUISS MASSAPEQUA, NY

START TO FINISH: 30 MIN.
MAKES: 6 SERVINGS

- 1½ cups fresh or frozen raspberries, thawed
- ⅓ cup orange juice
- 1 tablespoon confectioners' sugar
- 2 medium firm bananas, cut into ¾-inch slices
- 2 cups cubed fresh pineapple
- 2 large fresh plums, cut into ¾-inch pieces
- 24 large marshmallows
- 1 tablespoon lemon juice
- 1 tablespoon honey

1. Mash and strain the raspberries, reserving juice. Discard seeds. In a small bowl, combine the orange juice, sugar and raspberry juice; set aside.
2. On 12 metal or soaked wooden skewers, alternately thread fruit and marshmallows. Combine lemon juice and honey; brush over fruit.
3. Using long-handled tongs, moisten a paper towel with cooking oil and lightly coat the grill rack. Prepare grill for indirect heat. Place kabobs over drip pan and grill over indirect medium heat for 2-4 minutes or until marshmallows are golden, turning frequently. Serve with raspberry sauce.

Honey-Beer Braised Ribs

Honey-Beer Braised Ribs

Braised in beer with a sweet honey finish, these tender, flavor-rich ribs will be the talk of the table. Serve them with baked potatoes, green beans and a salad for a memorable meal.
—TERRY SERENA MCMURRAY, PA

PREP: 3½ HOURS • **GRILL:** 10 MIN.
MAKES: 6 SERVINGS

- ½ cup packed brown sugar
- 1 teaspoon pepper
- ¾ teaspoon salt
- 6 pounds pork baby back ribs
- ¼ cup honey
- 1 bottle (12 ounces) dark beer or beef broth
- ¼ cup cider vinegar
- 1 bottle (18 ounces) barbecue sauce

1. Combine the brown sugar, pepper and salt; rub over ribs. Place ribs bone side down on a rack in a foil-lined large shallow roasting pan. Drizzle with honey. Combine beer and vinegar; pour around ribs. Spoon some of the beer mixture over ribs.
2. Cover tightly with foil and bake at 325° for 1 hour. Reduce heat to 250°; bake 2 hours longer or until tender.
3. Moisten a paper towel with cooking oil; using long-handled tongs, rub on grill rack to coat lightly. Drain ribs. Grill, covered, over medium heat for 10-15 minutes or until browned, turning and basting occasionally with barbecue sauce. Serve with the remaining barbecue sauce.

Citrus Berry
Shortcake

Citrus Berry Shortcake

Sometimes, I'll sprinkle a few blueberries over the top, too, for a patriotic finish!
—**MERYL HERR** GRAND RAPIDS, MI

PREP: 30 MIN. • **BAKE:** 20 MIN. + COOLING
MAKES: 8 SERVINGS

- 1⅓ cups all-purpose flour
- ½ cup sugar
- 2 teaspoons baking powder
- ¼ teaspoon salt
- ⅔ cup buttermilk
- ¼ cup butter, melted
- 1 egg
- 1 tablespoon orange juice
- 1 teaspoon grated orange peel
- 1 teaspoon vanilla extract
- 1 cup sliced fresh strawberries

TOPPING

- 1½ cups sliced fresh strawberries
- 1 tablespoon lemon juice
- 1 teaspoon sugar
- 2 cups whipped topping
- 2 teaspoons orange liqueur or orange juice

1. Preheat oven to 350°. Line bottom of a greased 9-in. round baking pan with parchment paper; grease paper.
2. In a bowl, whisk flour, sugar, baking powder and salt. In another bowl, whisk buttermilk, melted butter, egg, orange juice, orange peel and vanilla. Stir into dry ingredients just until moistened. Fold in 1 cup of sliced strawberries. Transfer to prepared pan.
3. Bake 20-25 minutes or until a toothpick inserted in center comes out clean. Cool in pan 10 minutes before removing from pan to a wire rack; remove paper. Cool completely.
4. For topping, in a small bowl, toss strawberries with lemon juice and sugar. Refrigerate until serving. In another bowl, mix whipped topping and liqueur; spread over cake. Drain strawberries; arrange over top.

Nectarine Barbecued Cornish Hen

Nectarine Barbecued Cornish Hen

Mildly sweet and tangy, nectarine sauce is especially good with grilled poultry or pork. It adheres nicely to Cornish hens, adding more flavor to every bite.
—**TASTE OF HOME TEST KITCHEN**

PREP: 15 MIN. • **GRILL:** 20 MIN.
MAKES: 2 SERVINGS

- 2 medium nectarines, peeled and sliced
- 2 tablespoons ketchup
- 2 teaspoons thawed orange juice concentrate
- 1 teaspoon sugar
- ⅛ teaspoon chili powder
- 2 tablespoons finely chopped red onion
- 1 teaspoon olive oil
- 1 garlic clove, minced
- 1 Cornish game hen (20 to 24 ounces), split lengthwise
- ¼ teaspoon salt
- ⅛ teaspoon pepper

1. In a food processor, combine the first five ingredients; cover and process until smooth.
2. In a small skillet, saute the onion in oil until tender. Add the garlic; cook 1 minute longer. Stir in the nectarine mixture and bring to a boil; cook and stir for 1 minute.
3. Sprinkle hen with salt and pepper. Moisten a paper towel with cooking oil; using long-handled tongs, rub on grill rack to coat lightly. Grill hen, covered, over medium heat for 20-25 minutes or until a thermometer reads 180° in the thigh; turn and baste occasionally with sauce.

IN THE BACKYARD!

Grilled Peaches & Pound Cake

FAST FIX ▸ Grilled Peaches & Pound Cake

If you do not have a grill wok or basket for this no-fuss dessert, use a disposable foil pan. Poke holes in the bottom of the pan with a meat fork to allow liquid to drain.

—JOY PENDLEY ORTONVILLE, MI

START TO FINISH: 20 MIN.
MAKES: 6 SERVINGS

- 3 medium peaches, sliced
- 1 tablespoon balsamic vinegar
- 1 loaf (10¾ ounces) frozen pound cake, thawed
- ¼ cup packed brown sugar
- 2 tablespoons butter, melted
- 6 scoops vanilla ice cream

1. Brush the peaches with vinegar and place in a grill wok or basket. Grill, uncovered, over medium heat for 10-12 minutes or until the peaches are tender, stirring frequently.

2. Cut pound cake into six slices. In a small bowl, combine brown sugar and butter; brush over both sides of cake slices. Grill, uncovered, over medium heat for 1-2 minutes on each side or until light golden brown. Place cake slices on serving plates and top with peaches and ice cream.

top tip

Removing Peach Skin

Not everyone likes the texture of peach skin. To remove, plunge peaches into boiling water for about 30-40 seconds or until the skin splits, then into ice water to cool the fruit. Peel off the skin easily with a paring knife.

Rhubarb Tart with Shortbread Crust

Here's a perfect ending to a grilled summer meal! Between the creamy texture, the pretty color and the buttery crust, this dessert is simply delightful.

—EMILY SEEFELDT RED WING, MN

PREP: 40 MIN. • **BAKE:** 15 MIN. + CHILLING
MAKES: 12 SERVINGS

- 3¾ cups chopped fresh rhubarb (about 1¼ pounds)
- ¼ cup sugar
- 2 tablespoons water

CRUST

- 1 cup all-purpose flour
- ½ cup ground pecans
- ½ cup cold butter, cubed
- ⅓ cup confectioners' sugar
- ¼ teaspoon salt

CURD

- 6 egg yolks
- ½ cup sugar
- 1 tablespoon lemon juice
- 1½ teaspoons grated lemon peel
- 5 tablespoons butter, cubed
- 4 drops red food coloring, optional
  Additional confectioners' sugar

Rhubarb Tart with Shortbread Crust

1. In a saucepan, bring rhubarb, sugar and water to a boil. Reduce heat; cook and stir until thickened and rhubarb is tender. Cool slightly. Transfer to a food processor; cover and process until mixture is smooth; set aside.
2. For crust, place the flour, pecans, butter, confectioners' sugar and salt in a food processor; cover and process until crumbly. Press onto the bottom and up the sides of an ungreased 9-in. tart pan with removable bottom. Bake crust at 350° for 18-20 minutes or until lightly browned.
3. Meanwhile, in a small heavy saucepan over medium heat, whisk the egg yolks, sugar, lemon juice, peel and rhubarb mixture until blended. Add butter; cook until butter is melted, whisking constantly. Stir in food coloring if desired; pour into the prepared crust.
4. Bake at 350° 12-15 minutes longer or until center is almost set. Cool completely on a wire rack. Refrigerate for at least 1 hour. Just before serving, dust with confectioners' sugar.

FAST FIX ▶ White Bean and Spinach Salads

This is one of my favorite hot-weather salads. Fresh parsley, tarragon and chives give the homemade dressing special flavor.

—ELISABETH LARSEN
PLEASANT GROVE, UT

START TO FINISH: 20 MIN.
MAKES: 4 SERVINGS

- ¼ cup olive oil
- 2 tablespoons white wine vinegar
- 2 teaspoons minced fresh parsley
- 2 teaspoons minced fresh tarragon
- 2 teaspoons lemon juice
- 1 teaspoon minced chives
- 1 teaspoon Dijon mustard
- ½ teaspoon sugar
- ½ teaspoon salt
- ⅛ teaspoon pepper
- 1 can (15 ounces) cannellini or white kidney beans, rinsed and drained
- ½ cup julienned carrot
- ¼ cup roasted sweet red peppers, chopped
- 2 tablespoons chopped red onion
- 4 cups fresh baby spinach

1. In a small bowl, whisk the first 10 ingredients. In another bowl, combine the beans, carrot, red peppers and onion. Add dressing and toss to coat.
2. Divide spinach among four serving plates. Top with bean mixture.

Couscous Tuna Tower, page 59; Pasta with Mozzarella, Tomatoes and Fresh Basil, page 60; Marinated Cucumber Pasta Salad, page 59; Apricot Chicken Drumsticks, page 60

Vegetable Beef
Kabobs, page 70

IT'S TIME TO BARBECUE...

BY THE
Pool!

When hosting a poolside soiree, finger foods and **refreshing bites** take top priority. This summer, slap on suntan lotion, fire up the grill, mix some beverages and toss a few salads that will **whet appetites** as friends and family keep cool by the pool.

Marinated Steak & Pepper Fajitas

These are the best fajitas ever, and a much healthier version of the typically pan-fried fajitas you find in restaurants. I also serve them in flatbreads instead of tortillas.

—**ERIN MICHNIACKI** MANHATTAN, KS

PREP: 25 MIN. + MARINATING
GRILL: 20 MIN. • **MAKES:** 8 SERVINGS

- ½ cup tequila or reduced-sodium beef broth
- ½ cup lime juice
- 4 garlic cloves, sliced
- 1 teaspoon grated lime peel
- 1 teaspoon chili powder
- ¾ teaspoon salt
- ¾ teaspoon pepper
- 4 poblano peppers or medium sweet red peppers, halved and seeded
- 4 jalapeno peppers, halved and seeded
- 1 large sweet onion, cut crosswise into ¾-inch-thick slices
- 1½ pounds beef skirt steaks or flank steak
- 8 whole wheat tortillas (8 inches), warmed
- ½ cup shredded Mexican cheese blend

Marinated Steak & Pepper Fajitas

1. In a small bowl, whisk the first seven ingredients until blended. Divide marinade between two large resealable plastic bags. Add peppers and onion to one bag; seal bag and turn gently to coat. Cut skirt steaks in half and add to the second bag; seal bag and turn to coat. Refrigerate vegetables and beef 8 hours or overnight.

2. Drain the vegetables and beef, discarding marinade. Grill onion and poblanos, covered, over medium heat 4-6 minutes on each side or until tender. Grill jalapenos 2-3 minutes on each side or until crisp-tender. Grill the steaks, covered, over medium heat 4-6 minutes on each side or until the meat reaches desired doneness (for medium-rare, a thermometer should read 145°; medium, 160°; well-done, 170°). Let steaks stand 5 minutes.

3. Cut peppers into strips; coarsely chop onion. Thinly slice steaks across the grain. Serve vegetables and beef on tortillas; top with cheese.

NOTE *Wear disposable gloves when cutting hot peppers; the oils can burn skin. Avoid touching your face.*

 Pool-Party Provisions

To make guests comfortable at your pool-side barbecue, set out a basket of sunny-day supplies, including beach towels, sunscreen, spray bottles filled with water and bottled drinking water.

Corn with Cilantro Butter

I created a lime butter especially for grilled corn and use the fresh cilantro from my garden to add a nice twist.
—**ANDREA REYNOLDS** ROCKY RIVER, OH

PREP: 15 MIN. + CHILLING • **GRILL:** 15 MIN.
MAKES: 12 SERVINGS

- ½ **cup butter, softened**
- ¼ **cup minced fresh cilantro**
- 1 **tablespoon lime juice**
- 1½ **teaspoons grated lime peel**
- 12 **medium ears sweet corn, husks removed**
     Grated cotija cheese, optional

1. In a small bowl, mix butter, cilantro, lime juice and lime peel. Shape into a log; wrap in plastic wrap. Refrigerate 30 minutes or until firm. Wrap each ear of corn with a piece of heavy-duty foil (about 14 in. square).

2. Grill corn, covered, over medium heat 15-20 minutes or until tender, turning occasionally. Meanwhile, cut lime butter into 12 slices. Remove corn from grill. Carefully open foil, allowing steam to escape. Serve corn with butter and, if desired, cheese.

Corn with
Cilantro Butter

FAST FIX ▶ Sweet & Spicy Pineapple Salsa

There's a definite punch to this fruity combination, which makes a colorful topping for tortilla chips or grilled chicken, pork or fish.
—**DONNA KELLY** PROVO, UT

START TO FINISH: 30 MIN.
MAKES: 2 CUPS

- ½ **fresh pineapple, peeled, cored and cut into ½-inch slices**
- 2 **jalapeno peppers**
- 1 **medium mango, peeled and finely chopped**
- ¼ **cup finely chopped onion**
- 2 **green onions, finely chopped**
- 3 **tablespoons minced fresh cilantro**
- 3 **tablespoons lime juice**
- 2 **tablespoons olive oil**
- 2 **tablespoons honey**
- ⅛ **teaspoon salt**
- ⅛ **teaspoon pepper**
- ⅛ **teaspoon hot pepper sauce**

1. Moisten a paper towel with cooking oil; using long-handled tongs, rub on grill rack to coat lightly. Grill pineapple, covered, over medium heat for 3 to 5 minutes on each side or until golden brown. Grill jalapenos until tender, turning occasionally.

2. Let pineapple and peppers cool slightly; finely chop and transfer to a large bowl. Add remaining ingredients. Refrigerate at least 2 hours. Before serving, allow the salsa to come to room temperature.

NOTE *Wear disposable gloves when cutting hot peppers; the oils can burn skin. Avoid touching your face.*

Greek Grilled Chicken Pitas

I switched up my mom's recipe to create this variation that takes advantage of summer veggies and keeps my kitchen nice and cool.

—BLAIR LONERGAN ROCHELLE, VA

PREP: 20 MIN. + MARINATING
GRILL: 10 MIN. • **MAKES:** 4 SERVINGS

- ½ cup balsamic vinaigrette
- 1 pound boneless skinless chicken breast halves

CUCUMBER SAUCE
- 1 cup plain Greek yogurt
- ½ cup finely chopped cucumber
- ¼ cup finely chopped red onion
- 1 tablespoon minced fresh parsley
- 1 tablespoon lime juice
- 1 garlic clove, minced
- ¼ teaspoon salt
- ⅛ teaspoon pepper

PITAS
- 8 pita pocket halves
- ½ cup sliced cucumber
- ½ cup grape tomatoes, chopped
- ½ cup sliced red onion
- ½ cup crumbled feta cheese

1. Pour the vinaigrette into a large resealable plastic bag. Add the chicken; seal bag and turn to coat. Refrigerate for at least 4 hours or overnight. In a small bowl, combine the sauce ingredients; chill until serving.
2. Drain and discard marinade. If grilling the chicken, moisten a paper towel with cooking oil; using long-handled tongs, rub on grill rack to coat lightly. Grill chicken, covered, over medium heat or broil 4 in. from the heat for 4-7 minutes on each side or until a meat thermometer reads 165°.
3. Cut chicken into strips. Fill each pita half with chicken, cucumber, tomatoes, onion and cheese; drizzle with sauce.

Greek Grilled Chicken Pitas

FAST FIX **BLT Catfish Sandwiches**

A classic gets a rockin' new twist with lemon-grilled catfish and tangy chili sauce instead of mayo. I serve these sandwiches with sweet red pepper strips and grilled potato wedges. They're always a huge hit!

—MARY ANN DELL PHOENIXVILLE, PA

START TO FINISH: 30 MIN.
MAKES: 4 SERVINGS

- 2 tablespoons chili sauce
- 2 tablespoons ketchup
- ¼ teaspoon hot pepper sauce
- 4 tablespoons lemon juice, divided
- 4 catfish fillets (6 ounces each)
- ½ teaspoon lemon-pepper seasoning
- ¼ teaspoon salt
- 8 slices whole wheat bread, toasted
- 8 cooked bacon strips
- 4 lettuce leaves
- 4 thin slices tomato
- 4 slices red onion

1. In a small bowl, combine the chili sauce, ketchup, pepper sauce and 2 tablespoons lemon juice; set aside.
2. Drizzle remaining lemon juice over fillets; sprinkle with lemon-pepper and salt. Moisten a paper towel with cooking oil; using long-handled tongs, rub on grill rack to coat lightly.
3. Grill catfish, covered, over medium-hot heat or broil 4 in. from the heat for 3-5 minutes on each side or until fish flakes easily with a fork.
4. Layer four slices of toast with catfish, bacon, lettuce, tomato and onion. Spread sauce mixture over remaining toast slices; place on top.

Blackberry Cheesecake Bars

Blackberry Cheesecake Bars

Sugar cookie dough is a speedy way to turn ricotta and mascarpone cheeses topped with blackberries into pretty bars.

—**TERRI CRANDALL** GARDNERVILLE, NV

PREP: 30 MIN. • **BAKE:** 20 MIN. + COOLING
MAKES: 12 SERVINGS

- 1 tube (16½ ounces) refrigerated sugar cookie dough
- 1½ cups ricotta cheese
- 1 carton (8 ounces) mascarpone cheese
- ½ cup sugar
- 2 eggs, lightly beaten
- 3 teaspoons vanilla extract
- 2 teaspoons grated lemon peel
- 1 teaspoon lemon juice
- 1 teaspoon orange juice
- 1 tablespoon amaretto, optional
- 1 cup seedless blackberry spreadable fruit
- 2⅔ cups fresh blackberries

1. Preheat oven to 375°. Let cookie dough stand at room temperature 5 minutes to soften. Press dough onto bottom and 1 in. up sides of a greased 13x9-in. baking dish. Bake for 12-15 minutes or until golden brown. Cool on a wire rack.

2. Meanwhile, in a large bowl, beat ricotta cheese, mascarpone cheese and sugar until blended. Add eggs; beat on low speed just until combined. Stir in vanilla, lemon peel, citrus juices and, if desired, amaretto. Pour into crust.

3. Bake 20-25 minutes or until the center is almost set. Cool for 1 hour on a wire rack.

4. Place spreadable fruit in a small microwave-safe bowl; microwave on high for 30-45 seconds or until melted. Spread over cheesecake layer; top with blackberries. Refrigerate until serving.

BY THE POOL!

Martha's Fish Tacos

We can't get enough barbecued fish at our house. This recipe can be made in advance and served cold, or eaten hot off the grill. It's fantastic either way!

—MARTHA BENOIT
PROCTORSVILLE, VT

PREP: 25 MIN. • **GRILL:** 10 MIN.
MAKES: 6 SERVINGS

- 2 **large ears sweet corn**
- 1 **teaspoon butter, softened**
- ⅛ **teaspoon salt**
- ⅛ **teaspoon pepper**
- 1 **haddock fillet (8 ounces)**
- 2 **teaspoons chili powder, divided**
- 2 **cups shredded lettuce**
- 2 **medium tomatoes, seeded and chopped**
- 1 **medium sweet red pepper, chopped**
- 1 **medium ripe avocado, peeled and chopped**
- 3 **tablespoons taco sauce**
- 2 **tablespoons lime juice, divided**
- 1 **tablespoon minced fresh cilantro**
- 1½ **teaspoons grated lime peel**
- 12 **flour tortillas (8 inches)**

1. Spread corn with butter and sprinkle with salt and pepper. Grill, covered, over medium heat for 10-12 minutes or until tender, turning occasionally.

2. Meanwhile, sprinkle fish with 1 teaspoon chili powder. Moisten a paper towel with cooking oil; using long-handled tongs, rub on grill rack to coat lightly. Grill fish, covered, over medium heat for 7-9 minutes or until fish flakes easily with a fork.

3. Cool corn slightly; remove kernels from cobs. Place in a large bowl. Add the lettuce, tomatoes, red pepper, avocado, taco sauce, 1 tablespoon lime juice, cilantro, lime peel and remaining chili powder.

4. Drizzle remaining lime juice over fish; cut into ½-in. cubes. Add to corn mixture. Spoon ½ cup mixture over each tortilla. Serve immediately.

Banana Cream Pie

FAST FIX ▸ Banana Cream Pie

This no-bake pie is full of old-fashioned flavor, with only a fraction of the work. Because it uses instant pudding, it's ready in just minutes!

—PERLENE HOEKEMA LYNDEN, WA

START TO FINISH: 10 MIN.
MAKES: 8 SERVINGS

- 1 **cup cold 2% milk**
- ½ **teaspoon vanilla extract**
- 1 **package (3.4 ounces) instant vanilla pudding mix**
- 1 **carton (12 ounces) frozen whipped topping, thawed, divided**
- 1 **graham cracker crust (9 inches)**
- 2 **medium firm bananas, sliced**
  Additional banana slices, optional

1. In a large bowl, whisk milk, vanilla and pudding mix for 2 minutes (mixture will be thick). Fold in 3 cups whipped topping.

2. Pour 1⅓ cups of pudding mixture into pie crust. Layer with banana slices and remaining pudding mixture. Top with remaining whipped topping. Garnish with additional banana slices if desired. Refrigerate until serving.

FAST FIX ▸ Spicy Cajun Salsa Burgers

I use a few on-hand seasonings like Creole, red pepper flakes and garlic powder to create these flavorful and juicy burgers.

—**DAVID DALTON** ORLEANS, IN

START TO FINISH: 20 MIN.
MAKES: 4 SERVINGS

- ½ cup salsa
- 1 teaspoon Creole seasoning
- ½ teaspoon garlic powder
- ½ teaspoon crushed red pepper flakes
- ½ teaspoon pepper
- 1 pound ground beef
- 4 kaiser rolls, split and toasted

1. In a large bowl, combine the first five ingredients. Add beef; mix lightly but thoroughly. Shape into four ½-in.-thick patties.

2. Grill the burgers, covered, over medium heat or broil 4 in. from heat 4-5 minutes on each side or until a thermometer reads 160°. Serve on the rolls.

NOTE *The following spices may be substituted for 1 teaspoon Creole seasoning: ¼ teaspoon each salt, garlic powder and paprika; and a pinch each of dried thyme, ground cumin and cayenne pepper.*

Salmon with Tangy Raspberry Sauce

FAST FIX ▸ Salmon with Tangy Raspberry Sauce

Salmon is a favorite at my house and I'm always finding new ways to make it. This one turned out so well! The raspberry sauce adds a nice sweetness.

—**ANNA-MARIE WILLIAMS**
LEAGUE CITY, TX

START TO FINISH: 25 MIN.
MAKES: 4 SERVINGS

- 1 teaspoon smoked paprika
- ¼ teaspoon salt
- ¼ teaspoon pepper
- 4 salmon fillets (6 ounces each)
- 2 tablespoons olive oil
- 2 tablespoons red raspberry preserves
- 1 tablespoon white vinegar
- 1 tablespoon honey

1. Combine the paprika, salt and pepper; sprinkle over salmon. Drizzle with oil. Moisten a paper towel with cooking oil; using long-handled tongs, rub on grill rack to coat lightly. Place salmon skin side down on grill rack.

2. Grill, covered, over medium heat or broil 4 in. from the heat for 10-12 minutes or until fish flakes easily with a fork. In a small bowl, whisk the preserves, vinegar and honey; spoon over fillets.

Spicy Cajun Salsa Burgers

French Onion Pizza au Gratin

French Onion Pizza au Gratin

I love a hot bowl of French onion soup and am also a big fan of pizza. I combined the two classics into this unforgettable meal!

—BONNIE LONG LAKEWOOD, OH

PREP: 30 MIN. • **BAKE:** 10 MIN.
MAKES: 8 SLICES

- 1 large onion, sliced
- 2 tablespoons brown sugar
- 2 tablespoons olive oil, divided
- 3 tablespoons balsamic vinegar
- 3 garlic cloves, minced
- 1 tablespoon bourbon, optional
- 1 cup sliced fresh mushrooms
- ¼ pound thickly sliced deli roast beef, coarsely chopped
- 1 prebaked 12-inch pizza crust
- ¾ cup French onion dip
- ¾ cup shredded part-skim mozzarella cheese
- 1 medium sweet red pepper, chopped
- ¾ cup shredded Gruyere or Swiss cheese
- 1 teaspoon minced fresh rosemary

1. In a skillet, saute onion with brown sugar in 1 tablespoon oil until softened. Reduce heat to medium-low; cook, stirring occasionally, for 30 minutes or until deep golden brown. Stir in vinegar and garlic. Remove from the heat; add bourbon if desired. Continue cooking until liquid is nearly evaporated.
2. In another skillet, saute mushrooms in remaining oil until tender; add roast beef and heat through.
3. Place crust on a pizza pan; spread with French onion dip. Layer with mozzarella cheese, onion mixture, red pepper, mushroom mixture and Gruyere cheese.
4. Bake at 425° for 10-15 minutes or until the cheese is melted. Sprinkle with rosemary.

FAST FIX ▸ Aunt Frances' Lemonade

My sister and I used to spend a week each summer with our Aunt Frances, who always had this thirst-quenching lemonade in a stoneware crock in the refrigerator. It makes a refreshing drink during a hot day.

—DEBBIE REINHART
NEW CUMBERLAND, PA

START TO FINISH: 15 MIN.
MAKES: 12-16 SERVINGS (1 GALLON)

- 5 **lemons**
- 5 **limes**
- 5 **oranges**
- 3 **quarts water**
- 1½ **to 2 cups sugar**

1. Squeeze the juice from four of the lemons, limes and oranges; pour into a gallon container.
2. Thinly slice remaining fruit and set aside for garnish. Add water and sugar; mix well. Store in the refrigerator. Serve over ice with fruit slices.

Sliced Tomato Salad

Aunt Frances' Lemonade

FAST FIX ▸ Sliced Tomato Salad

Grandmother gave me this salad idea, and it's the perfect platter to serve with burgers or hot sandwiches.

—KENDAL TANGEDAL
PLENTYWOOD, MT

START TO FINISH: 25 MIN.
MAKES: 12 SERVINGS

- 8 **large tomatoes, cut into ¼-inch slices**
- 2 **large sweet onions, halved and thinly sliced**
- ⅓ **cup olive oil**
- 2 **tablespoons lemon juice**
- 1 **teaspoon dried oregano**
- ¾ **teaspoon salt**
- ¼ **teaspoon pepper**
- 2 **tablespoons minced fresh parsley**

Arrange tomatoes and onions on a large rimmed serving platter. In a small bowl, whisk oil, lemon juice, oregano, salt and pepper. Drizzle over the top. Sprinkle with parsley.

Lemon Raspberry
Smoothies

Fruit Kabobs with
Margarita Dip

FAST FIX Lemon Raspberry Smoothies

Summers get pretty hot here in Arizona, so we're always looking for a cool treat to enjoy while hanging out around the pool. My love of raspberry lemonade inspired me to create this recipe.
—**LAURINDA NELSON** PHOENIX, AZ

START TO FINISH: 5 MIN.
MAKES: 4 SERVINGS

- 2 **cups frozen unsweetened raspberries**
- 2 **cups lemonade**
- 1 **cup raspberry yogurt**

Place half of the raspberries, lemonade and yogurt in a blender; cover and process until blended. Pour into chilled glasses; repeat with the remaining ingredients. Serve immediately.

FAST FIX Fruit Kabobs with Margarita Dip

Your adult guests will love the margarita flavor of this cool and creamy dip. Serve the kabobs either as a snack or a dessert.
—**MICHELLE ZAPF** KINGSLAND, GA

START TO FINISH: 25 MIN.
MAKES: 6 KABOBS (1½ CUPS DIP)

- 1 **package (3 ounces) cream cheese, softened**
- ½ **cup sour cream**
- ¼ **cup confectioners' sugar**
- 1 **tablespoon lime juice**
- 1 **tablespoon thawed orange juice concentrate**
- 1 **tablespoon tequila**
- ½ **cup heavy whipping cream**
- 12 **fresh strawberries**
- 6 **pineapple chunks**
- 1 **medium mango, peeled and cubed**
- 6 **seedless red grapes**
- 2 **slices pound cake, cubed**

In a large bowl, combine the first six ingredients. Beat in whipping cream until fluffy. Alternately, thread fruits and cake on metal or wooden skewers. Serve with dip.

Couscous Tuna Tower

These attractive tuna towers are sure to impress your guests. Better yet, the cost of ingredients is easy on the wallet!
—**JENNIFER HONEYCUTT**
NASHVILLE, TN

PREP: 25 MIN. • **COOK:** 10 MIN.
MAKES: 8 SERVINGS

- 1 **small onion, chopped**
- 1 **tablespoon canola oil**
- ⅔ **cup uncooked couscous**
- 1¼ **cups water**
- 2 **cans (6 ounces each) light water-packed tuna, drained and flaked**
- ⅓ **cup minced fresh parsley**
- 2 **tablespoons capers, drained**
- 2 **tablespoons sliced ripe olives, drained**
- 1 **tablespoon grated lemon peel**
- 1 **tablespoon lemon juice**
   Dash salt and pepper
- 1 **tablespoon red wine vinaigrette**
- 2 **cups torn curly endive**
- 8 **thick slices red tomatoes**
- 8 **thick slices yellow tomatoes**

1. In a small skillet, saute onion in oil until tender. Add couscous; saute 1-2 minutes longer or until couscous is lightly browned. Add water; bring to a boil. Reduce heat; cover and simmer for 8 minutes. Cool slightly.
2. In a large bowl, combine couscous mixture, tuna, parsley, capers, olives, lemon peel, lemon juice, salt and pepper; set aside.
3. Pour vinaigrette over endive; toss to coat. On each of eight serving plates, layer a red tomato slice, a yellow tomato slice, ½ cup couscous mixture and ¼ cup endive leaves.

Marinated Cucumber Pasta Salad

The sweet-and-sour dressing for this pasta salad makes a nice change of pace from more traditional varieties. My nursing supervisor shared the recipe with me...and I'm glad she did!
—**SUE DORRANCE** WEST BEND, WI

PREP: 20 MIN. + MARINATING
MAKES: 16 SERVINGS

- 1 **package (16 ounces) mostaccioli**
- 1 **medium cucumber, thinly sliced**
- 6 **green onions, chopped**

MARINADE
- 1 **cup sugar**
- 1 **cup white vinegar**
- ¼ **cup canola oil**
- 1 **jar (2 ounces) diced pimientos, drained**
- 1 **tablespoon minced fresh parsley**
- 2 **teaspoons Dijon mustard**
- 1 **teaspoon salt**
- 1 **teaspoon garlic powder**
- ½ **teaspoon pepper**

1. Cook mostaccioli according to the package directions; drain and rinse in cold water. In a large bowl, combine the mostaccioli, cucumber and onions.
2. In a jar with a tight-fitting lid, combine the marinade ingredients; shake well. Pour over pasta mixture; toss to coat. Cover and refrigerate overnight, stirring occasionally. Serve with a slotted spoon.

top tip Trimming Tip

Here's a simple idea for mincing fresh parsley. Place washed parsley in a small glass container and snip the sprigs with kitchen shears until minced.

Pasta with Mozzarella, Tomatoes and Fresh Basil

During the growing season, I like to prepare this pasta salad with garden-fresh tomatoes and basil.

—KEN CHURCHES KAILUA-KONA, HI

PREP: 20 MIN. + STANDING
COOK: 15 MIN. • **MAKES:** 6 SERVINGS

- 12 **ounces fresh mozzarella cheese, cubed**
- 6 **tablespoons olive oil**
- 4 **teaspoons minced garlic**
- 1 **teaspoon salt**
- 1 **teaspoon pepper**
- 1 **package (16 ounces) uncooked linguine**
- 1 **cup chopped fresh basil leaves**
- 3 **medium tomatoes, chopped**

1. In a large bowl, combine the cheese, oil, garlic, salt and pepper; let stand at room temperature for 1 hour.
2. Meanwhile, cook the linguine according to package directions; drain and rinse in cold water. Add to cheese mixture. Stir in basil and tomatoes. Serve at room temperature or chilled.

Apricot Chicken Drumsticks

Throughout the summer, you'll find my family gathered around the grill enjoying delicious entrees like this.

—MARY ANN SKLANKA BLAKELY, PA

PREP: 10 MIN. • **GRILL:** 15 MIN. + CHILLING
MAKES: 6 SERVINGS

- 12 **chicken drumsticks (3 pounds)**
- 1 **teaspoon salt**
- ¼ **teaspoon pepper**
- ¼ **cup canola oil**
- ¼ **cup apricot jam, warmed**
- ¼ **cup prepared mustard**
- 1 **tablespoon brown sugar**

1. Sprinkle chicken with salt and pepper. For sauce, in a small bowl, combine the remaining ingredients.

Apricot Chicken Drumsticks

2. Moisten a paper towel with cooking oil; using long-handled tongs, rub on grill rack to coat lightly. Grill chicken, covered, over medium heat for 15-20 minutes or until a thermometer reads 180°, turning and basting occasionally with sauce. Cool for 5 minutes.
3. Serve warm or chilled.

NOTE *To bake drumsticks, coat a foil-lined baking sheet with cooking spray. Arrange drumsticks in a single layer. Baste with sauce. Bake at 400° for 25 minutes or until a thermometer reads 180°. Serve warm or chilled.*

Strawberry-Mango Daiquiri Pops

When hosting a summer party for adults, offer them a grown-up frosty treat!

—TASTE OF HOME TEST KITCHEN

PREP: 20 MIN. + FREEZING
MAKES: 20 SERVINGS

- 1 **cup water**
- ½ **cup mango nectar**
- ¼ **cup light rum**
- 3 **tablespoons lime juice**
- 1 **pound halved fresh strawberries**
- 1 **cup coarsely chopped peeled mango**
- ⅓ **cup sugar**
- 20 **freezer pop molds or 3-ounce paper cups and wooden pop sticks**

Place half of the water, mango nectar, rum, lime juice, strawberries, mango and sugar in a blender; cover and process until blended. Fill 10 molds or cups with ¼ cup mixture each; top molds with holders. If using cups, top with foil and insert sticks through foil. Freeze until firm. Repeat with the remaining ingredients.

Caribbean Fruit Soup

This fruit soup is a delicious, refreshing way to begin a warm-weather meal. Jerk seasoning gives each spoonful a little kick.
—CHERYL PERRY HERTFORD, NC

PREP: 35 MIN. + CHILLING
MAKES: 12 SERVINGS (2 QUARTS)

- 1 cup each chopped peeled fresh peaches, nectarines, papaya and mango
- 1 cup chopped fresh pineapple
- 1 cup diced cantaloupe
- 1 cup chopped seeded peeled cucumber
- 1 cup chopped sweet red pepper
- ¼ cup thinly sliced green onions
- 2 cups frozen nonalcoholic pina colada mix, thawed
- 1 cup passion fruit or mango nectar
- ¼ cup minced fresh cilantro
- 2 tablespoons plus 2 teaspoons lime juice, divided
- 1 tablespoon sugar
- 1 tablespoon Caribbean jerk seasoning
- 1 teaspoon salt
- 1 teaspoon grated fresh gingerroot
- 1 teaspoon minced seeded jalapeno pepper
- 2 medium bananas, sliced
- 1 cup flaked coconut

1. In a bowl, mix peaches, nectarines, papaya, mango, pineapple, cantaloupe, cucumber, red pepper and onions. In a blender or food processor, place half the fruit mixture; cover and puree.

2. Transfer to a large bowl; stir in the remaining fruit mixture, pina colada mix, nectar, cilantro, 2 tablespoons lime juice, sugar, jerk seasoning, salt, ginger and jalapeno. Cover and refrigerate for 3 hours or until chilled.

3. Toss bananas with the remaining lime juice. Garnish soup with bananas and coconut.

Grilled Halibut with Salsa Verde

Roasting the vegetables for the salsa in these fish tacos intensifies the flavors and provides a wonderful smoky taste.
—MICHELLE ANDERSON EAGLE, ID

PREP: 40 MIN. + MARINATING
GRILL: 10 MIN. • **MAKES:** 8 SERVINGS

- 1 pound tomatillos, husks removed
- 1 small sweet onion, cut into ½-inch slices
- 4 garlic cloves, unpeeled
- ½ cup fresh cilantro leaves
- 1 serrano pepper, seeded
- 1 tablespoon lime juice
  Dash salt and pepper

TACOS
- ¼ cup lime juice
- ¼ cup olive oil
- 1 tablespoon salt
- 1 tablespoon garlic powder
- 1 tablespoon ground coriander
- 2 teaspoons ground cumin
- ½ teaspoon cayenne pepper
- 2 pounds halibut steaks
- 8 corn tortillas (6 inches)
- 2½ cups shredded cabbage

1. Moisten a paper towel with cooking oil; using long-handled tongs, rub on grill rack to lightly coat. For salsa, place the tomatillos, onion and garlic on a grilling grid; place on a grill rack. Grill, covered, over medium heat until tender and browned, turning frequently. Cool to room temperature.

2. Remove skin from garlic. Transfer grilled vegetables to a food processor. Add the cilantro, serrano pepper, lime juice, salt and pepper. Cover and pulse until chunky. Refrigerate until serving.

3. In a large resealable plastic bag, combine the lime juice, oil, salt, garlic powder, coriander, cumin and cayenne; add halibut. Seal bag and turn to coat; refrigerate for up to 1 hour.

4. Drain and discard marinade from fish. Grill the halibut, covered, over medium heat for 4-6 minutes on each side or until fish flakes easily with a fork. Flake fish into 1½-in. pieces; cool to room temperature.

5. To serve, top tortillas with fish, cabbage and salsa.

NOTE *If you do not have a grilling grid, use a disposable foil pan. Poke holes in the bottom of the pan with a meat fork to allow liquid to drain. Wear disposable gloves when cutting hot peppers; the oils can burn skin. Avoid touching your face.*

Grilled Halibut with Salsa Verde

Chili-Rubbed Steak & Bread Salad

We love skirt steak at our house. To make it a meal, I created a ranch-inspired bread salad with the best flavor combinations—creamy, tangy, sweet and fresh.

—DEVON DELANEY WESTPORT, CT

PREP: 35 MIN. + STANDING
GRILL: 15 MIN. • **MAKES:** 6 SERVINGS

- 2 **teaspoons chili powder**
- 2 **teaspoons brown sugar**
- ½ **teaspoon salt**
- ½ **teaspoon pepper**
- 1 **beef top sirloin steak (1 inch thick and 1¼ pounds)**
- 2 **cups cubed multigrain bread**
- 2 **tablespoons olive oil**
- 1 **cup ranch salad dressing**
- 2 **tablespoons finely grated horseradish**
- 1 **tablespoon prepared mustard**
- 3 **large tomatoes, cut into 1-inch pieces**
- 1 **medium cucumber, cut into 1-inch pieces**
- 1 **small red onion, halved and thinly sliced**

1. Mix chili powder, brown sugar, salt and pepper; rub over steak. Let stand 15 minutes.

2. Meanwhile, toss bread cubes with oil. In a large skillet, toast bread over medium heat 8-10 minutes or until crisp and lightly browned, stirring frequently. In a small bowl, whisk salad dressing, horseradish and mustard.

3. Grill steak, covered, over medium heat or broil 4 in. from heat 6-8 minutes on each side or until meat reaches desired doneness (for medium-rare, a thermometer should read 145°; medium, 160°; well-done, 170°). Let stand 5 minutes.

4. In a large bowl, combine tomatoes, cucumber, onion and toasted bread. Add ½ cup dressing mixture; toss to coat. Slice steak; serve with salad and remaining dressing.

Chili-Rubbed Steak & Bread Salad

Poolside Lemon Bars

The recipe for these tangy lemon bars comes from my cousin Bernice, a farmer's wife famous for cooking up feasts.

—MILDRED KELLER ROCKFORD, IL

PREP: 10 MIN. • **BAKE:** 40 MIN. + COOLING
MAKES: 4 DOZEN

- ¾ **cup butter, softened**
- ⅔ **cup confectioners' sugar**
- 1½ **cups plus 3 tablespoons all-purpose flour, divided**
- 3 **eggs, lightly beaten**
- 1½ **cups sugar**
- ¼ **cup lemon juice**
  Additional confectioners' sugar

1. Preheat oven to 350°. In a large bowl, beat butter and confectioners' sugar until blended. Gradually beat in 1½ cups flour. Press onto bottom of a greased 13x9-in. baking pan. Bake 18-20 minutes or until golden brown.

2. Meanwhile, in a small bowl, whisk eggs, sugar, lemon juice and remaining flour until frothy; pour over hot crust.

3. Bake 20-25 minutes longer or until topping is set and lightly browned. Cool completely on a wire rack. Dust with additional confectioners' sugar. Cut into bars. Refrigerate leftovers.

Poolside Lemon Bars

Dreamy S'more Pie

Desserts are my specialty, and I was looking for a way to use hazelnut spread when I came up with this recipe. I wanted something that could be prepped quickly. The results were simply wonderful!

—**KAREN BOWLDEN** BOISE, ID

PREP: 10 MIN. + CHILLING • **BROIL:** 5 MIN.
MAKES: 8 SERVINGS

- 1 package (8 ounces) cream cheese, softened
- 1¼ cups heavy whipping cream
- 1 jar (13 ounces) Nutella
- 1 graham cracker crust (9 inches)
- 3 cups miniature marshmallows

1. In a large bowl, beat cream cheese and cream until thickened. Add the Nutella; beat just until combined. Spoon into crust. Cover and refrigerate for at least 3 hours.
2. Just before serving, top with the marshmallows; press gently into filling. Broil 6 in. from the heat for 1-2 minutes or until marshmallows are golden brown.

Raspberry Sorbet

I rely on this dessert to help use up the abundant crop of fresh raspberries from my backyard. It makes a tasty, no-fuss frozen treat.

—**KAREN BAILEY** GOLDEN, CO

PREP: 5 MIN. + FREEZING
MAKES: 6 SERVINGS

- ¼ cup plus 1½ teaspoons fresh lemon juice
- 3¾ cups fresh or frozen unsweetened raspberries
- 2¼ cups confectioners' sugar

In a blender or food processor, combine all ingredients; cover and process until smooth. Transfer to a freezer container; freeze until firm.

Barbecued Chicken Pizzas

So fast and so easy with refrigerated pizza crust, this entree will bring raves with its hot-off-the-grill, rustic flavor. Perfect for a spur-of-the-moment barbecue!

—**ALICIA TREVITHICK** TEMECULA, CA

PREP: 25 MIN. • **GRILL:** 10 MIN.
MAKES: 2 PIZZAS (4 PIECES EACH)

- 2 boneless skinless chicken breast halves (6 ounces each)
- ¼ teaspoon salt
- ¼ teaspoon pepper
- 1 cup barbecue sauce, divided
- 1 tube (13.8 ounces) refrigerated pizza crust
- 2 teaspoons olive oil
- 1 medium red onion, thinly sliced
- 2 cups (8 ounces) shredded Gouda cheese
- ¼ cup minced fresh cilantro

1. Sprinkle chicken with salt and pepper. Moisten a paper towel with cooking oil; using long-handled tongs, rub on grill rack to coat lightly. Grill, covered, over medium heat or broil 4 in. from the heat for 5-7 minutes on each side or until a thermometer reads 165°, basting frequently with ½ cup barbecue sauce. Set aside; keep warm.
2. Divide dough in half. On a lightly floured surface, roll each portion into a 12-in. x 10-in. rectangle. Lightly brush both sides of dough with oil; place on grill. Cover and grill over medium heat for 1-2 minutes or until the bottom is lightly browned.
3. Remove from grill. Cut the chicken into ½-in. cubes. Spread the grilled side of each pizza with ¼ cup barbecue sauce; layer with chicken, onion, cheese and cilantro. Return to grill. Cover and cook each pizza for 4-5 minutes or until the bottom is lightly browned and cheese is melted.

Barbecued Chicken Pizzas

BY THE POOL!

Grilled Cheese & Tomato Flatbreads

Grilled Cheese & Tomato Flatbreads

This is a combination of grilled pizza and a cheesy flatbread recipe I discovered years ago. It's a great appetizer or main dish.

—TINA REPAK MIRILOVICH
JOHNSTOWN, PA

PREP: 30 MIN. • **GRILL:** 5 MIN.
MAKES: 2 FLATBREADS
(12 SERVINGS EACH)

- 1 package (8 ounces) cream cheese, softened
- ⅔ cup grated Parmesan cheese, divided
- 2 tablespoons minced fresh parsley, divided
- 1 tablespoon minced chives
- 2 garlic cloves, minced
- ½ teaspoon minced fresh thyme
- ¼ teaspoon salt
- ¼ teaspoon pepper
- 1 tube (13.8 ounces) refrigerated pizza crust
- 2 tablespoons olive oil
- 3 medium tomatoes, thinly sliced

1. In a small bowl, beat the cream cheese, ⅓ cup Parmesan cheese, 1 tablespoon parsley, chives, garlic, thyme, salt and pepper until blended.
2. Unroll pizza crust and cut in half. On a lightly floured surface, roll out each portion into a 12-in. x 6-in. rectangle; brush each side with oil. Grill, covered, over medium heat for 1-2 minutes or until bottoms are lightly browned. Remove from the grill.
3. Spread grilled sides with cheese mixture. Sprinkle with remaining Parmesan cheese; top with tomatoes. Return to the grill. Cover and cook for 2-3 minutes or until crust is lightly browned and cheese is melted, rotating halfway through cooking to ensure an evenly browned crust. Sprinkle with remaining parsley.

Mint Watermelon Salad

I invented this refreshing fruit salad one sultry afternoon while my friends were gathered around my pool. It was quick to prepare, and the colorful salad disappeared from their plates even quicker. Even the kids ate it up!
—ANTOINETTE DUBECK
HUNTINGDON VALLEY, PA

START TO FINISH: 20 MIN.
MAKES: 8 SERVINGS

- 1 **tablespoon lemon juice**
- 1 **tablespoon olive oil**
- 2 **teaspoons sugar**
- 6 **cups cubed seedless watermelon**
- 2 **tablespoons minced fresh mint**
  Lemon wedges, optional

In a small bowl, whisk the lemon juice, oil and sugar. In a large bowl, combine watermelon and mint. Drizzle with lemon juice mixture; toss to coat. Serve with lemon wedges if desired.

Mushroom-Stuffed Cheeseburgers

No need to call my family twice when these burgers are on the menu. For added convenience, stuff the patties ahead of time, then grill them later.
—JOYCE GUTH MOHNTON, PA

PREP: 30 MIN. • **GRILL:** 10 MIN.
MAKES: 8 SERVINGS

- 2 **bacon strips, finely chopped**
- 2 **cups chopped fresh mushrooms**
- ¼ **cup chopped onion**
- ¼ **cup chopped sweet red pepper**
- ¼ **cup chopped green pepper**
- 2 **pounds lean ground beef (90% lean)**
- 2 **tablespoons steak sauce**
- ½ **teaspoon seasoned salt**
- 4 **slices provolone cheese, halved**
- 8 **kaiser rolls, split**

1. In a large skillet, cook bacon over medium heat until crisp, stirring occasionally. Remove with a slotted spoon; drain on paper towels. Cook and stir the mushrooms, onion and peppers in bacon drippings until vegetables are tender. Using a slotted spoon, remove to a small bowl; cool completely. Stir in bacon.
2. In a large bowl, combine beef, steak sauce and seasoned salt, mixing lightly but thoroughly. Shape into 16 thin patties. Top eight of the patties with cheese, folding over cheese to fit within ¾ inch of edge. Spread with the mushroom mixture. Top with the remaining patties, pressing edges to enclose filling.
3. Grill burgers, uncovered, over medium-high heat or broil 4 in. from heat 5-6 minutes on each side or until a thermometer inserted in meat portion reads 160°. Serve on rolls.

Mushroom-Stuffed Cheeseburgers

BY THE POOL!

Mini Burgers with
the Works

Guacamole
Appetizer
Squares

FAST FIX ▶ Mini Burgers with the Works

I started making these mini burgers several years ago as a way to use up bread crusts. Their tiny size makes them irresistible!

—**LINDA LANE** BENNINGTON, VT

START TO FINISH: 30 MIN.
MAKES: 1 DOZEN

- ¼ **pound ground beef**
- 3 **slices process American cheese**
- 4 **slices white bread (heels of loaf recommended)**
- 2 **tablespoons prepared Thousand Island salad dressing**
- 2 **pearl onions, thinly sliced**
- 4 **baby dill pickles, thinly sliced**
- 3 **cherry tomatoes, thinly sliced**

1. Shape beef into twelve 1-in. patties. Place on a microwave-safe plate lined with paper towels. Cover with another paper towel; microwave on high for 1 minute until meat is no longer pink. Cut each slice of cheese into fourths.
2. Using a 1-in. round cookie cutter, cut out six circles from each slice of bread. Spread half of the bread circles with dressing. Layer with burgers, cheese, onions, pickles and tomatoes. Top with remaining bread circles; secure with toothpicks.
NOTE *This recipe was tested in a 1,100-watt microwave.*

Guacamole Appetizer Squares

My cold appetizer pizza is a tradition at family functions. I know you'll love it, too.
—**LAURIE PESTER** COLSTRIP, MT

PREP: 20 MIN. • **BAKE:** 10 MIN. + COOLING
MAKES: ABOUT 3 DOZEN

- 2 **tubes (8 ounces each) refrigerated crescent rolls**
- 1½ **teaspoons taco seasoning**
- 1 **package (1 pound) sliced bacon, diced**
- 1 **package (8 ounces) cream cheese, softened**
- 1½ **cups guacamole**
- 3 **plum tomatoes, chopped**
- 1 **can (3.8 ounces) sliced ripe olives, drained**

1. Unroll both tubes of crescent dough and pat into an ungreased 15-in. x 10-in. x 1-in. baking pan; seal seams and perforations. Build up edges. Prick dough with a fork; sprinkle with taco seasoning. Bake at 375° for 10-12 minutes or until golden brown. Cool completely on a wire rack.
2. In a skillet, cook bacon over medium heat until crisp. Using a slotted spoon, remove to paper towels. In a bowl, beat cream cheese and guacamole until smooth. Spread cream cheese mixture over crust. Sprinkle with bacon, tomatoes and olives. Refrigerate until serving. Cut into squares.

Watermelon Slice Cookies

When I made these butter cookies for an event, a neighbor thought they were so attractive, she froze one to show friends!
—**SUE ANN BENHAM** VALPARAISO, IN

PREP: 25 MIN. + CHILLING
BAKE: 10 MIN./BATCH
MAKES: ABOUT 3 DOZEN

- ¾ **cup butter, softened**
- ¾ **cup sugar**
- 1 **egg**
- ½ **teaspoon almond extract**
- 2 **cups all-purpose flour**
- ¼ **teaspoon baking powder**
- ⅛ **teaspoon salt**
  Red and green gel food coloring
- ⅓ **cup miniature semisweet chocolate chips or raisins, chopped**
- 1 **teaspoon sesame seeds, optional**

1. In a large bowl, cream butter and sugar until light and fluffy. Beat in egg and extract. In another bowl, whisk the flour, baking powder and salt; gradually beat into creamed mixture. Reserve 1 cup dough.
2. Tint remaining dough red; shape into a 3½-in.-long roll. Wrap in plastic wrap. Tint ⅓ cup of reserved dough green; wrap in plastic wrap. Wrap remaining plain dough. Refrigerate 2 hours or until firm.
3. On a lightly floured surface, roll plain dough into an 8½x3½-in. rectangle. Unwrap red dough and place on a short end of the plain dough; roll up.
4. Roll green dough into a 10x3½-in. rectangle. Place red and plain roll on a short end of the green dough; roll up. Wrap in plastic wrap; refrigerate overnight.
5. Preheat oven to 350°. Unwrap and cut dough into ³⁄₁₆-in. slices (just less than ¼ in.). Place 2 in. apart on ungreased baking sheets. If desired, lightly press chocolate chips into red dough to resemble watermelon seeds.
6. Bake 9-11 minutes or until firm. Immediately cut cookies in half. Remove to wire racks to cool.

Watermelon Slice Cookies

BY THE POOL!

FAST FIX ▶ Fruit Salsa with Cinnamon Chips

I made this fresh, fruity salsa for a family get-together. Now, someone makes this juicy snack for just about every gathering!

—JESSICA ROBINSON INDIAN TRAIL, NC

START TO FINISH: 30 MIN.
MAKES: 2½ CUPS SALSA (80 CHIPS)

- 1 cup finely chopped fresh strawberries
- 1 medium navel orange, peeled and finely chopped
- 3 medium kiwifruit, peeled and finely chopped
- 1 can (8 ounces) unsweetened crushed pineapple, drained
- 1 tablespoon lemon juice
- 1½ teaspoons sugar

CINNAMON CHIPS

- 10 flour tortillas (8 inches)
- ¼ cup butter, melted
- ⅓ cup sugar
- 1 teaspoon ground cinnamon

1. In a small bowl, combine the first six ingredients. Cover and refrigerate until serving.
2. For chips, brush tortillas with butter; cut each into eight wedges. Combine sugar and cinnamon; sprinkle over tortillas. Place on ungreased baking sheets.
3. Bake at 350° for 5-10 minutes or just until crisp. Serve with fruit salsa.

Fruit Salsa with Cinnamon Chips

Refreshing Grilled Chicken Salad

Refreshing Grilled Chicken Salad

Combining my favorite power foods— blueberries, walnuts and olive oil—into this light and zippy salad, I created the perfect dish for luncheon with friends.

—DENISE RASMUSSEN SALINA, KS

PREP: 20 MIN. + MARINATING
GRILL: 10 MIN. • **MAKES:** 4 SERVINGS

- ½ cup lime juice
- 2 tablespoons honey
- 4 teaspoons olive oil
- ½ teaspoon salt
- ½ teaspoon pepper
- 4 boneless skinless chicken breast halves (4 ounces each)
- 6 cups spring mix salad greens
- 2 cups cubed seedless watermelon
- 1 cup fresh blueberries
- 1 medium sweet yellow pepper, cut into 1-inch pieces
- ⅓ cup chopped walnuts, toasted

1. In a small bowl, combine the lime juice, honey, oil, salt and pepper. Pour ⅓ cup into a large resealable plastic bag; add chicken. Seal bag and turn to coat; refrigerate for at least 1 hour. Cover and refrigerate remaining lime juice mixture for dressing.
2. Drain and discard marinade. Using long-handled tongs, moisten a paper towel with cooking oil and lightly coat the grill rack. Grill chicken, covered, over medium heat or broil 4 in. from the heat for 4-7 minutes on each side or until a thermometer reads 170°.
3. In a large bowl, combine the salad greens, watermelon, blueberries and yellow pepper; add reserved dressing and toss to coat. Divide among four serving plates. Slice chicken; serve with salads. Sprinkle each serving with 4 teaspoons of walnuts.

FAST FIX Halibut Soft Tacos

Here's a warm-weather favorite that's quick, colorful and full of nutrients. I sometimes serve the fish wrapped in lettuce instead of tortillas. The mango salsa is great served alongside.

—**KRISTIN KOSSAK** BOZEMAN, MT

START TO FINISH: 25 MIN.
MAKES: 4 SERVINGS

- 1 medium mango, peeled and cubed
- ½ cup cubed avocado
- ¼ cup chopped red onion
- 2 tablespoons chopped seeded jalapeno pepper
- 1 tablespoon minced fresh cilantro
- 3 teaspoons olive oil, divided
- 1 teaspoon lemon juice
- 1 teaspoon honey
- 1 pound halibut steaks (¾ inch thick)
- ½ teaspoon salt
- ¼ teaspoon pepper
- 4 Bibb lettuce leaves
- 4 flour tortillas (6 inches), warmed
- 4 teaspoons sweet Thai chili sauce

1. In a small bowl, combine mango, avocado, onion, jalapeno, cilantro, 2 teaspoons oil, lemon juice and honey; set aside. Brush halibut with remaining oil; sprinkle with salt and pepper.

2. Moisten a paper towel with cooking oil; using long-handled tongs, rub on grill rack to coat lightly. Grill halibut, covered, over high heat or broil 3-4 in. from the heat for 3-5 minutes on each side or until fish flakes easily with a fork.

3. Place lettuce leaves on tortillas; top with fish and mango mixture. Drizzle with chili sauce.

NOTE *Wear disposable gloves when cutting hot peppers; the oils can burn skin. Avoid touching your face.*

Halibut Soft Tacos

Asian Quinoa

I love to cook and come up with new recipes. I serve this dish at least once a month and sometimes more. For a different twist, I'll occasionally add a scrambled egg or use soy sauce instead of the rice vinegar.

—**SONYA LABBE** WEST HOLLYWOOD, CA

PREP: 20 MIN.
COOK: 20 MIN. + STANDING
MAKES: 4 SERVINGS

- 1 cup water
- 2 tablespoons rice vinegar
- 2 tablespoons plum sauce
- 2 garlic cloves, minced
- 1 teaspoon minced fresh gingerroot
- 1 teaspoon sesame oil
- ¼ teaspoon salt
- ¼ teaspoon crushed red pepper flakes
- ½ cup quinoa, rinsed
- 1 medium sweet red pepper, chopped
- ½ cup sliced water chestnuts, chopped
- ½ cup fresh sugar snap peas, trimmed and halved
- 2 green onions, thinly sliced

1. In a large saucepan, combine the first eight ingredients; bring to a boil. Add quinoa. Reduce heat; cover and simmer for 12-15 minutes or until water is absorbed.

2. Remove from the heat. Add the red pepper, water chestnuts, peas and onions; fluff with a fork. Cover and let stand for 10 minutes.

NOTE *Look for quinoa in the cereal, rice or organic food aisle.*

Chilled Mixed Berry Soup

For a lovely addition to a poolside menu, try this cool, fruity soup. It features three kinds of berries.
—TASTE OF HOME TEST KITCHEN

PREP: 45 MIN. + CHILLING
MAKES: 4 SERVINGS

- 1 cup sliced fresh strawberries
- ½ cup fresh raspberries
- ½ cup fresh blackberries
- 1 cup unsweetened apple juice
- ½ cup water
- ¼ cup sugar
- 2 tablespoons lemon juice
  Dash ground nutmeg
- 1½ cups (12 ounces) raspberry yogurt

1. In a heavy saucepan, combine the berries, apple juice, water, sugar, lemon juice and nutmeg. Cook, uncovered, over low heat for 20 minutes or until berries are softened. Strain, reserving juice. Press berry mixture through a fine meshed sieve; discard seeds. Add the pulp to reserved juice; cover and refrigerate until chilled.
2. Place the berry mixture in a food processor or blender; add the yogurt. Cover and process until smooth. Pour into bowls.

Vegetable Beef Kabobs

Vegetable Beef Kabobs

I like to grill outdoors, and this dish makes good use of our delicious Kansas beef.
—MYNIE LOU GRIFFITH
HUTCHINSON, KS

PREP: 10 MIN. + MARINATING
GRILL: 15 MIN. • **MAKES:** 6 SERVINGS

- 1½ pounds beef top sirloin steak
- ⅔ cup white wine or beef broth
- ⅓ cup soy sauce
- 2 tablespoons canola oil
- 1 teaspoon minced fresh gingerroot or ¼ teaspoon ground ginger
- 1 garlic clove, minced
- ½ teaspoon dried tarragon
- 18 small whole onions
- 3 to 4 small zucchini, cut in 1-inch slices
- 2 large sweet red peppers, cut in 1-inch pieces

1. Cut beef in 1¼-in. cubes; place in large resealable plastic bag. In a 2-cup measuring cup, combine the wine, soy sauce, oil, ginger, garlic and tarragon; pour ⅔ cup marinade over beef. Seal bag; let stand at room temperature for 30 minutes. Set aside remaining marinade for basting.
2. Drain and discard marinade from beef. Thread meat, onions, zucchini and peppers alternately on six metal or soaked wooden skewers.
3. Grill over medium-hot heat for 10-12 minutes or until meat reaches desired doneness, turning and basting occasionally with reserved marinade.

Watermelon Shark

Take a bite out of summer boredom with this kid-friendly food project!
—**TASTE OF HOME TEST KITCHEN**

PREP: 1 HOUR • **MAKES:** 32 SERVINGS

- 1 **large watermelon**
- 2 **cups seedless red grapes**
- 1 **medium cantaloupe, peeled, seeded and cubed**
- 2 **cups fresh blueberries**
- 2 **medium oranges**
- 1 **jar (12 ounces) pineapple preserves**

1. Using a large sharp knife, cut off one end of watermelon so that watermelon stands at an angle. Using a razor blade or small knife, score an opening for the mouth. With knife, cut out and remove mouth. Cut out triangles for teeth; remove rind from teeth.

2. For shark fin, cut a triangle from removed rind; attach to shark with toothpicks. For eyes, attach two grapes with toothpicks.

3. Remove the fruit from inside the watermelon; cut into cubes. In a large bowl, combine the watermelon, cantaloupe, blueberries and remaining grapes. Finely grate peel from oranges and squeeze juice. In a small bowl, mix preserves, orange juice and peel; add to fruit and toss gently.

4. Stand shark on a platter. Fill the opening with some of the fruit mixture; add a few Swedish Fish if desired. Serve with remaining fruit.

Watermelon Shark

FAST FIX Spinach Penne Toss

Spinach provides a delicious base for all the wonderful flavor combinations found in this hearty salad.
—**KIERSTE WADE** MIDLAND, MI

START TO FINISH: 25 MIN.
MAKES: 10 SERVINGS

- 2 **cups uncooked penne pasta**
- 1 **medium sweet red pepper, julienned**
- 1 **medium onion, sliced**
- 1 **tablespoon plus ¼ cup olive oil, divided**
- 1 **package (6 ounces) fresh baby spinach**
- ¾ **cup crumbled cooked bacon**
- ½ **cup crumbled feta cheese**
- ½ **cup oil-packed sun-dried tomatoes, chopped**
- 2 **tablespoons cider vinegar**
- ¼ **teaspoon pepper**
- ⅛ **teaspoon salt**

1. Cook pasta according to the package directions. Meanwhile, in a skillet, saute red pepper and onion in 1 tablespoon oil for 3-4 minutes or until tender.

2. Drain the pasta and place in a serving bowl. Add the red pepper mixture, spinach, bacon, feta cheese and the tomatoes.

3. In a small bowl, whisk the vinegar, pepper, salt and remaining oil. Drizzle over pasta mixture; toss to coat.

BY THE POOL!

**Sugar Cookie
Fruit Pizzas**

Macadamia Key Lime Pie

I make my Key lime pie at least four times a month during summer, it's so refreshing. The shortbread crust adds richness.
—**BRYNN LEMAIRE** GUEYDAN, LA

PREP: 20 MIN. + CHILLING
MAKES: 8 SERVINGS

- 1 **cup crushed shortbread cookies**
- ½ **cup finely chopped macadamia nuts**
- ¼ **cup sugar**
- ⅓ **cup butter, melted**

FILLING
- 1 **package (8 ounces) cream cheese, softened**
- 1 **can (14 ounces) sweetened condensed milk**
- ½ **cup Key lime juice or lime juice**
- 1 **cup heavy whipping cream**
- ¼ **cup coarsely chopped macadamia nuts**

1. In a small bowl, mix cookie crumbs, macadamia nuts and sugar; stir in the butter. Press onto bottom and up sides of a greased 9-in. pie plate. Refrigerate 30 minutes.
2. In a large bowl, beat cream cheese until smooth. Beat in milk and lime juice until blended. Transfer to crust. Refrigerate, covered, at least 4 hours.
3. In a small bowl, beat cream until soft peaks form; spoon or pipe onto pie. Top with macadamia nuts.

Macadamia Key Lime Pie

Sugar Cookie Fruit Pizzas

Purchased sugar cookies create a sweet "crust" for these colorful pizzas. Make them throughout the year using a variety of fresh and canned fruits.
—**MARGE HODEL** ROANOKE, IL

PREP: 45 MIN. + CHILLING
MAKES: 1 DOZEN

- ½ **cup sugar**
- 1 **tablespoon cornstarch**
- ½ **cup unsweetened pineapple juice**
- ¼ **cup water**
- 2 **tablespoons lemon juice**
- 4 **ounces cream cheese, softened**
- ¼ **cup confectioners' sugar**
- 1¾ **cups whipped topping**
- 12 **sugar cookies (3 inches)**
- 1 **cup fresh blueberries**
- 1 **cup chopped peeled kiwifruit**
- ½ **cup chopped fresh strawberries**

1. For glaze, in a small saucepan, combine the sugar, cornstarch, pineapple juice, water and lemon juice until smooth. Bring to a boil; cook and stir for 2 minutes or until thickened. Transfer to a small bowl; refrigerate until cooled but not set.
2. In a small bowl, beat cream cheese and confectioners' sugar until smooth; fold in whipped topping. Spread over tops of cookies. Arrange fruit on top; drizzle with glaze. Refrigerate for 1 hour or until chilled.

Cookie Dough Cupcakes with Ganache Frosting

Rich chocolaty frosting adds extra flavor to this unbeatable dessert.

—MORGAN PHILLIPS
CHARLOTTESVILLE, VA

PREP: 25 MIN. + CHILLING • **BAKE:** 20 MIN.
MAKES: 2 DOZEN

- 1 package yellow cake mix (regular size)
- 1 cup milk
- 3 eggs
- ½ cup butter, melted
- 1 teaspoon vanilla extract
- 1 tube (16½ ounces) refrigerated chocolate chip cookie dough

FROSTING

- 2 cups (12 ounces) semisweet chocolate chips
- 1 cup heavy whipping cream
- ½ cup miniature semisweet chocolate chips

Creamy
Watermelon
Pie

1. In a large bowl, combine the cake mix, milk, eggs, butter and vanilla; beat on low speed for 30 seconds. Beat on medium for 2 minutes.
2. Fill paper-lined muffin cups one-third full. Roll tablespoonfuls of cookie dough into balls. Drop into center of each cupcake. Top with remaining batter.
3. Bake at 350° for 15-20 minutes or until a toothpick comes out clean. Cool for 10 minutes before removing from pans to wire racks to cool completely.
4. For frosting, in a saucepan, melt chocolate chips with cream over low heat; stir until blended. Transfer to a bowl. Cover and chill for 45-60 minutes or until mixture reaches spreading consistency; stir every 15 minutes.
5. Cut a small hole in the corner of pastry or plastic bag; insert #20 star pastry tip. Fill bag with chocolate mixture; pipe onto cupcakes. Sprinkle with miniature chocolate chips.

FAST FIX ▶ Lemon Mint Spritzer

Mint adds a delightful touch to this citrusy spritzer! It's wonderful for sipping at a grilling party or while lounging by the pool.

—LAURA NIX ELLIJAY, GA

START TO FINISH: 10 MIN.
MAKES: 12 SERVINGS (1 CUP EACH)

- 2 medium lemons
- 2 cans (12 ounces each) frozen lemonade concentrate, thawed
- ¼ cup confectioners' sugar
- ¼ cup fresh mint leaves, chopped
- 2 bottles (1 liter each) carbonated water, chilled
  Ice cubes

1. Cut lemons into wedges and squeeze the juice into a large pitcher. Stir in the lemonade concentrate, confectioners' sugar and mint; add lemon wedges. Chill until serving.
2. Just before serving, stir in carbonated water. Serve over ice.

Creamy Watermelon Pie

Here's a pie that's so refreshing, it never lasts long on warm summer days. Watermelon and a few convenience items add up to a change-of-pace dessert that couldn't be easier!

—VELMA BECK CARLINVILLE, IL

PREP: 15 MIN. + CHILLING
MAKES: 6-8 SERVINGS

- 1 package (3 ounces) watermelon gelatin
- ¼ cup boiling water
- 1 carton (12 ounces) frozen whipped topping, thawed
- 2 cups cubed seeded watermelon
- 1 graham cracker crust (9 inches)

In a large bowl, dissolve the gelatin in boiling water. Cool to room temperature. Whisk in the whipped topping; fold in watermelon. Spoon into crust. Refrigerate for 2 hours or until set.

Lemon-Berry Ice Cream Pie

½ teaspoon Worcestershire sauce
½ teaspoon prepared horseradish
¼ teaspoon garlic powder
¼ teaspoon pepper
   Ice cubes

In a small pitcher, mix together the first 12 ingredients; serve over ice.

Patriotic Pops

My kids love homemade ice pops, and I love knowing that they're enjoying frozen treats that are good for them. We whip up a big batch with multiple flavors so they have many choices, but these are always a surefire hit!
—**SHANNON CARINO** FRISCO, TX

PREP: 15 MIN. + FREEZING
MAKES: 1 DOZEN

1¼ cups sliced fresh strawberries, divided
1¾ cups (14 ounces) vanilla yogurt, divided
1¼ cups fresh or frozen blueberries, divided
12 freezer pop molds or 12 paper cups (3 ounces each) and wooden pop sticks

1. In a blender, combine 1 cup of the strawberries and 2 tablespoons yogurt; cover and process until blended. Transfer to a small bowl. Chop the remaining strawberries; stir into strawberry mixture.
2. In same blender, combine 1 cup of the blueberries and 2 tablespoons yogurt; cover and process until blended. Stir in remaining blueberries.
3. Layer 1 tablespoon strawberry mixture, 2 tablespoons yogurt and 1 tablespoon blueberry mixture in each of 12 molds or paper cups. Top molds with holders. If using cups, top with foil and insert sticks through foil. Freeze until firm.

Lemon-Berry Ice Cream Pie

Refreshing and cool, this make-ahead dessert is perfect for summer parties.
—**ROXANNE CHAN** ALBANY, CA

PREP: 15 MIN. + FREEZING
MAKES: 8 SERVINGS

1 pint strawberry ice cream, softened
1 graham cracker crust (9 inches)
1 cup lemon curd
2 cups frozen whipped topping, thawed
1 pint fresh strawberries, halved

1. Spoon ice cream into pie crust; freeze 2 hours or until firm.
2. Spread lemon curd over ice cream; top with whipped topping. Freeze, covered, 4 hours or until firm.

3. Remove from freezer 10 minutes before serving. Top with strawberries.

FAST FIX ▶ Firecracker Mary

While cleaning out my fridge, a lot of the ingredients for a Bloody Mary just jumped out at me. I couldn't resist combining them into this spicy Mary.
—**JIMMY CABABA** WEST ALLIS, WI

START TO FINISH: 10 MIN.
MAKES: 2 SERVINGS

1½ cups tomato juice
2 ounces vodka
3 tablespoons beef broth
2 teaspoons dill pickle juice
2 teaspoons stone-ground mustard
1 teaspoon lemon juice
1 teaspoon lime juice
½ teaspoon hot pepper sauce

FAST FIX Grilled Sirloin Kabobs with Peach Salsa

Peaches, peach preserves and peach salsa star in these beef kabobs that deliver a classic combo of spicy and sweet flavors.

—BETH ROYALS RICHMOND, VA

START TO FINISH: 25 MIN.
MAKES: 6 SERVINGS

- 3 tablespoons peach preserves
- 1 tablespoon finely chopped seeded jalapeno pepper
- 1 beef top sirloin steak (1½ pounds), cut into 1-inch cubes
- ½ teaspoon salt
- ¼ teaspoon pepper
- 3 medium peaches, cut into sixths
- 1½ cups peach salsa

1. In a small bowl, mix preserves and jalapeno. Season beef with salt and pepper. Alternately thread beef and peaches onto six metal or soaked wooden skewers.

2. Moisten a paper towel with cooking oil; using long-handled tongs, rub on grill rack to coat lightly. Grill kabobs, covered, over medium heat or broil 4 in. from heat for 6-8 minutes or until the beef reaches desired doneness, turning occasionally. Remove from grill; brush with the preserves mixture. Serve with the salsa.

NOTE *Wear disposable gloves when cutting hot peppers; the oils can burn skin. Avoid touching your face.*

**Grilled Sirloin
Kabobs with
Peach Salsa**

Grilled Clam Bake, page 87; Cheddar Drop
Biscuits, page 87; New England Iced Tea, page 87

**Mango Shrimp
Pitas, page 95**

IT'S TIME TO BARBECUE...

AT THE
Beach!

Seafood is a must when **celebrating seaside!** Whether at the beach or grilling up a few coastal favorites at home, turn here for **shrimp and fish staples** as well as clam bakes, oysters and other sensations that bring the beach to your table.

FAST FIX ▶ Turkey Burgers with Mango Salsa

This is the cookout recipe that will have everyone talking. The secret is mixing a creamy, spreadable cheese into the turkey patties. It gives them a rich taste without overpowering the burger.

—**NANCEE MELIN** TUCSON, AZ

START TO FINISH: 30 MIN.
MAKES: 6 SERVINGS

- ½ cup dry bread crumbs
- ⅓ cup reduced-fat garlic-herb spreadable cheese
- 2 green onions, chopped
- 4½ teaspoons lemon juice
- 1½ teaspoons grated lemon peel
- 1 teaspoon minced fresh thyme or ¼ teaspoon dried thyme
- ½ teaspoon salt
- ½ teaspoon pepper
- 1½ pounds lean ground turkey
- 6 whole wheat hamburger buns, split
- ¾ cup mango salsa

1. In a large bowl, combine the first eight ingredients. Crumble the turkey over mixture and mix well. Shape into six patties.

2. Moisten a paper towel with cooking oil; using long-handled tongs, rub on grill rack to coat lightly. Grill burgers, covered, over medium heat or broil 4 in. from the heat for 4-6 minutes on each side or until a thermometer reads 165° and juices run clear.

3. Grill the buns, uncovered, for 1-2 minutes or until toasted. Place burgers on bun bottoms. Top with the salsa. Replace bun tops.

Pesto Grilled Salmon

FAST FIX ▶ Pesto Grilled Salmon

Buttery, colorful and flaky, this simple but impressive salmon will be a family favorite in moments! Five smart ingredients, and your dinner entree is done.

—**SONYA LABBE** WEST HOLLYWOOD, CA

START TO FINISH: 30 MIN.
MAKES: 12 SERVINGS

- 1 salmon fillet (3 pounds)
- ½ cup prepared pesto
- 2 green onions, finely chopped
- ¼ cup lemon juice
- 2 garlic cloves, minced

1. Moisten a paper towel with cooking oil, using long-handled tongs, rub on grill rack to lightly coat. Place salmon skin side down on grill rack. Grill, covered, over medium heat or broil 4 in. from the heat for 5 minutes.

2. In a small bowl, combine the pesto, onions, lemon juice and garlic. Carefully spoon some of the pesto mixture over salmon. Grill 15-20 minutes longer or until fish flakes easily with a fork, basting occasionally with remaining pesto mixture.

Shrimp 'n' Scallops Tropical Salad

A fruity dressing drapes this zippy salad. Served on a bed of greens, the scrumptious combination of grilled seafood, veggies and macadamia nuts is the perfect way to celebrate a special summer occasion.

—JACKIE PRESSINGER STUART, FL

PREP: 35 MIN. • **COOK:** 5 MIN.
MAKES: 2 SERVINGS

- 2 tablespoons diced peeled mango
- 1 tablespoon diced fresh pineapple
- 1½ teaspoons mango chutney
- 1½ teaspoons olive oil
- 1 teaspoon rice vinegar
- ¾ teaspoon lime juice
  Dash salt
  Dash crushed red pepper flakes
- 3 cups torn Bibb or Boston lettuce
- 1 cup chopped peeled cucumber
- ½ medium ripe avocado, peeled and sliced
- 2 tablespoons coarsely chopped macadamia nuts, toasted
- 1 tablespoon finely chopped red onion
- 1 tablespoon minced fresh cilantro
- 2 tablespoons canola oil
- 1½ teaspoons Caribbean jerk seasoning
- 6 uncooked large shrimp, peeled and deveined
- 6 sea scallops, halved

1. Place the first eight ingredients in a blender. Cover and process until blended; set aside. Divide the lettuce, cucumber, avocado, nuts, onion and cilantro between two serving plates.

2. In a small bowl, combine oil and jerk seasoning. Thread the shrimp and scallops onto two metal or soaked wooden skewers; brush with the oil mixture.

3. Grill, covered, over medium heat for 2-3 minutes on each side or until shrimp turn pink and scallops are firm and opaque. Place on salads; drizzle with dressing.

Cilantro Couscous Salad

FAST FIX ## Cilantro Couscous Salad

I always make this refreshing salad for potlucks. My daughter likes it so much, we served it at her birthday party.

—CINDY GIFFORD CEDAR CITY, UT

START TO FINISH: 25 MIN.
MAKES: 12 SERVINGS (⅔ CUP EACH)

- 1 package (10 ounces) couscous
- 1 medium cucumber, finely chopped
- 2 medium tomatoes, seeded and finely chopped
- ⅔ cup minced fresh cilantro
- ⅓ cup olive oil
- ¼ cup lemon juice
- 3 garlic cloves, minced
- 1 package (8 ounces) feta cheese, crumbled

1. Prepare couscous according to package directions; let cool to room temperature.

2. In a large serving bowl, combine the cucumber, tomatoes, cilantro and couscous. In a small bowl, whisk the oil, lemon juice and garlic. Drizzle over salad; toss to coat. Add cheese and toss gently to combine. Chill until serving.

Shrimp 'n' Scallops Tropical Salad

AT THE BEACH!

Carolina Crab Boil

Carolina Crab Boil

With sausage, crab legs, corn and potatoes, this pot will satisfy hearty appetites at barbecues, picnics, tailgates or other outdoor celebrations.
—**MELISSA HASS** GILBERT, SC

PREP: 15 MIN. • **COOK:** 35 MIN.
MAKES: 4 SERVINGS

- 2 teaspoons canola oil
- 1 package (14 ounces) smoked turkey sausage, cut into ½-inch slices
- 2 cartons (32 ounces each) reduced-sodium chicken broth
- 4 cups water
- 1 can (12 ounces) light beer or 1½ cups additional reduced-sodium chicken broth
- ¼ cup seafood seasoning
- 5 bay leaves
- 4 medium ears sweet corn, cut into 2-inch pieces
- 1 pound fingerling potatoes
- 1 medium red onion, quartered
- 2 pounds cooked snow crab legs Pepper to taste

1. In a stockpot, heat oil over medium-high heat; brown sausage. Stir in the broth, water, beer, seafood seasoning and bay leaves.
2. Add the vegetables; bring to a boil. Reduce heat; simmer, uncovered, 20-25 minutes or until the potatoes are tender.
3. Add the crab; heat through. Drain; remove the bay leaves. Transfer to a serving bowl; season with pepper.

Pineapple Shrimp Packets

Your family and friends will delight in receiving these individual grilled shrimp packets. The foil makes cleanup so simple.

—NANCY ZIMMERMAN
CAPE MAY COURT HOUSE, NJ

START TO FINISH: 25 MIN.
MAKES: 6 SERVINGS

- 6 **canned pineapple slices**
- 1½ **pounds uncooked medium shrimp, peeled and deveined**
- ⅓ **cup chopped sweet red pepper**
- ⅓ **cup packed brown sugar**
- 1 **tablespoon seafood seasoning**
- 3 **tablespoons butter, cubed**

1. For each packet, place a pineapple slice on a double thickness of heavy-duty foil (about 12 in. square). Top with shrimp and red pepper. Combine the brown sugar and seafood seasoning; sprinkle over shrimp. Dot with butter. Fold foil around mixture and seal tightly.

2. Grill, covered, over medium heat for 10-15 minutes or until the shrimp turn pink. Open foil carefully to allow steam to escape.

Lemon Grilled
Salmon

**Pineapple
Shrimp Packets**

Lemon Grilled Salmon

Mom proudly serves this tender, flaky fish to family and guests alike. The savory marinade with dill gives the salmon its mouthwatering flavor. Since it can be grilled or broiled, we enjoy it year-round!

—AELITA KIVIRIST GLENVIEW, IL

PREP: 10 MIN. + MARINATING
BAKE: 15 MIN. • **MAKES:** 6 SERVINGS

- 2 **teaspoons snipped fresh dill or ¾ teaspoon dill weed**
- ½ **teaspoon lemon-pepper seasoning**
- ½ **teaspoon salt, optional**
- ¼ **teaspoon garlic powder**
- 1 **salmon fillet (1½ pounds)**
- ¼ **cup packed brown sugar**
- 3 **tablespoons chicken broth**
- 3 **tablespoons canola oil**
- 3 **tablespoons reduced-sodium soy sauce**
- 3 **tablespoons finely chopped green onions**
- 1 **small lemon, thinly sliced**
- 2 **onion slices, separated into rings**

1. Sprinkle dill, lemon-pepper, salt if desired, and garlic powder over salmon. In a large resealable plastic bag, mix brown sugar, broth, oil, soy sauce and green onions; add salmon. Seal bag and turn to coat. Cover and refrigerate for 1 hour, turning once.

2. Drain and discard marinade. Grill salmon, skin side down, over medium heat; arrange lemon and onion slices over the top. Cover and cook for 15-20 minutes or until fish flakes easily with a fork.

NOTE *Salmon can be broiled instead of grilled. Place the fillet on a greased broiler pan. Broil 3-4 in. from the heat for 6-8 min. or until fish flakes easily with a fork.*

Polynesian Kabobs

FAST FIX

With their tongue-tingling flavors and textures, these kabobs make a quick yet satisfying starter. I've also served them as an entree.

—CHRIS ANDERSON MORTON, IL

START TO FINISH: 30 MIN.
MAKES: 14 KABOBS

- 1 can (8 ounces) unsweetened pineapple chunks
- 1 package (14 ounces) breakfast turkey sausage links, cut in half
- 1 can (8 ounces) whole water chestnuts, drained
- 1 large sweet red pepper, cut into 1-inch chunks
- 2 tablespoons honey
- 2 teaspoons reduced-sodium soy sauce
- ⅛ teaspoon ground nutmeg
  Dash of pepper

1. Drain the pineapple, reserving 1 tablespoon juice (discard remaining juice or save for another use). Thread sausages, water chestnuts, pineapple and red pepper alternately onto 14 metal or soaked wooden skewers.

2. In a small bowl, combine honey, soy sauce, nutmeg, pepper and reserved pineapple juice.

3. Grill the kabobs, uncovered, over medium-hot heat for 6-7 minutes on each side or until the sausages are browned, basting occasionally with the marinade.

Polynesian Kabobs

Grilled Wasabi Oysters

My recipe for grilled oysters is easy to make, but incredibly impressive. The wasabi-flavored butter makes it a go-to appetizer for your next barbecue.

—PERRY PERKINS WILSONVILLE, OR

PREP: 30 MIN. • **GRILL:** 5 MIN.
MAKES: 1½ DOZEN

- ½ cup white wine
- 1 shallot, finely chopped
- 1 tablespoon white wine vinegar
- 1 tablespoon wasabi mustard
- 1½ teaspoons reduced-sodium soy sauce
- ½ cup butter, cubed
- ½ cup minced fresh cilantro
- ⅛ teaspoon salt
  Rock salt
- 18 fresh oysters in the shell, washed

1. In a small saucepan, combine the wine, shallot and vinegar. Bring to a boil; cook until liquid is reduced by half. Strain liquid, discarding shallot.

2. Return to pan; stir in mustard and soy sauce. Cook and stir over low heat. Add butter and whisk until melted. Stir in cilantro and salt; set aside.

3. Spread rock salt into an ungreased 15-in. x 10-in. x 1-in. baking pan; set aside. Place oysters, flat side up, on grill rack. Grill, covered, over high heat for 3-6 minutes or until shells open.

4. Transfer to prepared pan. To loosen oysters, cut muscles from top shell; place on bottom shell in juices. Discard the top shell.

5. Spoon 2 teaspoons of the butter mixture over each oyster. Serve immediately.

AT THE BEACH!

California Quinoa

Spring Pilaf with Salmon & Asparagus

Here's a salad that's ideal for outdoor dining. Fresh asparagus, carrots, lemon and chives perfectly complement leftover cooked salmon in this simple dish.

—**STEVE WESTPHAL** WIND LAKE, WI

PREP: 15 MIN. • **COOK:** 30 MIN.
MAKES: 4 SERVINGS

- 2 **medium carrots, sliced**
- 1 **medium sweet yellow pepper, chopped**
- ¼ **cup butter, cubed**
- 1½ **cups uncooked long grain rice**
- 4 **cups reduced-sodium chicken broth**
- ½ **teaspoon salt**
- ¼ **teaspoon pepper**
- 2½ **cups cut fresh asparagus (1-inch pieces)**
- 12 **ounces fully cooked salmon chunks**
- 2 **tablespoons lemon juice**
- 2 **tablespoons minced fresh chives, divided**
- 1 **teaspoon grated lemon peel**

1. Saute the carrots and yellow pepper in butter in a large saucepan until crisp-tender. Add rice; cook and stir for 1 minute or until lightly toasted.

2. Stir in the broth, salt and pepper. Bring to a boil. Reduce heat; cover and simmer for 20 minutes. Stir in the asparagus. Cook, uncovered, 3-4 minutes longer or until rice is tender.

3. Stir in the salmon, lemon juice, 1 tablespoon chives and lemon peel; heat through. Fluff with a fork. Sprinkle with remaining chives.

FAST FIX ## California Quinoa

I'm always changing up this salad. Here I used tomato, zucchini and olives for a Greek-inspired flavor. Try adding a few more favorite fresh veggies that you know your family will love. It's just as good served chilled as it is warm!

—**ELIZABETH LUBIN**
HUNTINGTON BEACH, CA

START TO FINISH: 30 MIN.
MAKES: 4 SERVINGS

- 1 **tablespoon olive oil**
- 1 **cup quinoa, rinsed and well drained**
- 2 **garlic cloves, minced**
- 1 **medium zucchini, chopped**
- 2 **cups water**
- ¾ **cup garbanzo beans or chickpeas, rinsed and drained**
- 1 **medium tomato, finely chopped**
- ½ **cup crumbled feta cheese**
- ¼ **cup finely chopped Greek olives**
- 2 **tablespoons minced fresh basil**
- ¼ **teaspoon pepper**

In a large saucepan, heat oil over medium-high heat. Add quinoa and garlic; cook and stir 2-3 minutes or until quinoa is lightly browned. Stir in the zucchini and water; bring to a boil. Reduce heat; simmer, covered, 12-15 minutes or until liquid is absorbed. Stir in the remaining ingredients; heat through.

Spring Pilaf with Salmon & Asparagus

Sesame Chicken with Creamy Satay Sauce

Sesame Chicken with Creamy Satay Sauce

These exotic skewers are surprisingly simple to make but taste like they came from an Asian restaurant. Before grilling, just marinate the chicken strips in a sesame salad dressing.

—KATHI JONES-DELMONTE
ROCHESTER, NY

PREP: 20 MIN. + MARINATING
GRILL: 10 MIN. • **MAKES:** 4 SERVINGS

- ¾ **cup Asian toasted sesame salad dressing**
- 1 **pound boneless skinless chicken breast halves, cut into 1-inch strips**
- ½ **cup reduced-fat cream cheese**
- ¼ **cup coconut milk**
- 3 **tablespoons creamy peanut butter**
- 2 **tablespoons lime juice**
- 1 **tablespoon reduced-sodium soy sauce**
- ½ **teaspoon crushed red pepper flakes**
- 1 **tablespoon minced fresh cilantro**

1. Pour salad dressing into a large resealable plastic bag. Add the chicken; seal bag and turn to coat. Refrigerate for 4 hours or overnight.
2. Drain and discard marinade from chicken. Thread chicken onto metal or soaked wooden skewers. Moisten a paper towel with cooking oil; using long-handled tongs, rub on grill rack to coat lightly.
3. Grill skewers, covered, over medium heat or broil 4 in. from the heat for 10-15 minutes or until no longer pink, turning once.
4. Meanwhile, in a small bowl, mix the cream cheese, coconut milk, peanut butter, lime juice, soy sauce and pepper flakes; sprinkle with cilantro. Serve chicken with sauce.

Fruity Halibut Steaks

FAST FIX ▶ Fruity Halibut Steaks

My friends and family rave about this special entree every time I serve it! When I have time, I make and refrigerate the salsa early so the flavors can blend.

—PATRICIA NIEH PORTOLA VALLEY, CA

START TO FINISH: 30 MIN.
MAKES: 6 SERVINGS

- 1 **cup chopped fresh pineapple**
- 1 **cup chopped peeled mango**
- ⅔ **cup chopped sweet red pepper**
- 1 **medium tomato, seeded and chopped**
- ⅓ **cup chopped seeded peeled cucumber**
- ¼ **cup minced fresh cilantro**
- 2 **tablespoons chopped seeded jalapeno pepper**
- 2 **tablespoons lime juice**
- 6 **halibut steaks (8 ounces each)**
- 2 **tablespoons olive oil**
- ½ **teaspoon salt**
- ½ **teaspoon pepper**

1. In a small bowl, combine the first eight ingredients; chill until serving.
2. Brush halibut with oil; sprinkle with salt and pepper. Moisten a paper towel with cooking oil; using long-handled tongs, rub on grill rack to coat lightly. Grill the halibut, covered, over high heat or broil 3-4 in. from the heat for 3-5 minutes on each side or until the fish flakes easily with a fork. Serve with the salsa.
NOTE *Wear disposable gloves when cutting hot peppers; the oils can burn skin. Avoid touching your face.*

Seafood Chowder

Chock-full of fish, shrimp and scallops, this comforting chowder has been pleasing my family for many years. The seasoned oyster crackers add a nice bit of spice.

—**VIRGINIA ANTHONY** JACKSONVILLE, FL

PREP: 45 MIN. • **COOK:** 25 MIN.
MAKES: 12 SERVINGS (4½ QUARTS)

- 1 tablespoon unsalted butter, melted
- 1 tablespoon marinade for chicken
- 1 teaspoon hot pepper sauce
- ¼ teaspoon curry powder
- ¼ teaspoon paprika
- 1¼ cups oyster crackers

CHOWDER

- 8 bacon strips, chopped
- 1½ pounds red potatoes, cut into ½-inch cubes
- 2 cups thinly sliced leeks (white portion only)
- ¼ cup all-purpose flour
- ¾ teaspoon dried thyme
- 1 carton (32 ounces) reduced-sodium chicken broth
- 4 cups clam juice
- 1 package (12 ounces) frozen corn
- 1½ cups diced zucchini
- 1 pound grouper or tilapia fillets, cut into 1-inch cubes
- ¾ pound uncooked medium shrimp, peeled and deveined
- ½ pound bay scallops
- 1 cup half-and-half cream
- 1 teaspoon salt
- ¼ teaspoon white pepper

1. In a small bowl, combine the butter, marinade for chicken, pepper sauce, curry and paprika. Add the crackers; toss to coat.

2. Transfer to a greased 15-in. x 10-in. x 1-in. baking pan. Bake at 350° for 8-10 minutes or until golden brown, stirring twice. Set aside.

3. Meanwhile, in a stockpot, cook bacon over medium heat until crisp. Using a slotted spoon, remove to paper towels to drain.

4. Saute the potatoes and leeks in the drippings; stir in flour and thyme until blended. Gradually whisk in broth and clam juice. Bring to a boil, stirring constantly. Cook and stir 1-2 minutes longer. Reduce heat; cover and simmer for 10 minutes or until the potatoes are tender.

5. Add the corn, zucchini, grouper, shrimp and scallops; cook for 2-4 minutes or until fish flakes easily with a fork. Stir in the cream, salt and pepper; heat through. Serve with crackers and bacon.

NOTE *This recipe was tested with Lea & Perrins Marinade for Chicken.*

Seafood Chowder

Lobster Rolls

Mayonnaise infused with dill and lemon lends a zippy flavor to these sandwiches.

—**TASTE OF HOME TEST KITCHEN**

PREP/TOTAL: 30 MIN.
MAKES: 8 SERVINGS

- 1 cup chopped celery
- ⅓ cup mayonnaise
- 2 tablespoons lemon juice
- ½ teaspoon dill weed
- 5 cups cubed cooked lobster meat (about 4 small lobsters)
- 8 hoagie rolls, split and toasted

In a large bowl, combine the celery, mayonnaise, lemon juice and dill weed. Gently stir in lobster. Serve on rolls.

FAST FIX ▸ Cheddar Drop Biscuits

Bakers of any skill level can make these savory biscuits because there's no rolling or cutting. The heavenly biscuits are filled with fabulous flavors of cheese, butter and garlic.
—**MARLANA BAROUSSE** CARRIERE, MS

START TO FINISH: 30 MIN.
MAKES: 1½ DOZEN

- 1¼ cups self-rising flour
- ¾ cup cake flour
- 1 tablespoon sugar
- ¾ teaspoon baking powder
- ½ teaspoon salt
- ¼ teaspoon garlic powder
- ⅛ teaspoon baking soda
- ¼ cup cold butter
- 1¼ cups heavy whipping cream
- 1 cup (4 ounces) shredded sharp cheddar cheese

OIL MIXTURE

- ⅓ cup olive oil
- 1 teaspoon garlic powder
- 1 teaspoon dried parsley flakes
- ¼ teaspoon salt

1. In a small bowl, combine the first seven ingredients. Cut in butter until mixture resembles coarse crumbs. Stir in the cream and cheese just until moistened.
2. Drop dough by ⅛ cupfuls 2 in. apart onto a greased 15-in. x 10-in. x 1-in. baking pan. In a small bowl, combine the remaining ingredients. Brush half of oil mixture over biscuits.
3. Bake at 450° for 8-10 minutes or until golden brown. Brush with remaining oil mixture. Serve warm.
NOTE *As a substitute for each cup of self-rising flour, place 1½ teaspoons baking powder and ½ teaspoon salt in a measuring cup. Add all-purpose flour to measure 1 cup.*

Grilled Clam Bake

With clams and crab legs, this entree looks impressive but is quite easy to prepare on the grill. The addition of corn and potatoes makes it a meal in one bowl.
—**TASTE OF HOME TEST KITCHEN**

PREP: 20 MIN. • **GRILL:** 25 MIN.
MAKES: 6 SERVINGS

- 18 fresh littleneck clams
- 4 medium ears sweet corn, husks removed and cut into thirds
- 8 medium red potatoes, cut into ½-inch cubes
- 2 medium onions, cut into 2-inch pieces
- 1 cup white wine or chicken broth
- 1 cup minced fresh parsley
- ¼ cup minced fresh basil
- ½ cup olive oil
- 2 garlic cloves, minced
- 1 teaspoon coarsely ground pepper
- 1 teaspoon hot pepper sauce
- ½ teaspoon salt
- 3 bay leaves
- 3 pounds uncooked snow crab legs
- ¼ cup butter, cubed
  French bread, optional

1. Tap the clams; discard any that do not close.
2. In a large disposable roasting pan, layer clams, corn, potatoes, onions, wine, herbs, oil, garlic, pepper, pepper sauce, salt and bay leaves. Grill, covered, over medium heat for 15 minutes.
3. Add crab; cook until potatoes are tender, about 25-30 minutes. Discard bay leaves; stir in butter. Serve with bread if desired.

FAST FIX ▸ New England Iced Tea

While growing up in Massachusetts, I spent summers with my family at our cottage. Clam bakes on the beach would always include these cocktails for all the adults at the party.
—**ANN LIEBERGEN** BROOKFIELD, WI

START TO FINISH: 10 MIN.
MAKES: 1 SERVING

- 2 tablespoons sugar
- 1 ounce vodka
- 1 ounce light rum
- 1 ounce gin
- 1 ounce Triple Sec
- 1 ounce lime juice
- 1 ounce tequila
- 1 to 1½ cups ice cubes
- 2 ounces cranberry juice
  Lemon slice, optional

1. In a mixing glass or tumbler, combine the sugar, vodka, rum, gin, Triple Sec, lime juice and tequila; stir until sugar is dissolved.
2. Place ice in a highball glass; pour in the sugar mixture. Top with cranberry juice. Garnish with lemon if desired.
LONG ISLAND ICED TEA *Substitute cola for the cranberry juice.*

New England Iced Tea

FAST FIX ▶ Grilled Halibut Steaks

No one would guess you use convenient ingredients like brown sugar, soy sauce and lemon juice in this delicious recipe.
—**MARY ANN DELL** PHOENIXVILLE, PA

START TO FINISH: 25 MIN.
MAKES: 4 SERVINGS

- 2 **tablespoons brown sugar**
- 2 **tablespoons butter**
- 1 **tablespoon lemon juice**
- 2 **teaspoons soy sauce**
- 1 **teaspoon minced garlic**
- ½ **teaspoon pepper**
- 4 **halibut steaks (5 ounces each)**

1. In a small saucepan, combine the first six ingredients. Cook and stir until butter is melted. Remove from the heat; set aside.

2. Moisten a paper towel with cooking oil; using long-handled tongs, rub on grill rack to coat lightly. Grill the halibut, covered, over medium-hot heat or broil 4 in. from the heat for 4-5 minutes on each side or until the fish flakes easily with a fork, basting frequently with butter mixture.

Colorful Coleslaw

Although raspberry vinegar may seem like an odd ingredient in coleslaw, it adds such fresh, fruity flavor!
—**KATHY RAIRIGH** MILFORD, IN

PREP: 20 MIN. + CHILLING
MAKES: 9 SERVINGS

- 7 **cups shredded cabbage**
- 1 **cup cherry tomatoes, halved**
- ½ **cup chopped fresh broccoli**
- ½ **cup chopped zucchini**
- ¼ **cup chopped red onion**
- ¼ **cup chopped sweet red pepper**
- ½ **cup white wine vinegar**
- ½ **cup canola oil**
- ⅓ **cup sugar**
- 2 **teaspoons Dijon mustard**
- 1 **teaspoon salt**
- 1 **teaspoon celery seed**
- 1 **teaspoon mustard seed**
- 1 **teaspoon raspberry vinegar**

In a large bowl, combine the first six ingredients. In a small bowl, whisk the remaining ingredients; pour over salad and toss to coat. Cover and refrigerate for at least 4 hours; stir occasionally.

FAST FIX ▶ Spiced Grilled Corn

This wonderful spice blend doesn't add heat—just great taste—to the corn.
—**TASTE OF HOME TEST KITCHEN**

START TO FINISH: 20 MIN.
MAKES: 8 SERVINGS

- 2 **teaspoons ground cumin**
- 2 **teaspoons ground coriander**
- 1 **teaspoon salt**
- 1 **teaspoon dried oregano**
- ½ **teaspoon ground ginger**
- ¼ **teaspoon ground cinnamon**
- ¼ **teaspoon pepper**
- ⅛ **teaspoon ground cloves**
- 2 **tablespoons olive oil**
- 8 **medium ears sweet corn, husks removed**

1. In a small bowl, combine the first eight ingredients. Brush oil over corn; sprinkle with spice mixture. Place each ear on a double thickness of heavy-duty foil (about 14 in. x 12. in.). Fold foil over corn and seal tightly.

2. Grill corn, covered, over medium heat for 10-12 minutes or until tender, turning occasionally. Open foil carefully to allow steam to escape.

Grilled Halibut Steaks

Steamed Veggie Bundles

In late summer, when we have an abundance of garden produce, we enjoy this medley of fresh veggies.
—**TERRI MULE** ANGOLA, NY

PREP: 20 MIN. • **GRILL:** 20 MIN.
MAKES: 6 SERVINGS

- 1 medium yellow summer squash, halved and cut into ¾-inch slices
- 1 medium zucchini, cut into ¾-inch slices
- 6 large fresh mushrooms, quartered
- 2 large tomatoes, cut into wedges
- 1 medium sweet red pepper, julienned
- 1 medium green pepper, julienned
- ½ cup fresh baby carrots, quartered lengthwise
- ¼ cup prepared ranch salad dressing
- ¼ cup prepared Italian salad dressing

1. Divide vegetables between two pieces of double thickness heavy-duty foil (about 18 in. square). Fold foil around vegetables and seal tightly. Grill, covered, over medium heat for 10-13 minutes on each side or until vegetables are tender.

2. Open foil carefully to allow steam to escape. With a slotted spoon, remove vegetables to a serving dish. Combine the salad dressings; drizzle over vegetables and toss to coat.

Did you know?

Summer and winter squash are members of the gourd family. The skin and seeds of summer squash are edible, while the skin is hard on winter squash.

Steamed Veggie Bundles

AT THE BEACH!

FAST FIX ▶ Crunchy Cool Coleslaw

This recipe is my take on the Honey Roasted Peanut Slaw at Lucille's Smokehouse BBQ, which I love. I think it's a pretty close match!

—**ELAINE HOFFMANN** SANTA ANA, CA

START TO FINISH: 30 MIN.
MAKES: 16 SERVINGS

- 2 **packages (16 ounces each) coleslaw mix**
- 2 **medium Honey Crisp apples, julienned**
- 1 **large carrot, shredded**
- ¾ **cup chopped red onion**
- ½ **cup chopped green pepper**
- ½ **cup cider vinegar**
- ⅓ **cup canola oil**
- 1½ **teaspoons sugar**
- ½ **teaspoon celery seed**
- ½ **teaspoon salt**
- ½ **cup coarsely chopped dry roasted peanuts or cashews**

1. In a bowl, combine the first five ingredients. In a small bowl, whisk the vinegar, oil, sugar, celery seed and salt.

2. Just before serving, pour dressing over salad; toss to coat. Sprinkle with the peanuts.

Tropical Chicken Packets

Crunchy Cool Coleslaw

Tropical Chicken Packets

Yum! These quick-and-easy chicken packets are destined to become your family's new favorite. The chicken is tender and laced with sweet pineapple and tropical flavors. These would be perfect for camping or dinner on the beach!

—**JACQUELINE CORREA** LANDING, NJ

PREP: 15 MIN. • **GRILL:** 20 MIN.
MAKES: 4 SERVINGS

- 4 **boneless skinless chicken breast halves (6 ounces each)**
- ⅛ **teaspoon pepper**
- 1 **can (20 ounces) unsweetened pineapple chunks, drained**
- 1 **medium sweet red pepper, julienned**
- 1 **small onion, sliced and separated into rings**
- ¼ **cup packed brown sugar**
- ¼ **cup reduced-sodium teriyaki sauce**
- 1 **teaspoon minced fresh gingerroot**

1. Sprinkle chicken breasts with pepper; place each on a double thickness of heavy-duty foil (about 18 in. x 12 in.). Top with pineapple, red pepper and onion. Combine the remaining ingredients; spoon over vegetables. Fold foil around mixture and seal tightly.

2. Grill, covered, over medium heat for 20-25 minutes or until chicken juices run clear. Open foil carefully to allow the steam to escape.

Cajun Shrimp Skewers

Fresh herbs and Cajun seasoning enhance these delicious shrimp, which are paired with a spicy Cajun butter sauce. You can serve them as an entree or as appetizers. Either way, you'll love them!

—**DWAYNE VERETTO** ROSWELL, NM

PREP: 20 MIN. + MARINATING
GRILL: 5 MIN. • **MAKES:** 8 SERVINGS

- ¾ cup canola oil
- 1 medium onion, finely chopped
- 2 tablespoons Cajun seasoning
- 6 garlic cloves, minced
- 2 teaspoons ground cumin
- 1 teaspoon minced fresh rosemary
- 1 teaspoon minced fresh thyme
- 2 pounds uncooked large shrimp, peeled and deveined

CAJUN BUTTER

- 1 cup butter, cubed
- 1 teaspoon minced fresh basil
- 1 teaspoon minced fresh tarragon
- 1 teaspoon Cajun seasoning
- ½ teaspoon garlic powder
- 3 drops hot pepper sauce

1. In a small bowl, combine the first seven ingredients. Place the shrimp in a large resealable plastic bag; add half of the marinade. Seal bag and turn to coat; refrigerate for 1-2 hours. Cover and refrigerate the remaining marinade for basting.
2. In a small saucepan, combine the Cajun butter ingredients; heat until butter is melted. Keep warm.
3. Drain and discard marinade from shrimp. Thread shrimp onto eight metal or soaked wooden skewers. Grill, uncovered, over medium heat for 2-4 minutes on each side or until shrimp turn pink, basting once with reserved marinade. Serve with Cajun butter.

Grilled Snapper with Caper Sauce

I often use snapper in this recipe, but if you prefer a different fish, try mahi-mahi.
—**ALAINA SHOWALTER** CLOVER, SC

PREP: 20 MIN. + MARINATING
GRILL: 10 MIN. • **MAKES:** 4 SERVINGS

- ⅓ cup lime juice
- 1 jalapeno pepper, seeded
- 3 garlic cloves, peeled
- 1¼ teaspoons fresh thyme leaves or ¼ teaspoon dried thyme
- 1 teaspoon salt
- 1 teaspoon pepper
- 4 red snapper fillets (6 ounces each)

SAUCE

- 3 tablespoons lime juice
- 3 tablespoons olive oil
- 2 tablespoons water
- 2 teaspoons red wine vinegar
- ½ cup fresh cilantro leaves
- 1 shallot, peeled
- 1 tablespoon capers, drained
- 1½ teaspoons chopped seeded jalapeno pepper
- 1 garlic clove, peeled and halved
- ¼ teaspoon pepper

1. In a food processor, combine the first six ingredients; cover and process until blended. Pour into a resealable plastic bag. Add the fillets; seal bag and turn to coat. Refrigerate for 30 minutes.
2. Drain and discard marinade. Moisten a paper towel with cooking oil; using long-handled tongs, rub on grill rack to coat lightly. Grill fillets, covered, over medium heat or broil 4 in. from the heat for 3-5 minutes on each side or until fish flakes easily with a fork.
3. Combine the sauce ingredients in a small food processor. Cover and process until blended. Serve with fish.

NOTE *Wear disposable gloves when cutting hot peppers; the oils can burn skin. Avoid touching your face.*

Cajun Shrimp Skewers

Cajun Shrimp Spread

Grilled Shrimp Appetizer Kabobs

This simple combination of pineapple, onion and marinated shrimp has turned me into a fan of seafood appetizers.

—**MICHELE TUNGETT** ROCHESTER, IL

PREP: 15 MIN. + MARINATING
GRILL: 5 MIN. • **MAKES:** 10 SERVINGS

- ⅓ cup tomato sauce
- ⅓ cup olive oil
- 3 tablespoons minced fresh basil
- 3 tablespoons red wine vinegar
- 5 garlic cloves, minced
- ¾ teaspoon salt
- ½ teaspoon cayenne pepper
- 10 uncooked jumbo shrimp, peeled and deveined (8-10 ounces)
- 10 fresh pineapple chunks
- 1 small onion, cut into 1-inch chunks

1. In a large bowl, whisk the first seven ingredients until blended. Reserve ¼ cup marinade for basting. Add the shrimp to remaining marinade; toss to coat. Refrigerate, covered, 30 minutes.

2. On each of 10 metal or soaked wooden appetizer skewers, alternately thread one shrimp, one pineapple chunk and onion. Grill, covered, over medium heat or broil 4 in. from heat 4-6 minutes or until shrimp turn pink, turning occasionally and basting with the reserved marinade during the last 2 minutes.

FAST FIX Cajun Shrimp Spread

Just for fun, I mixed my favorite recipes for spinach dip and shrimp spread together in one bowl. My snack-loving family is crazy about the Cajun-flavored combination!

—**LISA HUFF** WILTON, CT

START TO FINISH: 15 MIN.
MAKES: 4½ CUPS

- 1 package (8 ounces) cream cheese, softened
- ⅔ cup sour cream
- ⅔ cup mayonnaise
- 2 garlic cloves, minced
- 1½ teaspoons Cajun seasoning
  Dash hot pepper sauce
- 2 cups chopped cooked peeled shrimp
- 1 package (10 ounces) frozen chopped spinach, thawed and squeezed dry
- 2 tablespoons chopped sweet red pepper
- 2 tablespoons chopped green onion
  Assorted crackers

In a large bowl, beat the first six ingredients until blended. Stir in the shrimp, spinach and red pepper. Chill until serving. Sprinkle with green onion. Serve with crackers.

Grilled Shrimp Appetizer Kabobs

Grilled Greek Fish

Crisp & Spicy Cucumber Salad

Sweet-hot Asian flavors from rice vinegar, sesame oil and cayenne will light up your taste buds—and this salad!
—**ALIVIA DOCKERY** PARKER, CO

PREP: 25 MIN. + MARINATING
MAKES: 6 SERVINGS

- 2 small English cucumbers, thinly sliced
- 2 medium carrots, thinly sliced
- 1 large sweet red pepper, julienned
- ½ medium red onion, thinly sliced
- 2 green onions, sliced
- ½ serrano or jalapeno pepper, seeded and thinly sliced, optional

MARINADE
- ⅓ cup sugar
- ⅓ cup rice vinegar
- ⅓ cup water
- 1 teaspoon each salt, garlic powder and pepper
- 1 teaspoon sesame oil
- 1 teaspoon reduced-sodium soy sauce
- 1 small garlic clove, minced
- ½ teaspoon minced fresh gingerroot
- ¼ teaspoon cayenne pepper, optional
  Optional toppings: minced fresh cilantro, chopped peanuts and additional sliced green onion

1. In a large bowl, combine the first six ingredients. In a small bowl, mix the marinade ingredients, stirring to dissolve sugar. Pour over vegetables; toss to combine. Refrigerate, covered, 30 minutes or overnight.
2. Serve with a slotted spoon. If desired, sprinkle with toppings.
NOTE *Wear disposable gloves when cutting hot peppers; the oils can burn skin. Avoid touching your face.*

Grilled Greek Fish

Living in Tampa with the abundance of seafood, we eat a lot of fresh fish, mostly grouper, mahi-mahi and tilapia—all sweet white fish that go well with my marinade.
—**JUDY BATSON** TAMPA, FL

PREP: 15 MIN. + MARINATING
GRILL: 10 MIN. • **MAKES:** 4 SERVINGS

- ⅓ cup lemon juice
- 3 tablespoons olive oil
- 2 tablespoons minced fresh oregano
- 2 tablespoons minced fresh mint
- 1 garlic clove, minced
- ½ teaspoon grated lemon peel
- ½ teaspoon Greek seasoning
- 4 tilapia fillets (6 ounces each)

1. In a large resealable plastic bag, combine the first seven ingredients. Add the tilapia; seal bag and turn to coat. Refrigerate for 30 minutes. Drain and discard marinade.
2. Moisten a paper towel with cooking oil; using long-handled tongs, lightly coat the grill rack. Grill tilapia, covered, over medium heat or broil 4 in. from the heat for 4-5 minutes on each side or until fish flakes easily with a fork.

Dilly Red Potato Bundles

Here's a hearty side that came about when I attempted to cook an entire meal on the outdoor grill. Fresh dill adds wonderful flavor and a heavenly aroma.
—**DONNA GIBLIN** MIDDLETOWN, NJ

PREP: 15 MIN. • **GRILL:** 30 MIN.
MAKES: 8 SERVINGS

- 8 medium red potatoes, cubed
- ⅓ cup chopped onion
- ¼ cup snipped fresh dill
- ½ teaspoon salt
- ½ teaspoon pepper
- ¼ cup butter, cubed

1. In a large bowl, combine the first five ingredients. For each of four bundles, place 2 cups potato mixture on a double thickness of heavy-duty foil (about 18 in. x 12 in.). Dot with butter. Fold foil around potato mixture and seal tightly.
2. Grill, covered, over medium heat for 30-35 minutes or until potatoes are tender. Open foil carefully to allow the steam to escape.

**Maple Teriyaki
Salmon Fillets**

Maple Teriyaki Salmon Fillets

Maple syrup and apple juice provide a mildly sweet marinade that forms a nice glaze on these fillets when they're basted.
—**KATHY SCHRECENGOST** OSWEGO, NY

PREP: 10 MIN. + MARINATING
GRILL: 10 MIN. • **MAKES:** 4 SERVINGS

- ⅓ **cup apple juice**
- ⅓ **cup maple syrup**
- 3 **tablespoons reduced-sodium soy sauce**
- 2 **tablespoons finely chopped onion**
- 2 **garlic cloves, minced**
- 4 **salmon fillets (6 ounces each)**

1. In a small bowl, whisk the first five ingredients until blended. Remove ½ cup for basting; cover and refrigerate. Pour the remaining marinade into a large resealable plastic bag. Add the salmon; seal bag and turn to coat. Refrigerate for 1-3 hours.

2. Drain salmon, discarding marinade in bag. Moisten a paper towel with cooking oil; using long-handled tongs, rub on grill rack to coat lightly. Place salmon on grill rack, skin side down.

3. Grill, covered, over medium heat or broil 4 in. from the heat 10-12 minutes or until the fish flakes easily with a fork, basting frequently during the last 4 minutes.

Mango Shrimp Pitas

Mango, ginger and curry combine with a splash of lime juice to coat this juicy, grilled shrimp. Stuffed in pitas, the shrimp combo makes for an easy-to-hold, fabulous entree! You could also serve on a bed of rice for a less casual presentation.
—**BEVERLY OFERRALL** LINKWOOD, MD

PREP: 15 MIN. + MARINATING
GRILL: 10 MIN. • **MAKES:** 4 SERVINGS

- ½ **cup mango chutney**
- 3 **tablespoons lime juice**
- 1 **teaspoon grated fresh gingerroot**
- ½ **teaspoon curry powder**
- 1 **pound uncooked large shrimp, peeled and deveined**
- 2 **pita breads (6 inches), halved**
- 8 **Bibb or Boston lettuce leaves**
- 1 **large tomato, thinly sliced**

1. In a small bowl, combine the chutney, lime juice, ginger and curry. Pour ½ cup marinade into a large resealable plastic bag; add the shrimp. Seal bag and turn to coat; refrigerate for at least 15 minutes. Cover and refrigerate remaining marinade.

2. Drain and discard marinade from shrimp. Thread shrimp onto four metal or soaked wooden skewers. Moisten a paper towel with cooking oil; using long-handled tongs, rub on grill rack to coat lightly.

3. Grill shrimp, covered, over medium heat or broil 4 in. from the heat for 6-8 minutes or until shrimp turn pink, turning frequently.

4. Fill pita halves with lettuce, tomato and shrimp; spoon reserved chutney mixture over filling.

Mango Shrimp Pitas

FAST FIX Grilled Salmon Packets

I don't normally like plain salmon, but this recipe has a nice stir-fried flavor!

—**MIKE MILLER** CRESTON, IA

START TO FINISH: 25 MIN.
MAKES: 4 SERVINGS

- 4 salmon fillets (6 ounces each)
- 3 cups fresh sugar snap peas
- 1 small sweet red pepper, cut into strips
- 1 small sweet yellow pepper, cut into strips
- ¼ cup reduced-fat Asian toasted sesame salad dressing

1. Place each salmon fillet on a double thickness of heavy-duty foil (about 12 in. square). Combine sugar snap peas and peppers; spoon over salmon. Drizzle with salad dressing. Fold foil around mixture and seal tightly.

2. Grill, covered, over medium heat for 15-20 minutes or until fish flakes easily with a fork. Open foil carefully to allow steam to escape.

Grilled Shrimp with Cilantro Dipping Sauce

Grilled Salmon Packets

Grilled Shrimp with Cilantro Dipping Sauce

When my daughter grew a beautiful jalapeno plant last summer, I came up with this recipe. I already had cilantro in the garden, so it seemed like a great combo for a tasty seafood sauce.

—**ELIZABETH LUBIN**
HUNTINGTON BEACH, CA

PREP: 25 MIN. + MARINATING
GRILL: 5 MIN. • **MAKES:** 4 SERVINGS

- 2 tablespoons minced fresh cilantro
- 2 tablespoons olive oil
- 1 tablespoon minced fresh chives
- 1 garlic clove, minced
- 1 pound uncooked medium shrimp, peeled and deveined

DIPPING SAUCE

- 1 cup fresh cilantro leaves
- 1 cup fat-free mayonnaise
- 1 jalapeno pepper, seeded
- 1 garlic clove, peeled
- 1 tablespoon white vinegar
- 1 teaspoon sugar
  Dash cayenne pepper

1. In a large resealable plastic bag, combine the cilantro, oil, chives and garlic. Add the shrimp; seal bag and turn to coat. Cover and refrigerate for 1 hour.

2. In a blender, combine the sauce ingredients; cover and process until blended. Chill until serving.

3. Thread shrimp onto four metal or soaked wooden skewers. Grill, covered, over medium heat for 2-3 minutes on each side or until shrimp turn pink. Serve with sauce.

NOTE *Wear disposable gloves when cutting hot peppers; the oils can burn skin. Avoid touching your face.*

Grilled Vegetable Sandwich

Wow! Meat lovers won't even miss the meat, but they will rave about the simply fabulous flavor of this hearty grilled veggie sandwich. It's wonderful with ciabatta bread's crispy crust and light, airy texture.

—**DIANA TSEPERKAS** HAMDEN, CT

PREP: 20 MIN. + MARINATING
GRILL: 10 MIN. • **MAKES:** 4 SERVINGS

- 1 medium zucchini, thinly sliced lengthwise
- 1 medium sweet red pepper, quartered
- 1 small red onion, cut into ½-inch slices
- ¼ cup prepared Italian salad dressing
- 1 loaf ciabatta bread (14 ounces), halved lengthwise
- 2 tablespoons olive oil
- ¼ cup reduced-fat mayonnaise
- 1 tablespoon lemon juice
- 2 teaspoons grated lemon peel
- 1 teaspoon minced garlic
- ½ cup crumbled feta cheese

1. In a large resealable plastic bag, combine the zucchini, pepper, onion and salad dressing. Seal bag and turn to coat; refrigerate for at least 1 hour. Drain and discard marinade.
2. Brush cut sides of bread with oil; set aside. Place vegetables on grill rack. Grill, covered, over medium heat for 4-5 minutes on each side or until crisp-tender. Remove and keep warm. Grill bread, oil side down, over medium heat for 30-60 seconds or until toasted.
3. In a small bowl, combine the mayonnaise, lemon juice, peel and garlic. Spread over the bread bottom; sprinkle with the cheese. Top with vegetables and remaining bread. Cut into four slices.

Asian Pork Kabobs

Sweet and tangy, these kabobs have a delicious kick, thanks to the hot pepper sauce. My recipe can be adapted to add your favorite vegetables. It's great with rice and a fresh salad.

—**TRISHA KRUSE** EAGLE, ID

PREP: 10 MIN. + MARINATING
GRILL: 10 MIN. • **MAKES:** 4 SERVINGS

- ¼ cup teriyaki sauce
- 2 tablespoons balsamic vinegar
- 2 tablespoons sesame oil
- 2 tablespoons honey
- 2 teaspoons Sriracha Asian hot chili sauce or 1 teaspoon hot pepper sauce
- 1 pound pork tenderloin, cut into 1-inch cubes
- 1 medium onion, quartered
- 1 medium sweet red pepper, cut into 2-inch pieces

1. In a small bowl, combine the teriyaki sauce, vinegar, oil, honey and hot chili sauce. Pour ⅓ cup marinade into a large resealable plastic bag; add pork. Seal bag and turn to coat; refrigerate for at least 2 hours. Cover and refrigerate the remaining marinade for basting.
2. Drain and discard marinade from pork. On four metal or soaked wooden skewers, alternately thread the pork, onion and red pepper.
3. Grill kabobs, covered, over medium heat for 10-15 minutes or until the meat is tender, turning occasionally and basting frequently with the reserved marinade.

Grilled Vegetable Sandwich

Land and Sea Kabobs

FAST FIX Land and
Sea Kabobs

Create two flavor sensations with this one easy recipe. Basting with lime and curry adds a flavor flourish to these impressive kabobs that you don't want to miss!

—TERESA LAY ELKHART, IN

START TO FINISH: 30 MIN.
MAKES: 4 KABOBS

- 1 boneless pork loin chop (6 ounces), cut into 1-inch cubes
- 4 cubes fresh pineapple (1 inch)
- 1 medium plum, quartered
- 6 cubes papaya (1 inch)
- 4 uncooked jumbo shrimp, peeled and deveined
- 2 tablespoons canola oil
- 4 teaspoons lime juice
- 1½ teaspoons curry powder
- 1 small garlic clove, minced
- ¼ teaspoon salt
- ¼ teaspoon dried minced onion
- ¼ teaspoon grated lime peel

1. On two metal or soaked wooden skewers, alternately thread the pork, pineapple and plum. On two additional skewers, alternately thread papaya and shrimp. In a small bowl, combine the remaining ingredients; set aside.

2. Moisten a paper towel with cooking oil; using long-handled tongs, rub on grill rack to coat lightly. Grill kabobs, covered, over medium heat or broil 4 in. from the heat for 8-12 minutes or until pork juices run clear and shrimp turn pink, turning and basting frequently with lime mixture.

Sesame Spaghetti Salad with Peanuts

I love the sweet and spicy combination of this Asian-styled sauce. For convenience, it can be made a day ahead.
—**LEANN FUJIMOTO** NORMAL, IL

START TO FINISH: 30 MIN.
MAKES: 10 SERVINGS

- 1 package (1 pound) spaghetti
- ⅓ cup sesame oil
- ¼ cup canola oil
- 1 teaspoon crushed red pepper flakes
- ¼ cup reduced-sodium soy sauce
- 3 tablespoons honey
- 1½ teaspoons kosher salt
- ½ cup dry roasted peanuts, chopped
- ¼ cup minced fresh cilantro
- 2 tablespoons sesame seeds, toasted

1. Cook spaghetti according to the package directions.
2. Meanwhile, in a small saucepan over medium heat, heat the sesame oil, canola oil and pepper flakes until oil is fragrant. Remove from the heat. Stir in the soy sauce, honey and salt; set aside.
3. Drain spaghetti and rinse in cold water; transfer to a large bowl. Add the peanuts, cilantro, sesame seeds and oil mixture; toss to coat. Chill until serving.

Crab & Shrimp Stuffed Sole

The most casual cookout will seem elegant when it stars this delicate fish combined with seafood stuffing and a lemony sauce. Round out the meal with a salad and roll.
—**BRYN NAMAVARI** CHICAGO, IL

PREP: 25 MIN. • **GRILL:** 15 MIN.
MAKES: 4 SERVINGS

- 1 can (6 ounces) crabmeat, drained, flaked and cartilage removed

- ½ cup chopped cooked peeled shrimp
- ¼ cup soft bread crumbs
- ¼ cup butter, melted, divided
- 2 tablespoons whipped cream cheese
- 2 teaspoons minced chives
- 1 garlic clove, minced
- 1 teaspoon grated lemon peel
- 1 teaspoon minced fresh parsley
- 4 sole fillets (6 ounces each)
- 1½ cups cherry tomatoes
- 2 tablespoons dry white wine or chicken broth
- 2 tablespoons lemon juice
- ½ teaspoon salt
- ½ teaspoon pepper

1. In a small bowl, combine the crab, shrimp, bread crumbs, 2 tablespoons butter, cream cheese, chives, garlic, lemon peel and parsley. Spoon about ¼ cup stuffing onto each fillet; roll up and secure with toothpicks.
2. Place each fillet on a double thickness of heavy-duty foil (about 18 in. x 12 in.). Combine the tomatoes, wine, lemon juice, salt, pepper and remaining butter; spoon over fillets. Fold foil around fish and seal tightly.
3. Grill, covered, over medium heat for 12-15 minutes or until fish flakes easily with a fork. Open foil carefully to allow the steam to escape.

Crab & Shrimp Stuffed Sole

AT THE BEACH!

Shrimp on Rosemary Skewers

1 cup butter, softened
4 ounces cream cheese, softened
1¾ cups confectioners' sugar
½ cup thawed orange juice concentrate
4 teaspoons grated orange peel
½ teaspoon vanilla extract
2½ cups all-purpose flour
½ teaspoon baking soda
¼ teaspoon salt
10 drops yellow plus 2 drops red food coloring
Additional confectioners' sugar

FILLING

½ cup butter, softened
4 ounces cream cheese, softened
¼ teaspoon vanilla extract
2 cups confectioners' sugar
1 tablespoon orange juice concentrate
⅛ teaspoon grated orange peel

1. In a large bowl, cream butter and cream cheese until light and fluffy. Gradually beat in confectioners' sugar. Beat in the orange juice concentrate, peel and vanilla. Combine the flour, baking soda and salt; gradually add to creamed mixture and mix well. Stir in food coloring. (Dough will be soft.)
2. Drop by rounded tablespoonfuls 3 in. apart onto ungreased baking sheets. Flatten slightly with a glass dipped in confectioners' sugar.
3. Bake at 400° for 6-9 minutes or until edges begin to brown. Remove to wire racks to cool completely.
4. For filling, in a small bowl, cream the butter, cream cheese and vanilla until light and fluffy. Gradually beat in confectioners' sugar. Add orange juice concentrate and peel.
5. Spread filling on the bottoms of half of the cookies; top with remaining cookies. Store in the refrigerator.

Shrimp on Rosemary Skewers

Fresh sprigs of rosemary make the clever skewers for these tasty kabobs.
—**AMBER JOY NEWPORT** HAMPTON, VA

PREP: 30 MIN. • **GRILL:** 10 MIN.
MAKES: 8 SKEWERS

8 fresh rosemary sprigs, about 6 inches long
½ cup orange marmalade
½ cup flaked coconut, chopped
¼ teaspoon crushed red pepper flakes
¼ teaspoon minced fresh rosemary
1½ pounds uncooked large shrimp, peeled and deveined

1. Soak rosemary sprigs in water for 30 minutes. In a small bowl, combine the marmalade, coconut, pepper flakes and minced rosemary; set aside ¼ cup for sauce.

2. Thread shrimp onto rosemary sprigs. Moisten a paper towel with cooking oil; using long-handled tongs, rub on grill rack to coat lightly.
3. Grill, covered, over medium heat or broil 4 in. from the heat for 6-8 minutes or until shrimp turn pink, turning once and basting occasionally with remaining marmalade mixture. Serve with sauce.

Orange Sandwich Cookies

These cookies taste just like the orange Creamsicle treats you remember having had as a kid. Soft orange cookies are filled with a buttery smooth filling.
—**BENITA VILLINES** SPRING HILL, TN

PREP: 30 MIN.
BAKE: 10 MIN./BATCH + COOLING
MAKES: 28 COOKIES

Grilled Fan Potatoes

Wanting to do something different with grilled potatoes, I came upon this novel presentation. A foil packet means no muss or fuss with cleanup!

—**JEANNIE KLUGH** LANCASTER, PA

PREP: 10 MIN. • **GRILL:** 45 MIN.
MAKES: 2 SERVINGS

- 2 **medium potatoes**
- ¼ **cup butter, melted**
- 1 **tablespoon prepared horseradish**
- 1 **tablespoon V8 juice**
- 1 **teaspoon lime juice**
- 1 **teaspoon Worcestershire sauce**
- ¼ **teaspoon salt**
- ⅛ **teaspoon pepper**

1. With a sharp knife, slice potatoes but not all the way through, leaving slices attached at the bottom. Place each potato on a sheet of heavy-duty foil (about 18 in. x 12 in.). Fan potatoes slightly. Brush butter between slices.

2. Combine remaining ingredients; pour over potatoes. Fold foil around each potato and seal tightly. Grill, covered, over medium heat for 45-50 minutes or until tender.

Spicy Salmon Kabobs

Grilled Fan Potatoes

Spicy Salmon Kabobs

I first prepared these kabobs for a team of archaeologists excavating a site in the Aleutian Islands. We used fresh sockeye salmon, but other varieties of salmon work well, too.

—**TERRI MACH** HOMER, AK

PREP: 15 MIN. + MARINATING
GRILL: 10 MIN. • **MAKES:** 6 SERVINGS

- 1½ **pounds salmon fillets, cut into 1½-inch cubes**
- 1 **tablespoon brown sugar**
- 1 **teaspoon salt**
- 1 **teaspoon garlic powder**
- 1 **teaspoon celery seed**
- 1 **teaspoon pepper**
- 1 **teaspoon paprika**
- ½ **teaspoon onion powder**
- ½ **teaspoon cayenne pepper**
- ¼ **teaspoon chili powder**
- ⅛ **teaspoon fennel seed, crushed**
- ⅛ **teaspoon ground cumin**

1. Place salmon in a large resealable plastic bag. Combine the remaining ingredients; sprinkle over salmon. Seal bag and toss to coat; refrigerate for 30 minutes.

2. Thread the salmon onto six metal or soaked wooden skewers. Grill, covered, over medium heat or broil 4 in. from the heat for 4-6 minutes on each side or until fish flakes easily with a fork.

AT THE BEACH!

Grilled Chipotle Shrimp

3. Meanwhile, combine the sauce ingredients; chill until serving.
4. Drain and discard marinade. Thread shrimp onto metal or soaked wooden skewers. Moisten a paper towel with cooking oil; using long-handled tongs, rub on grill rack to coat lightly.
5. Grill shrimp, covered, over medium heat or broil 4 in. from the heat for 6-8 minutes or until shrimp turn pink, turning once. Serve with sauce.

Beach Ball Ice Cream Sandwiches

Who can resist creamy ice cream between homemade sugar cookies? These cheerful treats might be the perfect way to celebrate a get-away to the beach.

—**PATTIE ANN FORSSBERG** LOGAN, KS

PREP: 35 MIN. + FREEZING
MAKES: 2 DOZEN

- 3 tablespoons butter, softened
- 1½ cups confectioners' sugar
- ½ teaspoon vanilla extract
- 1 to 2 tablespoons 2% milk
  Red, blue, yellow and green food coloring
- 48 round sugar cookies
- 1 quart vanilla ice cream, softened

1. In a small bowl, combine the butter, confectioners' sugar, vanilla and enough milk to achieve spreading consistency. Divide frosting among five bowls; tint each a different color with red, blue, yellow and green food coloring. Leave one plain.
2. Frost tops of 24 sugar cookies with colored frostings to resemble beach balls. Let dry completely.
3. Spoon ice cream onto bottom of plain cookies; top with frosted cookies. Place in individual plastic bags; seal. Freeze until serving.

Grilled Chipotle Shrimp

I created this for a Cinco de Mayo party, and it was a hit! The creamy dipping sauce mellows out the shrimp's heat perfectly.

—**MANDY RIVERS** LEXINGTON, SC

PREP: 25 MIN. + MARINATING
GRILL: 10 MIN.
MAKES: ABOUT 5 DOZEN
(1¼ CUPS SAUCE)

- ¼ cup packed brown sugar
- 2 chipotle peppers in adobo sauce, chopped, plus ¼ cup adobo sauce
- 6 garlic cloves, minced
- 2 tablespoons water
- 2 tablespoons lime juice
- 1 tablespoon olive oil
- ¼ teaspoon salt

- 2 pounds uncooked large shrimp, peeled and deveined

CILANTRO CREAM SAUCE
- 1 cup sour cream
- ⅓ cup minced fresh cilantro
- 2 garlic cloves, minced
- 1½ teaspoons grated lime peel
- ¼ teaspoon salt
- ¼ teaspoon minced fresh mint

1. In a small saucepan, bring the first seven ingredients to a boil. Reduce heat; cook and stir 2 minutes longer. Remove from heat; cool completely.
2. Transfer the mixture to a large resealable plastic bag. Add the shrimp; seal bag and turn to coat. Refrigerate for up to 2 hours.

Grilled Chipotle Shrimp

Garlic-Ginger Salmon Packets

With minimal effort and mess, this tender salmon fillet has the makings of a dinnertime staple. Citrus, garlic and ginger bring out the best in this entree.

—LISA FINNEGAN FORKED RIVER, NJ

PREP: 20 MIN. • **GRILL:** 15 MIN.
MAKES: 4 SERVINGS

- 4 **salmon fillets (6 ounces each)**
- 1 **tablespoon minced fresh gingerroot**
- 1 **tablespoon minced fresh cilantro**
- 2 **garlic cloves, minced**
- 2 **teaspoons grated lemon peel**
- 2 **teaspoons grated orange peel**
- 1½ **teaspoons grated lime peel**
- 2 **tablespoons rice vinegar**
- 2 **tablespoons reduced-sodium soy sauce**
- ¼ **teaspoon pepper**

1. Place each salmon fillet on a double thickness of heavy-duty foil (about 12 in. square). Combine ginger, cilantro, garlic and peels; spoon over salmon.

2. In a bowl, combine the vinegar, soy sauce and pepper; drizzle over salmon. Fold foil around fish and seal tightly.

3. Grill, covered, over medium heat for 15-20 minutes or until fish flakes easily with a fork. Open foil carefully to allow the steam to escape.

Garlic-Ginger
Salmon Packets

top tip
Catching a Salmon

Choose fillets that have firm, moist-looking flesh and a mild odor. Keep salmon in the coldest part of your fridge. Use it within a day or two.

Grilled Shrimp Scampi

Grilled Shrimp Scampi

When I was in second grade, my class put together a cookbook. I saw this dish submitted by one of my friends, and I thought my mom would like it. I was right!

—PEGGY ROOS MINNEAPOLIS, MN

PREP: 15 MIN. + MARINATING
GRILL: 10 MIN. • **MAKES:** 6 SERVINGS

- 2 **tablespoons olive oil**
- 2 **tablespoons lemon juice**
- 3 **garlic cloves, minced**
- ¼ **teaspoon salt**
- ¼ **teaspoon pepper**
- 1½ **pounds uncooked jumbo shrimp, peeled and deveined**
  Hot cooked jasmine rice
  Minced fresh parsley

1. In a large bowl, whisk the first five ingredients. Add shrimp; toss to coat. Refrigerate, covered, 30 minutes.

2. Thread shrimp onto six metal or soaked wooden skewers. Grill, covered, over medium heat or broil 4 in. from heat 6-8 minutes or until shrimp turn pink, turning once. Serve with rice; sprinkle with parsley.

Brown-Sugar Salmon with Strawberries

I first tasted strawberries and cucumber together when living in the UK; now they make a delicious relish for salmon.

—JUDITH FOREMAN ALEXANDRIA, VA

PREP: 20 MIN. + CHILLING • **GRILL:** 10 MIN.
MAKES: 4 SERVINGS (2 CUPS RELISH)

- ⅓ **cup packed brown sugar**
- 1 **tablespoon canola oil**
- 1 **teaspoon ground mustard**
- 1 **teaspoon ground allspice**
- ½ **teaspoon salt**
- 4 **salmon fillets (5 ounces each)**

RELISH

- 1 **tablespoon minced fresh mint**
- 1 **tablespoon canola oil**
- 1 **tablespoon lemon juice**
- 2 **teaspoons grated lemon peel**
- ⅛ **teaspoon sugar**
- 1 **cup finely chopped fresh strawberries**
- 1 **small cucumber, finely chopped**

1. In a small bowl, mix the first five ingredients; rub over flesh side of salmon. Refrigerate, covered, 1 hour.

2. For relish, in another bowl, mix mint, oil, lemon juice, lemon peel and sugar. Add strawberries and cucumber; toss to coat.

3. Moisten a paper towel with cooking oil; using long-handled tongs, rub on grill rack to coat lightly. Place salmon on grill rack, skin side down. Grill, covered, over medium heat for 8-10 minutes or until fish flakes easily with a fork. Serve with relish.

Brown-Sugar Salmon with Strawberries

Fruit & Cereal Snack Mix, page 108; Puff Pastry Stars, page 108; Patriotic Cupcake Cones, page 108

Caribbean Jerk
Chicken, page 126

IT'S TIME TO BARBECUE...

IN THE
Park!

Summer offers fireworks, picnics and family reunions, accompanied by **grilled greats** perfect for sharing! Pack up your cooler, grab the kids and head outdoors with these dishes that travel well and turn **summer events** into memorable moments.

FAST FIX ▸ Fruit & Cereal Snack Mix

Tart dried cranberries and cherries make a nice contrast to the sweet cereal in this kid-friendly snack. It's a great take-along treat.

—JOHN LANCASTER UNION GROVE, WI

START TO FINISH: 10 MIN.
MAKES: 2½ QUARTS

- 8 cups Cinnamon Toast Crunch cereal
- 1¼ cups chopped dried apples
- ¾ cup dried cranberries
- ¾ cup raisins
- ½ cup dried cherries

In a large bowl, combine all ingredients. Store in an airtight container.

FAST FIX ▸ Puff Pastry Stars

We fashion festive star treats from convenient frozen puff pastry in this recipe. Feel free to change up the seasoning to suit your taste.

—TASTE OF HOME TEST KITCHEN

START TO FINISH: 30 MIN.
MAKES: 10 APPETIZERS

- 1 frozen puff pastry, thawed
- 2 tablespoons canola oil
- 1 tablespoon ranch salad dressing mix
- 3 tablespoons shredded Parmesan cheese

1. Unfold puff pastry. In a small bowl, combine oil and dressing mix; brush over pastry. Using a floured 3-in. star-shaped cookie cutter, cut out 10 stars. Place on a greased baking sheet. Sprinkle with the cheese.
2. Bake at 400° for 7-9 minutes or until the stars are puffy and golden brown. Serve warm.

Patriotic Cupcake Cones

Patriotic Cupcake Cones

Young and old alike will get a kick out of our cute cupcakes. The red-colored cake, white frosting and blue jimmies make for a perfect patriotic treat!

—TASTE OF HOME TEST KITCHEN

PREP: 40 MIN. • **BAKE:** 20 MIN. + COOLING
MAKES: 2 DOZEN

- ½ cup shortening
- 1½ cups sugar
- 2 eggs
- 1 bottle (1 ounce) red food coloring
- 3 teaspoons white vinegar
- 1 teaspoon butter flavoring
- 1 teaspoon vanilla extract
- 2½ cups cake flour
- ¼ cup baking cocoa
- 1 teaspoon baking soda
- 1 teaspoon salt
- 1 cup buttermilk
- 24 ice cream cake cones (about 3 inches tall)

FROSTING
- 1½ cups shortening
- 1½ teaspoons vanilla extract
- 6 cups confectioners' sugar
- 4 to 5 tablespoons milk
  Blue jimmies

1. In a large bowl, cream shortening and sugar until light and fluffy. Add eggs, one at a time, beating well after each addition. Beat in the food coloring, vinegar, butter flavoring and vanilla. Combine the flour, cocoa, baking soda and salt; add to the creamed mixture alternately with buttermilk, beating well after each addition. Pour batter into each cake cone to within ¾ in. of the top. Place in ungreased muffin cups.
2. Bake at 350° for 20-25 minutes or until a toothpick inserted near the center comes out clean. Cool.
3. In a large bowl, beat shortening and vanilla until fluffy; gradually add confectioners' sugar and beat until smooth. Add enough milk to achieve spreading consistency.
4. Cut a small hole in the corner of plastic bag; insert a large star tip. Fill the bag with frosting. Pipe onto cupcakes. Sprinkle with jimmies.

Peachy Pork Ribs

These meaty ribs are great picnic fare. Bake them first, to make them tender, then simply finish them off on the grill with a fruity basting sauce.

—TOM ARNOLD MILWAUKEE, WI

PREP: 20 MIN. • **COOK:** 2 HOURS 10 MIN.
MAKES: 4 SERVINGS

- 2 **racks pork baby back ribs (4 pounds), cut into serving-size pieces**
- ½ **cup water**
- 3 **medium ripe peaches, peeled and cubed**
- 2 **tablespoons chopped onion**
- 2 **tablespoons butter**
- 1 **garlic clove, minced**
- 3 **tablespoons lemon juice**
- 2 **tablespoons orange juice concentrate**
- 1 **tablespoon brown sugar**
- 2 **teaspoons soy sauce**
- ½ **teaspoon ground mustard**
- ¼ **teaspoon salt**
- ¼ **teaspoon pepper**

1. Place ribs in a shallow roasting pan; add water. Cover and bake at 325° for 2 hours.

2. Meanwhile, for sauce, place peaches in a blender; cover and process until blended. In a small saucepan, saute onion in butter until tender. Add garlic; cook 1 minute longer. Stir in the lemon juice, orange juice concentrate, brown sugar, soy sauce, mustard, salt, pepper and peach puree; heat through.

3. Drain ribs. Spoon some of the sauce over ribs. Moisten a paper towel with cooking oil; using long-handled tongs, lightly coat the grill rack. Grill ribs, covered, over medium heat for 8-10 minutes or until browned, turning occasionally and brushing with sauce.

Red and Blue Berry Lemonade Slush

Red and Blue Berry Lemonade Slush

Our tongue-tingling, fruity slush boasts fresh raspberries and blueberries. It's sure to cool you off on even the hottest summer day.

—TASTE OF HOME TEST KITCHEN

PREP: 15 MIN. + FREEZING
MAKES: 2 QUARTS

- 2 **cups lemon juice**
- 1½ **cups fresh raspberries**
- 1½ **cups fresh blueberries**
- 1 **to 1¼ cups sugar**
- 3 **cups cold water**

1. In a blender, combine the lemon juice, raspberries, blueberries and sugar. Cover and process until blended. Strain and discard seeds.

2. In a 2½-qt. pitcher, combine the berry mixture and water. Pour into a freezer container. Cover and freeze 8 hours or overnight.

3. Just before serving, remove from the freezer and let stand 45 minutes or until slushy.

Peachy Pork Ribs

Dad's Best Pork Chops

FAST FIX ▶ Dad's Best Pork Chops

My son, Kenneth, has loved pork chops since he was little, and he requests them often. He particularly likes this recipe because we pick the mint from our very own garden.
—GREG FONTENOT
THE WOODLANDS, TX

START TO FINISH: 25 MIN.
MAKES: 4 SERVINGS

- 2 medium tomatoes, chopped
- ¼ cup chopped onion
- 3 tablespoons minced fresh mint
- 1 jalapeno pepper, chopped
- 2 tablespoons Key lime juice
- 1½ teaspoons minced fresh rosemary
- 4 bone-in pork loin chops (¾ inch thick)
- ¼ teaspoon salt
- ¼ teaspoon pepper

1. In a small bowl, combine the first six ingredients. Chill until serving.
2. Sprinkle pork chops with salt and pepper. Grill chops, covered, over medium heat or broil 4-5 in. from the heat for 4-5 minutes on each side or until a thermometer reads 145°. Let meat stand for 5 minutes before serving. Serve with salsa.
NOTE *Wear disposable gloves when cutting hot peppers; the oils can burn skin. Avoid touching your face.*

Cajun Skewers

Add some veggies, like red and orange bell pepper rings, on a bed of salad greens, then top with the shrimp for an elegant meal. Red pepper flakes give some heat to the shrimp, but if you like your food a little tamer, cut back or omit them completely.
—BRIDGET CHESLOCK SAN DIEGO, CA

PREP: 20 MIN. + MARINATING
GRILL: 5 MIN. • **MAKES:** 8 SKEWERS

- 2 tablespoons olive oil
- 1 tablespoon onion powder
- 1 tablespoon paprika

Strawberry Salsa

- 1 tablespoon lemon juice
- 1 garlic clove, minced
- ½ teaspoon dried thyme
- ¼ teaspoon crushed red pepper flakes
- ¼ teaspoon coarsely ground pepper
- ¼ teaspoon cayenne pepper
- 1 pound uncooked jumbo shrimp, peeled and deveined
- 1 medium lemon, cut into wedges

1. In a large resealable plastic bag, combine the first nine ingredients. Add the shrimp; seal bag and turn to coat. Refrigerate for at least 30 minutes.
2. On eight metal or soaked wooden appetizer skewers, thread shrimp and lemon wedges. Grill, covered, over medium heat or broil 4 in. from the heat for 5-8 minutes or until shrimp turn pink, turning once.

FAST FIX ▶ Strawberry Salsa

Sweet and savory flavors combine in this summertime salsa. I like to serve it with tortilla chips for an appetizer, or as a side with grilled chicken or pork.
—AMY HINKLE TOPEKA, KS

START TO FINISH: 30 MIN.
MAKES: 6 CUPS

- 2 pints cherry tomatoes, quartered
- 1 pint fresh strawberries, chopped
- 8 green onions, chopped
- ½ cup minced fresh cilantro
- 6 tablespoons olive oil
- 2 tablespoons balsamic vinegar
- ½ teaspoon salt
  Tortilla chips

In a bowl, combine the tomatoes, strawberries, onions and cilantro. In a bowl, whisk the oil, vinegar and salt; gently stir into tomato mixture. Chill until serving. Serve with tortilla chips.

Grilled Three-Cheese Potatoes

While this side is delicious grilled, I've also cooked it in the oven at 350° for an hour. Add cubed ham to it and you can serve it as a full-meal main dish.

—**MARGARET RILEY** TALLAHASSEE, FL

PREP: 15 MIN. • **GRILL:** 35 MIN.
MAKES: 6-8 SERVINGS

- 6 **large potatoes, sliced ¼ inch thick**
- 2 **medium onions, chopped**
- ⅓ **cup grated Parmesan cheese**
- 1 **cup (4 ounces) shredded sharp cheddar cheese, divided**
- 1 **cup (4 ounces) shredded part-skim mozzarella cheese, divided**
- 1 **pound sliced bacon, cooked and crumbled**
- ¼ **cup butter, cubed**
- 1 **tablespoon minced chives**
- 1 **to 2 teaspoons seasoned salt**
- ½ **teaspoon pepper**

1. Divide the potatoes and onions equally between two pieces of heavy-duty foil (about 18 in. square) that have been coated with cooking spray.

2. Combine Parmesan cheese and ¾ cup each cheddar of and mozzarella; sprinkle over potatoes and onions. Top with bacon, butter, chives, seasoned salt and pepper. Bring opposite ends of foil together over filling and fold down several times. Fold unsealed ends toward filling and crimp tightly.

3. Grill, covered, over medium heat for 35-40 minutes or until potatoes are tender. Remove from the grill. Open foil carefully to allow steam to escape. Sprinkle with the remaining cheeses.

Honey Mustard Carrots

FAST FIX ► ## Honey Mustard Carrots

Wonderful color and flavor make fresh carrots a standout in this side dish. The bright orange julienned carrots add a pretty accent to any meat you are serving.

—**TRISHA KRUSE** EAGLE, ID

START TO FINISH: 20 MIN.
MAKES: 10 SERVINGS

- 4 **packages (10 ounces each) julienned carrots**
- ½ **cup honey**
- ¼ **cup honey mustard**
- 4 **teaspoons butter**
- ½ **teaspoon salt**

1. Place 1 in. of water in a large saucepan; add carrots. Bring to a boil. Reduce heat; cover and simmer for 3-4 minutes or until crisp-tender. Drain and set aside.

2. In a small saucepan, combine the remaining ingredients. Bring to a boil; cook and stir for 2-3 minutes or until slightly thickened. Pour over carrots; heat through.

Grilled Three-Cheese Potatoes

FAST FIX Grilled Waffle Treats

I made these super sandwiches for family and friends for the first time on the Fourth of July. Everyone loved the generous portions and shared their memories of making and eating s'mores while camping.

—**CHRIS SEGER** LOMBARD, IL

START TO FINISH: 15 MIN.
MAKES: 4 SERVINGS

- 8 **frozen waffles**
- 1 **cup miniature marshmallows**
- 1 **cup semisweet chocolate chips**

1. Place one waffle on a greased double thickness of heavy-duty foil (about 12 in. square). Sprinkle with ¼ cup each of marshmallows and chocolate chips; top with another waffle. Fold foil around sandwich and seal tightly. Repeat three times. Grill, covered, over medium heat for 8-10 minutes or until chocolate is melted, turning once. Open foil carefully to allow steam to escape.

FAST FIX Quick & Easy Honey Mustard

This fast, easy mustard with rice vinegar and honey has more flavor than any other honey-mustard dressing I have ever tried.

—**SHARON REHM** NEW BLAINE, AR

START TO FINISH: 5 MIN.
MAKES: 1 CUP

- ½ **cup stone-ground mustard**
- ¼ **cup honey**
- ¼ **cup rice vinegar**

In a small bowl, whisk all ingredients. Refrigerate until serving.

BBQ Hot Dog & Potato Packs

FAST FIX BBQ Hot Dog & Potato Packs

For these nifty foil packs, small hands make quick work of topping potato wedges with a hot dog, onions and cheese.

—**KELLY WESTPHAL** WIND LAKE, WI

START TO FINISH: 20 MIN.
MAKES: 4 SERVINGS

- 1 **package (20 ounces) refrigerated red potato wedges**
- 4 **hot dogs**
- 1 **small onion, cut into wedges**
- ¼ **cup shredded cheddar cheese**
- ½ **cup barbecue sauce**

1. Divide potato wedges among four pieces of heavy-duty foil (about 18 in. square). Top each with a hot dog, onion wedges and cheese. Drizzle with the barbecue sauce. Fold foil around the mixture, sealing tightly.

2. Grill, covered, over medium heat for 10-15 minutes or until heated through. Open the foil carefully to allow the steam to escape.

IN THE PARK!

Butterfinger Cookie Bars

Butterfinger Cookie Bars

My boys use Butterfingers in lots of treats. This bar was voted the best of the bunch.
—**BARBARA LEIGHTY** SIMI VALLEY, CA

PREP: 20 MIN. • **BAKE:** 25 MIN. + COOLING
MAKES: 3 DOZEN

- 1 package dark chocolate cake mix (regular size)
- 1 cup all-purpose flour
- 1 package (3.9 ounces) instant chocolate pudding mix
- 1 tablespoon baking cocoa
- ½ cup 2% milk
- ⅓ cup canola oil
- ⅓ cup butter, melted
- 2 eggs, divided
- 6 Butterfinger candy bars (2.1 ounces each), divided
- 1½ cups chunky peanut butter
- 1 teaspoon vanilla extract
- 1½ cups semisweet chocolate chips, divided

1. Preheat oven to 350°. In a large bowl, mix first four ingredients. Whisk milk, oil, butter and 1 egg until blended. Add to dry ingredients; stir just until moistened. Press half the mixture into a greased 15x10x1-in. baking pan. Bake for 10 minutes.

2. Chop two candy bars. Stir peanut butter, vanilla and remaining egg into remaining cake mix mixture. Fold in chopped bars and 1 cup chocolate chips.

3. Chop three additional candy bars; sprinkle over warm crust and press down gently. Cover with cake mix mixture; press down firmly with a metal spatula. Crush remaining candy bar; sprinkle crushed bar and the remaining chocolate chips over top.

4. Bake 25-30 minutes longer or until a toothpick inserted in center comes out clean. Cool on a wire rack. Cut into bars. Store in an airtight container.

Easy Refrigerator Pickles

Cola Hot Wings

These delectable wings are so easy to make—and offer year-round versatility, from summer cookouts to autumn tailgates. My husband likes them so much he'll stand out in the snow to grill them!

—LISA LINVILLE RANDOLPH, NE

PREP: 15 MIN. • **GRILL:** 40 MIN.
MAKES: ABOUT 2½ DOZEN

- 3 **pounds chicken wings**
- 1 **cup Louisiana-style hot sauce**
- 1 **can (12 ounces) cola**
- 1 **tablespoon soy sauce**
- ¼ **teaspoon cayenne pepper**
- ¼ **teaspoon pepper**
  Blue cheese salad dressing

1. Cut chicken wings into three sections; discard wing tip sections. In a small bowl, combine the hot sauce, cola, soy sauce, cayenne and pepper.
2. Prepare grill for indirect heat, using a drip pan. Moisten a paper towel with cooking oil; using long-handled tongs, rub on grill rack to coat lightly.
3. Grill chicken wings, covered, over indirect medium heat for 10 minutes. Grill 30-40 minutes longer, turning occasionally and basting frequently with sauce until wings are nicely glazed. Serve with salad dressing.
NOTE *Uncooked chicken wing sections (wingettes) may be substituted for whole chicken wings.*

Easy Refrigerator Pickles

In July, cucumbers are at their peak. Take advantage of garden extras by whipping up a few jars of pickles. My husband grows cucumbers, garlic and dill and eagerly waits for me to make these. My grandmother gave me the recipe.

—ANGELA LIENHARD BLOSSBURG, PA

PREP: 45 MIN. + CHILLING
MAKES: 4½ QUARTS

- 14 **pickling cucumbers**
- 40 **fresh dill sprigs**
- 4 **garlic cloves, sliced**
- 2 **quarts water**
- 1 **cup cider vinegar**
- ½ **cup sugar**
- ⅓ **cup salt**
- 1 **teaspoon mixed pickling spices**

1. Cut each cucumber lengthwise into six spears. In a large bowl, combine the cucumbers, dill and garlic; set aside.
2. In a Dutch oven, combine the remaining ingredients. Bring to a boil; cook and stir just until the sugar is dissolved. Pour over the cucumber mixture; cool.
3. Transfer to jars if desired and cover tightly. Refrigerate at least 24 hours. Store in the refrigerator up to 2 weeks.

Cola Hot Wings

Fresh Corn & Arugula Salad

This fresh-tasting salad is known as Aunt Pammy's salad in my family. It's so colorful that it always takes center stage.

—**PAMELA DAMM** SOUTH BELOIT, IL

PREP: 20 MIN.
GRILL: 10 MIN. + COOLING
MAKES: 6 SERVINGS

BASIL VINAIGRETTE
- ½ cup olive oil
- ¼ cup balsamic vinegar
- 3 tablespoons minced fresh basil
- 1 teaspoon chopped shallot
- 1 teaspoon minced fresh rosemary
- 1 teaspoon lemon juice
- ¼ teaspoon salt
- ¼ teaspoon pepper

SALAD
- 2 ears fresh corn, husked
- 1 teaspoon olive oil
- 8 cups fresh arugula or baby spinach
- 4 plum tomatoes, quartered
- ¼ cup pecan halves, toasted
- ¼ cup shaved Parmesan cheese

1. In a small bowl, whisk vinaigrette ingredients until blended.
2. Brush corn with oil; grill, covered, over medium heat until corn is crisp-tender and browned, turning occasionally. When cool enough to handle, cut corn off cobs and place in a large bowl.
3. Add arugula, tomatoes and pecans to corn. Drizzle with half of the vinaigrette; toss to coat. Top with the cheese; serve immediately. Cover and refrigerate remaining vinaigrette for later use.
NOTE *To toast nuts, spread in a 15x10x1-in. baking pan. Bake at 350° for 5-10 minutes or until lightly browned, stirring occasionally. Or, spread in a dry nonstick skillet and heat over low heat until lightly browned, stirring occasionally.*

Campfire Bundles

A family camping trip is where I made up this meal. I'd brought along a hodgepodge of ingredients, so I just threw them all together in a foil packet. Everyone said that the bundles were delicious!

—**LAURI KRAUSE** JACKSON, NE

PREP: 15 MIN. • **GRILL:** 1 HOUR
MAKES: 6 SERVINGS

- 1 large sweet onion, sliced
- 1 each large green, sweet red and yellow pepper
- 4 medium potatoes, cut into ¼-inch slices
- 6 medium carrots, cut into ¼-inch slices
- 1 small head cabbage, sliced
- 2 medium tomatoes, chopped
- 1 to 1½ pounds smoked Polish sausage, cut into ½-inch slices
- ½ cup butter, cubed
- 1 teaspoon salt
- ½ teaspoon pepper

1. Place the vegetables on three pieces of double-layered heavy-duty foil (about 18 in. square). Top with sausage; dot with butter. Sprinkle with salt and pepper. Fold foil around mixture and seal tightly.
2. Grill, covered, over medium heat for 30 minutes. Turn and grill 30 minutes or until vegetables are tender. Open foil carefully to allow steam to escape.

Campfire Bundles

Grilled Potato Packets

Grilled Teriyaki Pork Tenderloin

This recipe for pork tenderloin makes an elegant and scrumptious grilled entree!
—**TAHNIA FOX** TRENTON, MI

PREP: 10 MIN. + MARINATING
GRILL: 20 MIN. • **MAKES:** 4 SERVINGS

- ¾ cup honey mustard
- ¾ cup teriyaki marinade
- 1 pork tenderloin (1 pound)
- 2 garlic cloves, minced
- 1 green onion, chopped

1. In a bowl, combine mustard and teriyaki marinade; pour 1 cup into a large resealable plastic bag. Add pork and garlic; seal bag and turn to coat. Refrigerate 6 hours or overnight. Cover and refrigerate remaining marinade.
2. Prepare grill for indirect heat using a drip pan. Moisten a paper towel with cooking oil; using long-handled tongs, rub on grill rack to coat lightly. Drain and discard marinade from pork.
3. Place pork over drip pan. Grill, covered, over indirect medium-hot heat for 20-30 minutes or until a thermometer reads 145°, basting with reserved marinade and turning occasionally. Let stand 5 minutes before slicing. Sprinkle with onion.

Grilled Teriyaki Pork Tenderloin

Grilled Potato Packets

Potatoes require a little extra time on the grill, so give them first dibs on the flames.
—**ANNA BJORNN** REXBURG, ID

PREP: 20 MIN. • **GRILL:** 45 MIN.
MAKES: 8 SERVINGS

- 7 medium red potatoes
- 6 slices ready-to-serve fully cooked bacon, chopped
- ¼ cup thinly sliced green onions
- ¾ teaspoon salt
- ⅛ teaspoon pepper
- 2 tablespoons butter
- 1 cup (4 ounces) shredded cheddar cheese

1. Cut potatoes into wedges. In a large bowl, combine the potatoes, bacon, onions, salt and pepper. Divide between two double thicknesses of greased heavy-duty foil (about 18 in. square). Dot with butter.
2. Fold foil around mixture and seal tightly. Grill, covered, over medium heat for 40-45 minutes or until potatoes are tender, turning once.
3. Open foil carefully to allow steam to escape; sprinkle with the cheese. Grill 3-5 minutes longer or until the cheese is melted.

**Mojito
Marinated Fruit**

Mojito Marinated Fruit

All the flavors of the popular Mojito cocktail are featured in this fantastic salad. After you eat the fruit, you'll want to sip the luscious syrup down to the last drop!
—**MARCY GRIFFITH** EXCELSIOR, MN

PREP: 20 MIN. + CHILLING
MAKES: 8 SERVINGS

- ⅔ **cup sugar**
- ⅓ **cup water**
- ½ **cup light rum**
- 2 **tablespoons lime juice**
- 1 **teaspoon grated lime peel**
- 2 **cups each cantaloupe, honeydew and seedless watermelon balls**
- 2 **cups cubed fresh pineapple**
- 3 **mint sprigs**
  Fresh mint leaves, optional

1. In a saucepan, combine sugar and water; cook and stir over medium heat until sugar is dissolved. Remove from heat. Stir in rum, lime juice and peel. Cool completely.
2. In a large bowl, combine melons, pineapple and mint sprigs. Add rum mixture; toss to coat. Refrigerate, covered, overnight.
3. Discard mint sprigs. Spoon fruit with syrup into serving dishes. If desired, top with mint.

FAST FIX ▸ Garden Quinoa Salad

I enjoy this salad because it is chock-full of fresh vegetables and flavor. When you team them up with quinoa, the salad becomes a power-packed healthy dish!
—**PATRICIA NIEH** PORTOLA VALLEY, CA

START TO FINISH: 30 MIN.
MAKES: 4 SERVINGS

- 1½ **cups quinoa, rinsed and well drained**
- 3 **cups water**
- 1 **pound fresh asparagus, cut into 2-inch pieces**
- ½ **pound fresh sugar snap peas**
- ½ **pound fresh green beans, trimmed**
- 2 **tablespoons olive oil**
- 2 **tablespoons lemon juice**
- 2 **tablespoons minced fresh parsley**
- 1 **teaspoon grated lemon peel**
- ¾ **teaspoon salt**
- 1 **cup cherry tomatoes, halved**
- 3 **tablespoons salted pumpkin seeds or pepitas**

1. In a large saucepan, cook and stir quinoa over medium-high heat 3-5 minutes or until toasted. Add water; bring to a boil. Reduce heat; simmer, covered, 12-15 minutes or until liquid is absorbed. Transfer to a large bowl.
2. Meanwhile, in a large saucepan, bring 4 cups water to a boil. Add asparagus and snap peas; cook, uncovered, 2-4 minutes or just until crisp-tender. Remove vegetables and immediately drop into ice water.
3. Return water to a boil. Add green beans; cook 3-4 minutes or until crisp-tender. Remove beans and drop into ice water. Drain vegetables; pat dry.
4. In a small bowl, whisk oil, lemon juice, parsley, lemon peel and salt. Add tomatoes and blanched vegetables to quinoa; drizzle with dressing and toss to combine. Top with pumpkin seeds.

Garden Quinoa Salad

Keep 'em Cool

Set plastic bottles of water in the freezer until they are ice cold. Then, use the bottles to line picnic baskets to help keep chilled foods cold during transportation.

Pineapple Upside-Down Cupcakes

Pineapple Upside-Down Cupcakes

I have baked cupcakes for years—ever since I served as a room mother for my three children. These easy-to-make, jumbo treats make an attractive dessert for special events.

—BARBARA HAHN PARK HILLS, MO

PREP: 30 MIN. • **BAKE:** 30 MIN. + COOLING
MAKES: 1 DOZEN JUMBO CUPCAKES

- 6 **tablespoons butter, cubed**
- 1 **cup packed light brown sugar**
- 2 **tablespoons light corn syrup**
- 1 **small pineapple, peeled, cored and cut into ½-inch slices**
- 12 **maraschino cherries, well drained**
- 3 **eggs**
- 2 **cups sugar**
- 1 **cup canola oil**
- 1 **cup (8 ounces) sour cream**
- 2 **teaspoons vanilla extract**
- 2½ **cups all-purpose flour**
- ½ **teaspoon baking powder**
- ½ **teaspoon baking soda**
- ½ **teaspoon salt**
  Whipped topping, optional

1. Line the bottom of 12 greased jumbo muffin cups with waxed paper; grease the paper and set aside.
2. In a small saucepan, melt butter over low heat; stir in brown sugar and corn syrup. Cook and stir over medium heat until sugar is dissolved. Remove from the heat. Spoon 1 tablespoonful into each muffin cup; top each with a pineapple slice and a cherry.
3. In a large bowl, beat eggs and sugar until thickened and lemon-colored. Beat in the oil, sour cream and vanilla until smooth. Combine flour, baking powder, baking soda and salt. Add to egg mixture and mix well.
4. Fill muffin cups two-thirds full.

Bake at 350° for 28-32 minutes or until a toothpick inserted near the center comes out clean. Cool for 5 minutes before inverting onto wire racks to cool completely. Garnish with whipped topping if desired.

FAST FIX ▸ ## Seasoned T-Bones

A spicy seasoning rub and tender grilled steaks make a tasty match in this entree.
—TASTE OF HOME TEST KITCHEN

START TO FINISH: 20 MIN.
MAKES: 2 SERVINGS

- ½ **teaspoon salt**
- ½ **teaspoon dried oregano**
- ½ **teaspoon ground cinnamon**
- ¼ **teaspoon coarsely ground pepper**
- ¼ **teaspoon cayenne pepper**
- ¼ **teaspoon paprika**
- 2 **beef T-bone steaks (1 inch thick and ¾ pound each)**

1. In a small bowl, mix the seasonings. Rub over both sides of steaks.
2. Grill steaks, covered, over medium heat for 4-6 minutes on each side or until the meat reaches desired doneness (for medium-rare, a thermometer should read 145°; medium, 160°; well-done, 170°).

Seasoned T-Bones

IN THE PARK!

Sesame Chicken Kabobs

This colorful dish is a favorite of mine for entertaining. I marinate the chicken and cut up the peppers the night before. Then the next day, I just assemble the kabobs, grill, and dinner is ready!

—**CINDY NOVAK** ANTIOCH, CA

PREP: 15 MIN. + MARINATING
GRILL: 15 MIN. • **MAKES:** 6 SERVINGS

- ⅓ cup sherry or chicken broth
- ⅓ cup soy sauce
- 2 green onions, chopped
- 3 tablespoons apricot preserves
- 1 tablespoon canola oil
- 2 garlic cloves, minced
- 2 teaspoons minced fresh gingerroot
- ½ teaspoon hot pepper sauce
- 3 teaspoons sesame seeds, toasted, divided
- 1½ pounds boneless skinless chicken breasts, cut into 1-inch cubes
- 1 medium sweet red pepper, cut into 1-inch pieces
- 1 medium sweet yellow pepper, cut into 1-inch pieces

1. In a large bowl, combine the sherry or broth, soy sauce, onions, preserves, oil, garlic, ginger, hot pepper sauce and 1½ teaspoons sesame seeds. Pour ⅓ cup into another bowl for basting; cover and refrigerate. Pour remaining marinade into a large resealable plastic bag; add chicken. Seal bag and turn to coat; refrigerate for 2-3 hours or overnight, turning occasionally.

2. Drain and discard marinade from chicken. On metal or soaked wooden skewers, alternating, thread chicken and peppers. Grill, uncovered, over medium heat for 6 minutes, basting with reserved marinade. Grill 5-10 minutes longer or until meat juices run clear, turning and basting frequently. Sprinkle with remaining sesame seeds.

FAST FIX ▸ S'Moreos

My son introduced us to this twist on classic s'mores when we were camping. Have a jar of Nutella around? Slather it on the inside of the graham cracker halves before you build this one-of-a-kind treat.

—**CHRISTINA SMITH** SANTA ROSA, CA

START TO FINISH: 15 MIN.
MAKES: 4 SERVINGS

- 4 Oreo cookies
- 3 tablespoons creamy peanut butter
- 4 whole graham crackers, halved
- 1 milk chocolate candy bar (1.55 ounces), quartered
- 4 large marshmallows

1. Spread both sides of each Oreo cookie with peanut butter; place over half of the halved graham crackers. Top with chocolate.

2. Using a long metal skewer or long-handled fork, toast the marshmallows 6 in. from medium-hot heat until golden brown, turning occasionally. Place on chocolate; cover with remaining graham crackers. Serve immediately.

S'Moreos

Kansas City-Style Ribs

Our family recipe for ribs has evolved to near perfection. These country-style beauties are a legend in our close circle.
—**LINDA SCHEND** KENOSHA, WI

PREP: 1 HOUR + CHILLING
GRILL: 1 HOUR 25 MIN.
MAKES: 12 SERVINGS

- 1⅓ cups packed brown sugar
- 2 teaspoons each garlic powder, onion powder and smoked paprika
- 1¼ teaspoons each ground cumin, coarsely ground pepper and cayenne pepper
- 12 bone-in country-style pork ribs (about 7 pounds)

SAUCE

- 2 tablespoons canola oil
- 1 medium onion, finely chopped
- 1 cup tomato sauce
- ⅓ cup dark brown sugar
- ¼ cup ketchup
- ¼ cup molasses
- 1 tablespoon apple cider vinegar
- 2 teaspoons Worcestershire sauce
- 1 teaspoon salt
- 1 teaspoon ground mustard
- ¼ teaspoon smoked paprika
- ¼ teaspoon cayenne pepper

1. In a small bowl, mix brown sugar and seasonings; sprinkle over ribs. Refrigerate, covered, at least 1 hour.
2. For sauce, in a large saucepan, heat oil over medium heat. Add onion; cook and stir 5-6 minutes or until tender. Stir in remaining ingredients; bring to a boil, stirring occasionally. Remove from heat.
3. Wrap the ribs in a large piece of heavy-duty foil; seal edges of foil. Grill, covered, over indirect medium heat for 1¼ to 1¾ hours or until the ribs are tender.
4. Carefully remove ribs from foil. Place ribs over direct medium heat; baste with some sauce. Grill, covered, 8-10 minutes or until ribs are browned; turn and baste occasionally with remaining sauce.

Beer Cheese

I like to serve this zesty cheese spread with crackers and veggie dippers. It's great to take along to picnics and is also popular on my snack buffets.
—**PAT WARTMAN** BETHLEHEM, PA

PREP: 30 MIN. + CHILLING
MAKES: 3 CUPS

- ⅓ cup beer or nonalcoholic beer
- 4 ounces cream cheese, cubed
- 3 ounces crumbled blue cheese
- ¼ cup Dijon mustard
- 2 tablespoons grated onion
- ½ to 1 teaspoon hot pepper sauce
- 1 garlic clove, minced
- 3 cups (12 ounces) shredded cheddar cheese
  Assorted crackers

1. In a small saucepan, bring beer to a boil. Remove from the heat and cool to room temperature.
2. In a food processor, combine the beer, cream cheese, blue cheese, mustard, onion, pepper sauce and garlic. Add cheddar cheese; cover and process until well blended. Transfer to a bowl. Cover and chill overnight.
3. Let the cheese stand at room temperature for 30 minutes before serving. Serve with crackers.

Beer Cheese

Speedy Brownies

Caraway Coleslaw with Citrus Mayonnaise

The combination of caraway and orange keeps this slaw from being anything *but* run-of-the-mill. I always get requests to bring a batch to potlucks. I often like to make it a day ahead so the flavors can blend.

—**LILY JULOW** GAINESVILLE, FL

PREP: 20 MIN. + CHILLING
MAKES: 12 SERVINGS (⅔ CUP EACH)

- 1 **medium head cabbage, finely shredded**
- 1 **tablespoon sugar**
- 2 **teaspoons salt**

DRESSING

- ⅔ **cup reduced-fat mayonnaise**
- ⅓ **cup orange juice**
- 3 **tablespoons cider vinegar**
- 2 **tablespoons caraway seeds**
- 2 **teaspoons grated orange peel**
- ¼ **teaspoon salt**
- ¼ **teaspoon pepper**

1. Place cabbage in a colander over a plate. Sprinkle with sugar and salt; toss to coat. Let stand 1 hour.
2. In a small bowl, whisk the dressing ingredients until blended. Rinse cabbage and drain well; place in a large bowl. Add dressing; toss to coat. Refrigerate, covered, overnight.

Caraway Coleslaw with Citrus Mayonnaise

Speedy Brownies

Since you "dump" all the ingredients for these brownies together, they take very little time to prepare. But there's no mistaking the homemade goodness of a freshly baked batch—they're rich and fudgy!

—**DIANE HEIER** HARWOOD, ND

PREP: 15 MIN. • **BAKE:** 30 MIN.
MAKES: ABOUT 3 DOZEN

- 2 **cups sugar**
- 1¾ **cups all-purpose flour**
- ½ **cup baking cocoa**
- 1 **teaspoon salt**
- 5 **eggs**
- 1 **cup canola oil**
- 1 **teaspoon vanilla extract**
- 1 **cup (6 ounces) semisweet chocolate chips**

1. In a large bowl, beat the first seven ingredients. Pour into a greased 13-in. x 9-in. baking pan. Sprinkle with the chocolate chips.
2. Bake at 350° for 30 minutes or until a toothpick inserted near center comes out clean. Cool in pan on a wire rack.

IN THE PARK!

Sweet 'n' Salty
Party Mix

FAST FIX ## Faux Potato Salad

Cauliflower in potato salad? You bet—along with carrots, olives and a few other crunchy surprises.

—**MIKE SCHULZ** TAWAS CITY, MI

START TO FINISH: 30 MIN.
MAKES: 8 SERVINGS

- 1 **medium head cauliflower, broken into florets**
- 1 **medium carrot, chopped**
- 2 **hard-cooked eggs, chopped**
- 4 **green onions, chopped**
- 1 **celery rib, chopped**
- ¼ **cup pitted green olives, halved lengthwise**
- ¼ **cup thinly sliced radishes**
- ¼ **cup chopped dill pickle**
- ¼ **cup fat-free mayonnaise**
- 1 **tablespoon Dijon mustard**
- ¼ **teaspoon salt**
- ⅛ **teaspoon pepper**

1. In a large saucepan, bring 1 in. of water to a boil. Add cauliflower florets; cook, covered, 5-8 minutes or until tender. Drain and rinse in cold water. Pat dry and place in a large bowl. Add carrot, eggs, green onions, celery, olives, radishes and pickle.
2. In a small bowl, mix the remaining ingredients. Add to cauliflower mixture; toss to coat. Refrigerate until serving.

Sweet 'n' Salty Party Mix

These crunchy munchies are sure to rank high with your family and friends. The combination of sweet and salty flavors is just right!

—**CANDICE LUMLEY** CHARLES CITY, IA

PREP: 10 MIN.
BAKE: 1¼ HOURS + COOLING
MAKES: ABOUT 10 QUARTS

- 1 **package (12 ounces) Corn Chex**
- 1 **package (10 ounces) Cheerios**
- 1 **package (10 ounces) Honeycomb cereal**
- 1 **package (10 ounces) pretzel sticks, broken**
- 1¾ **cups sugar**
- 1½ **cups canola oil**
- 1¼ **cups butter, melted**
- 3 **tablespoons soy sauce**
- 2 **tablespoons garlic salt**

1. Preheat oven to 275°. In a large bowl, combine cereals and pretzels. In another bowl, mix the remaining ingredients until sugar is dissolved. Pour over cereal mixture; toss to coat.
2. Transfer to a large roasting pan. Bake, uncovered, 1¼ hours or until cereal is crisp, stirring every 15 minutes. Cool completely. Store the mix in an airtight container.

top tip

Picnic Pointer

To keep multiple dishes cold at picnics, I fill a flat under-bed storage container with ice and simply nestle in the dishes that need to be chilled.

—**JOYCE AMBER** OELWEIN, IA

Blueberry Angel Dessert

Make the most of angel food cake, pie filling and whipped topping by creating this light impressive dessert that doesn't keep you in the kitchen for hours.
—**CAROL JOHNSON** TYLER, TX

PREP: 10 MIN. + CHILLING
MAKES: 12 SERVINGS

- 1 **package (8 ounces) cream cheese, softened**
- 1 **cup confectioners' sugar**
- 1 **carton (8 ounces) frozen whipped topping, thawed**
- 1 **prepared angel food cake (8 to 10 ounces), cut into 1-inch cubes**
- 2 **cans (21 ounces each) blueberry pie filling**

In a large bowl, beat cream cheese and confectioners' sugar until smooth; fold in whipped topping and cake cubes. Spread evenly into an ungreased 13x9-in. dish; top with pie filling. Refrigerate, covered, at least 2 hours before serving.

FAST FIX ➤ Honey-Balsamic Goat Cheese Dip

This is so delicious, you can't stop eating it! You can find both the honey and goat cheese at your local farmers market.
—**JONI HILTON** ROCKLIN, CA

START TO FINISH: 10 MIN.
MAKES: 8 SERVINGS (¾ CUP DIP)

- 1 **cup crumbled goat cheese**
- ⅓ **cup fat-free mayonnaise**
- 2 **tablespoons honey**
- 1 **tablespoon balsamic vinegar**
- 1 **medium apple, sliced**
- 8 **slices French bread (¼ inch thick)**

In a bowl, beat the goat cheese, mayonnaise, honey and vinegar until smooth. Serve with slices of apple and French bread.

Blueberry Angel Dessert

Loaded-Up Pretzel Cookies

Coconut, M&M's and salty, crunchy pretzels make these loaded cookies unlike any you've ever tasted—they're irresistible!

—JACKIE RUCKWARDT

COTTAGE GROVE, OR

PREP: 20 MIN. • **BAKE:** 15 MIN./BATCH
MAKES: 2 DOZEN

- 1 **cup butter, softened**
- 1 **cup sugar**
- 1 **cup packed brown sugar**
- 2 **eggs**
- 2 **teaspoons vanilla extract**
- 2½ **cups all-purpose flour**
- 1 **teaspoon baking powder**
- 1 **teaspoon baking soda**
- 1 **teaspoon salt**
- 2 **cups miniature pretzels, broken**
- 1½ **cups flaked coconut**
- 1½ **cups milk chocolate M&M's**

1. Preheat oven to 350°. In a large bowl, cream butter and sugars until light and fluffy. Beat in eggs and vanilla. In another bowl, whisk flour, baking powder, baking soda and salt; gradually beat into creamed mixture. Stir in remaining ingredients.

2. Shape ¼ cupfuls of dough into balls; place 3 in. apart on ungreased baking sheets. Bake 12-14 minutes or until golden brown. Remove from pans to wire racks to cool.

Loaded-Up Pretzel Cookies

Caribbean Jerk Chicken

Caribbean Jerk Chicken

Get ready to rock the grill with this spicy and wonderfully fragrant chicken. The zippy marinade includes hints of cinnamon, cayenne and thyme. We like to think of this dish as "chicken with attitude."

—JUDY KAMALIEH NEBRASKA CITY, NE

PREP: 15 MIN. + MARINATING
GRILL: 35 MIN. • **MAKES:** 4 SERVINGS

- 4 **chicken leg quarters, skin removed**
- ¼ **cup olive oil**
- 2 **tablespoons brown sugar**
- 2 **tablespoons reduced-sodium soy sauce**
- 1 **envelope Italian salad dressing mix**
- 1 **teaspoon dried thyme**
- 1 **teaspoon ground cinnamon**
- ½ **teaspoon cayenne pepper**

1. With a sharp knife, cut leg quarters at the joints if desired. In a large resealable plastic bag, combine the remaining ingredients; add chicken. Seal bag and turn to coat; refrigerate for 2-4 hours.

2. Drain and discard marinade. Moisten a paper towel with cooking oil; using long-handled tongs, rub on grill rack to coat lightly. Grill chicken, covered, over medium heat for 35-45 minutes or until a thermometer reads 180°, turning occasionally.

Homemade Antipasto Salad

Here's a colorful salad that's tasty and will feed a huge crowd. Guests love the homemade dressing, which is a nice change from bottled Italian.
—**LINDA HARRINGTON** WINDHAM, NH

PREP: 1 HOUR + CHILLING
MAKES: 50 (¾ CUP) SERVINGS

- 2 packages (1 pound each) spiral pasta
- 4 cups chopped green peppers
- 4 cups chopped seeded tomatoes
- 3 cups chopped onions
- 2 cans (15 ounces each) garbanzo beans or chickpeas, rinsed and drained
- 1 pound thinly sliced Genoa salami, julienned
- 1 pound sliced pepperoni, julienned
- ½ pound provolone cheese, cubed
- 1 cup pitted ripe olives, halved

DRESSING
- 1 cup red wine vinegar
- ½ cup sugar
- 2 tablespoons dried oregano
- 2 teaspoons salt
- 1 teaspoon pepper
- 1½ cups olive oil

1. Cook pasta according to package directions. Drain; rinse with cold water. In several large bowls, combine the pasta with the next eight ingredients.

2. Place vinegar, sugar, oregano, salt and pepper in a blender. While processing, gradually add oil in a steady stream. Pour over pasta salads; toss to coat. Refrigerate, covered, for 4 hours or overnight.

Homemade Antipasto Salad

Caramelized Apple Hand Pies

Caramelized apples are tucked in a hand-held pie to make an ideal dessert.
—**EDWINA GADSBY** HAYDEN, ID

PREP: 25 MIN. + COOLING • **BAKE:** 20 MIN.
MAKES: 8 SERVINGS

- 2 tablespoons unsalted butter
- 3 medium apples, peeled and finely chopped
- ⅓ cup packed brown sugar
- ½ teaspoon cornstarch
- ⅛ teaspoon ground cinnamon
- 1 teaspoon lemon juice
- ½ teaspoon vanilla extract
- 1 package (14.1 ounces) refrigerated pie pastry

TOPPING
- ¼ cup coarse sugar
- 1 teaspoon ground cinnamon
- 3 tablespoons unsalted butter, melted

1. In a skillet, heat butter over medium heat. Add apples; cook and stir 5 minutes. Mix brown sugar, cornstarch and cinnamon; add to apples. Cook and stir 7-8 minutes longer or until apples begin to soften and caramelize. Remove from heat; stir in lemon juice and vanilla. Cool.

2. Preheat oven to 400°. On a lightly floured surface, unroll pastry sheets. Roll to ⅛-in. thickness; cut four 5-in. circles from each sheet. Place about 3 tablespoons filling on one half of each circle. Moisten pastry edges with water. Fold pastry over filling. Press edges with a fork to seal.

3. Transfer to greased baking sheets. Prick tops of pastry with a fork. Bake 20-25 minutes or until golden brown. Remove from pans to wire racks.

4. For topping, mix the sugar and cinnamon. Brush pies with melted butter; sprinkle with cinnamon-sugar. Serve warm or at room temperature.

Hot Quick
Banana Boats

FAST FIX ▶ Hot Quick Banana Boats

These delicious warm bananas are great on camp-outs or in the backyard. You can eat them right out of ther foil bowls.
—**SHEILA PARKER** RENO, NV

START TO FINISH: 20 MIN.
MAKES: 4 SERVINGS

- 4 **large unpeeled bananas**
- 8 **teaspoons semisweet chocolate chips**
- 8 **teaspoons trail mix**
- ¼ **cup miniature marshmallows**

1. Place each banana on a 12-in. square of foil; crimp and shape foil around bananas so they sit flat.
2. Cut each banana lengthwise about ½ in. deep, leaving ½ in. uncut at both ends. Gently pull each banana peel open, forming a pocket. Fill pockets with chocolate chips, trail mix and marshmallows.
3. Grill the bananas, covered, over medium heat for 4-5 minutes or until the marshmallows are melted and golden brown.

FAST FIX ▶ Granola Trail Mix

Whenever I make this snack for my family, it never lasts long. It is one of our favorite treats; whether we're watching a movie or going hiking, this tasty treat always comes along.
—**SHELLEY RIDDLESPURGER**
AMARILLO, TX

START TO FINISH: 10 MIN.
MAKES: ABOUT 3 QUARTS

- 1 **package (18 ounces) granola without raisins**
- 1 **package (15 ounces) raisins**
- 1 **package (14 ounces) milk chocolate M&M's**
- 1 **can (12 ounces) honey-roasted peanuts**

In a large bowl, combine all the ingredients. Store trail mix in an airtight container.

Hero Pasta Salad

Hide this salad until serving time, or you just might be surprised to find it gone! It's also great with kalamata olives, peppers or yellow tomatoes. Be creative!
—**ANGELA LEINENBACH**
MECHANICSVILLE, VA

PREP: 35 MIN. • **MAKES:** 4 SERVINGS

- 3 **tablespoons olive oil**
- 3 **tablespoons balsamic vinegar**
- 2 **small garlic cloves, minced**
- ⅛ **teaspoon salt**
- ⅛ **teaspoon pepper**

SALAD

- 2 **cups uncooked spiral pasta**
- 1 **small red onion, halved and thinly sliced**
- ¾ **cup sliced pepperoncini**
- 4 **ounces cubed provolone cheese**
- 2 **ounces thinly sliced deli ham, cut into strips (⅔ cup)**
- 2 **ounces thinly sliced hard salami, cut into strips (⅔ cup)**
- 5 **cups shredded lettuce**
- 1 **large tomato, coarsely chopped**
- ¾ **cup cherry tomatoes, halved**

1. In a small bowl, whisk the first five ingredients until blended. Cook pasta according to package directions. Drain pasta; rinse with cold water.
2. In a bowl, mix onion, pepperoncini, cheese, meats and pasta. Just before serving, add lettuce and tomatoes. Drizzle with dressing.

IN THE PARK!

FAST FIX **Bacon-Wrapped Hamburgers**

Since South Dakota summers are so short, we grill out as often as we can when the weather is warm. By mixing cheese right into these burgers, I know we'll get a little cheese in every bite.
—**DANA MATTHIES** PARKER, SD

START TO FINISH: 25 MIN.
MAKES: 6 SERVINGS

- ½ cup shredded cheddar cheese
- ½ cup finely chopped onion
- 1 egg, lightly beaten
- 2 tablespoons ketchup
- 1 tablespoon grated Parmesan cheese
- 1 tablespoon Worcestershire sauce
- ½ teaspoon salt
- ⅛ teaspoon pepper
- 1 pound ground beef
- 6 bacon strips
- 6 hamburger buns, split

1. In a large bowl, combine the first eight ingredients. Add beef; mix thoroughly.
2. Shape into six patties. Wrap a bacon strip around sides of each patty; secure with a toothpick.
3. Grill burgers, covered, over medium heat or broil 4 in. from heat for 5-6 minutes on each side or until a thermometer reads 160°. Discard toothpicks. Serve on buns.
NOTE *If you prefer, you can bake Bacon-Wrapped Hamburgers in a baking dish at 350° for 25 to 30 minutes or until a thermometer reads 160° and juices run clear.*

Tomatoes with Buttermilk Vinaigrette

FAST FIX **Tomatoes with Buttermilk Vinaigrette**

When tomatoes are plentiful, I like to make the most of them. One great way is to toss them in this old-fashioned homemade dressing with a fresh summery taste.
—**JUDITH FOREMAN** ALEXANDRIA, VA

START TO FINISH: 20 MIN.
MAKES: 12 SERVINGS (¾ CUP EACH)

- ¾ cup buttermilk
- ¼ cup minced fresh tarragon
- ¼ cup white wine vinegar
- 3 tablespoons canola oil
- 1½ teaspoons sugar
- ½ teaspoon ground mustard
- ¼ teaspoon celery salt
- ¼ teaspoon pepper
- 4 pounds cherry tomatoes, halved
- ⅓ cup minced fresh chives

1. In a small bowl, whisk the first eight ingredients until blended. Refrigerate, covered, until serving.
2. Just before serving, arrange the tomatoes on a platter; drizzle with vinaigrette. Sprinkle with chives.

Zesty Grilled Chops

These pork chops make a quick company dish. Our family enjoys them on the grill, as the summer weather in our part of the country is hot and muggy. In wintertime, they're wonderful prepared in the broiler.

—**BLANCHE BABINSKI** MINTO, ND

PREP: 10 MIN. + MARINATING
GRILL: 10 MIN. • **MAKES:** 6 SERVINGS

- ¾ cup soy sauce
- ¼ cup lemon juice
- 1 tablespoon chili sauce
- 1 tablespoon brown sugar
- 1 garlic clove, minced
- 6 bone-in pork loin or rib chops (about 1½ inches thick)

1. In a large resealable plastic bag, combine the first five ingredients; set aside ⅓ cup for basting. Add pork chops; seal bag and turn to coat. Refrigerate overnight.

2. Drain and discard marinade. Grill chops, covered, over medium heat or broil 4 in. from the heat for 12-16 minutes or until a thermometer reads 145°, turning once. Brush occasionally with reserved marinade. Let stand for 5 minutes before serving.

Saucy Barbecued Chicken

My aunt was affectionately called "The Barbecue Queen." As the aroma of her grilled chicken filled the air, folks in town would stop by just to sample her scrumptious food.

—**CHARLOTTE WITHERSPOON** DETROIT, MI

PREP: 65 MIN. • **GRILL:** 45 MIN.
MAKES: 4 SERVINGS

- 2 cups ketchup
- ½ cup water
- ½ cup corn syrup
- ½ cup tomato sauce
- ½ cup cola
- ¼ cup cider vinegar
- ¼ cup butter, cubed
- ¼ cup steak sauce
- 2 tablespoons soy sauce
- 1½ teaspoons sugar
- 1 teaspoon seasoned salt
- 1 teaspoon hot pepper sauce
- ½ teaspoon garlic powder
- ½ teaspoon onion powder
- ½ teaspoon liquid smoke, optional
- 1 broiler/fryer chicken (3 to 3½ pounds) cut up

1. In a large saucepan, combine the first 15 ingredients. Bring to a boil, stirring constantly. Reduce heat; simmer, uncovered, for 1 hour, stirring frequently.

2. Set aside 1 cup for basting. Store remaining sauce in the refrigerator for another use later.

3. Grill the chicken, covered, over medium heat for 30 minutes, turning occasionally. Baste with the marinade; grill 5-10 minutes longer or until a thermometer reads 180° and juices run clear, turning and basting frequently with marinade.

Zesty Grilled Chops

IN THE PARK!

Minty Tea Punch

Forget sugary (and boring) sodas for your next barbecue and treat your family and friends to a refreshing homemade punch. Serve up in mason jars with striped paper straws and really "wow" the crowd!

—**CRYSTAL BRUNS** ILIFF, CO

PREP: 15 MIN. + CHILLING
MAKES: 12 SERVINGS (¾ CUP EACH)

- 8 cups water, divided
- 12 mint sprigs
- 4 individual tea bags
- 1 cup orange juice
- ¼ cup lemon juice
- ½ cup sugar
  Ice cubes
  Orange and lemon slices, optional

1. In a large saucepan, bring 3 cups water to a boil. Remove from heat; add mint and tea bags. Steep, covered, 3-5 minutes according to taste. Discard mint and tea bags.
2. Stir in the orange and lemon juices, sugar and remaining water. Transfer to a pitcher; refrigerate until cold. Serve over ice; add orange and lemon slices if desired.

Honey Lime Chicken

Minty Tea Punch

Honey Lime Chicken

My grandfather used to grill this chicken. The simplicity of the recipe makes it nice for summer fun at a park, ballgame or any event where a grilled item is needed.

—**ANN NISEWONDER** DALLAS, TX

PREP: 10 MIN. + MARINATING
GRILL: 10 MIN. • **MAKES:** 4 SERVINGS

- 4 boneless skinless chicken breast halves (5 ounces each)
- 1 cup white wine
- ½ cup honey
- 2 tablespoons lime juice
- ¼ teaspoon ground ginger
- ¼ teaspoon garlic powder
- ¼ teaspoon salt
- ¼ teaspoon pepper
  Hot cooked couscous, optional

1. Place chicken in a large resealable plastic bag. In a small bowl, whisk wine, honey, lime juice and ginger; add to chicken. Seal bag and turn to coat. Refrigerate 2 hours, turning once.
2. Drain and discard marinade from chicken. Sprinkle chicken with garlic powder, salt and pepper.
3. Moisten a paper towel with cooking oil; using long-handled tongs, rub on grill rack to coat lightly. Grill chicken, covered, over medium heat or broil
4 in. from heat 5-6 minutes on each side or until a thermometer reads 165°. If desired, serve with couscous.

Marinated Pork Medallions

Serve this easy main dish with a green salad, corn and dinner rolls for a delicious, standout supper!
—**MELANIE MILLER** BASCOM, OH

PREP: 15 MIN. + MARINATING
GRILL: 10 MIN. • **MAKES:** 5 SERVINGS

- ½ cup packed brown sugar
- ½ cup Italian salad dressing
- ¼ cup unsweetened pineapple juice
- 3 tablespoons soy sauce
- 2 pork tenderloins (1 pound each), cut into ¾-inch slices

1. In a small bowl, combine first four ingredients. Pour ½ cup marinade into a large resealable plastic bag. Add pork; seal bag and turn to coat. Refrigerate overnight. Cover and refrigerate remaining marinade.

2. Drain and discard marinade from pork. Moisten a paper towel with cooking oil; using long-handled tongs, rub on grill rack to coat lightly.
3. Grill pork, covered, over medium heat 5-7 minutes on each side or until a thermometer reads 145°, basting occasionally with reserved marinade.

Lemon Nut Star Cookies

Family and friends will say "Hooray!" when they see these star-spangled cookies. Make these treats all year long by using different cookie cutters and food coloring.
—**TASTE OF HOME TEST KITCHEN**

PREP: 25 MIN. + CHILLING
BAKE: 10 MIN./BATCH + COOLING
MAKES: ABOUT 5½ DOZEN

- 1 cup butter, softened
- 2 cups confectioners' sugar
- 2 eggs
- 2 tablespoons lemon juice
- 4 teaspoons half-and-half cream
- 2 teaspoons grated lemon peel
- 3¼ cups all-purpose flour
- ½ cup ground almonds
- ½ teaspoon baking soda
- ⅛ teaspoon salt

GLAZE
- 2 cups confectioners' sugar
- ¼ cup light corn syrup
- 2 tablespoons lemon juice
  Red and blue food coloring

1. In a large bowl, cream butter and confectioners' sugar until light and fluffy. Add eggs, one at a time, beating well after each addition. Beat in the lemon juice, cream and lemon peel.
2. Combine the flour, almonds, baking soda and salt; gradually add to creamed mixture. Cover and refrigerate for 2 hours or until easy to handle.
3. On a lightly floured surface, roll out dough to ⅛-in. thickness. Cut with a floured star-shaped cookie cutter. Place 1 in. apart on ungreased baking sheets. Bake at 350° for 8-10 minutes or until lightly browned. Remove to wire racks to cool.
4. For glaze, in a small bowl, combine the confectioners' sugar, corn syrup and lemon juice until smooth. Divide into three bowls. Tint one portion red and one portion blue; leave the third portion white. Spread over cookies; let stand overnight for glaze to harden.

Marinated Pork Medallions

IN THE PARK!

Greek Three-Bean Salad

Citrus-Marinated Chicken

Citrus-Marinated Chicken

This juicy, zesty chicken stars in many of my family's summer meals. While there are a million ways to dress up poultry, you'll find yourself turning to this one again.

—DEBORAH GRETZINGER
GREEN BAY, WI

PREP: 10 MIN. + MARINATING
GRILL: 10 MIN. • **MAKES:** 6 SERVINGS

- ½ cup lemon juice
- ½ cup orange juice
- 6 garlic cloves, minced
- 2 tablespoons canola oil
- 1 teaspoon salt
- 1 teaspoon ground ginger
- 1 teaspoon dried tarragon
- ¼ teaspoon pepper
- 6 boneless skinless chicken breast halves (6 ounces each)

1. Combine the first eight ingredients in a large resealable plastic bag. Add the chicken; seal bag and turn to coat. Refrigerate for at least 4 hours.
2. Drain and discard marinade. Grill the chicken, covered, over medium heat or broil 4 in. from the heat for 5-7 minutes on each side or until a thermometer reads 165°.

FAST FIX ▶ Greek Three-Bean Salad

Thanks to the bold Mediterranean flavors, it's not hard to close your eyes and imagine yourself on a Greek island eating this salad.

—VIVIAN LEVINE SUMMERFIELD, FL

START TO FINISH: 25 MIN.
MAKES: 10 SERVINGS

- 2 cups frozen cut green beans, thawed
- 1 can (16 ounces) kidney beans, rinsed and drained
- 1 can (14½ ounces) cut wax beans, drained
- 1 medium red onion, halved and sliced

- 1 can (6 ounces) pitted ripe olives, drained
- ½ cup julienned green pepper
- ½ cup peeled, seeded and chopped cucumber
- ¾ cup bottled Greek vinaigrette
- 1 cup (4 ounces) crumbled feta cheese

Combine the first seven ingredients in a large salad bowl. Drizzle with the vinaigrette; toss to coat. Refrigerate until serving and sprinkle with cheese. Serve with a slotted spoon.

FAST FIX ▶ Vanilla Ice Cream In a Bag

Making homemade ice cream is an activity for the whole family. Just shake the bags until the liquid changes to ice cream!

—ERIN HOFFMAN CANBY, MN

START TO FINISH: 15 MIN.
MAKES: 1 CUP

- 1 cup milk
- 2 tablespoons sugar
- 2 tablespoons evaporated milk
- 1 teaspoon vanilla extract
- 4 cups coarsely crushed ice
- ¾ cup salt

1. In a small resealable plastic bag, combine the milk, sugar, evaporated milk and vanilla. Press out the air and seal. In a large resealable plastic bag, combine the ice and salt; add the sealed small bag.
2. Seal the large bag; place in another large resealable plastic bag and seal. Shake and knead for 5-7 minutes or until cream mixture is thickened. Serve immediately or freeze.

Picnic Berry Shortcakes

You can make this berry sauce in advance and keep chilled in the fridge. Then simply assemble the dessert before the picnic.

—TASTE OF HOME TEST KITCHEN

PREP: 20 MIN. + CHILLING
MAKES: 4 SERVINGS

- 2 tablespoons sugar
- ½ teaspoon cornstarch
- 2 tablespoons water
- 2 cups sliced fresh strawberries, divided
- ½ teaspoon grated lime peel
- 2 individual round sponge cakes
- 2 cups fresh blueberries

1. In a small saucepan, combine sugar and cornstarch. Stir in water. Add 1 cup strawberries; mash mixture. Bring to a boil; cook and stir for 1 minute or until thickened. Remove from the heat; stir in lime peel. Transfer to a small bowl; cover and refrigerate until chilled.
2. Cut sponge cakes in half widthwise; trim each to fit in the bottom of four wide-mouth half-pint canning jars. Combine blueberries and remaining strawberries; spoon over cakes. Top with sauce.

Picnic Berry Shortcakes

FAST FIX ▶ Scrum-Delicious Burgers

I'm not sure where this recipe originated, but it's one of my family's summertime favorites. I usually serve these juicy burgers when we have company. Guests rave about the flavorful cheesy topping. It's fun to serve a burger that's a little special yet easy.
—**WENDY SOMMERS** WEST CHICAGO, IL

START TO FINISH: 30 MIN.
MAKES: 6 SERVINGS

- 1½ **pounds ground beef**
- 3 **tablespoons finely chopped onion**
- ½ **teaspoon garlic salt**
- ½ **teaspoon pepper**
- 1 **cup (4 ounces) shredded cheddar cheese**
- ⅓ **cup canned sliced mushrooms**
- 6 **bacon strips, cooked and crumbled**
- ¼ **cup mayonnaise**
- 6 **hamburger buns, split**
  Lettuce leaves and tomato slices, optional

1. In a large bowl, combine the beef, onion, garlic salt and pepper. Shape into six patties, ¾ in. thick.
2. In a small bowl, combine the cheese, mushrooms, bacon and mayonnaise; chill.
3. Grill burgers, covered, over medium heat for 5-7 minutes on each side or until a meat thermometer reads 160°. During the last 3 minutes, spoon ¼ cup of the cheese mixture onto each burger. Serve on buns with lettuce and tomato if desired.

BLT Macaroni Salad

Scrum-Delicious Burgers

FAST FIX ▶ BLT Macaroni Salad

A friend served this salad, and I just had to get the recipe. My husband loves BLT sandwiches, so this has become a favorite of his. It's nice to serve on hot and humid days, which we frequently get during summer here in Virginia.
—**MRS. HAMILTON MYERS JR.**
CHARLOTTESVILLE, VA

START TO FINISH: 30 MIN.
MAKES: 6 SERVINGS

- ½ **cup mayonnaise**
- 3 **tablespoons chili sauce**
- 2 **tablespoons lemon juice**
- 1 **teaspoon sugar**
- 3 **cups cooked elbow macaroni**
- ½ **cup chopped seeded tomato**
- 2 **tablespoons chopped green onions**
- 3 **cups shredded lettuce**
- 4 **bacon strips, cooked and crumbled**

In a large bowl, combine the first four ingredients. Add macaroni, tomatoes and onions; toss to coat. Cover and refrigerate. Just before serving, add lettuce and bacon; toss to coat.

IN THE PARK!

Grilled Vegetable Cheese Bread

Here in the Deep South, tomatoes are really delicious by the Fourth of July. They're super on this bread, which is good any time you fire up the grill.

—SUNDRA HAUCK BOGALUSA, LA

PREP: 20 MIN. • **GRILL:** 15 MIN.
MAKES: 8 SERVINGS

- 1 loaf (1 pound) French bread, sliced lengthwise
- ¼ cup olive oil
- 3 large tomatoes, thinly sliced
- 2 cups thinly sliced zucchini
- 1 cup (4 ounces) shredded cheddar cheese
- 1 jar (4 ounces) sliced pimientos, drained
- 1 can (4¼ ounces) chopped ripe olives, drained
- 2 teaspoons Creole seasoning
- ¼ cup grated Parmesan cheese

1. Brush cut sides of bread with oil. Layer with tomatoes and zucchini; sprinkle with the cheddar cheese, pimientos, olives and seasoning.
2. Prepare grill for indirect heat. Place bread on grill rack. Grill, covered, over indirect medium heat for 10-12 minutes or until zucchini is crisp-tender. Sprinkle with Parmesan cheese; grill 2-4 minutes longer or until cheese is melted.

NOTE *The following spices may be substituted for 1 teaspoon Creole seasoning: ¼ teaspoon each salt, garlic powder and paprika; and a pinch each of dried thyme, ground cumin and cayenne pepper.*

Picnic Beans with Dip

Try this fun way to enjoy fresh-picked beans...with a creamy well-seasoned dip. I first enjoyed it at a friend's house and have made it for several years. Try the dip with other vegetables, too, such as broccoli, celery and carrots.

—MARTHA BERGMAN
CLEVELAND HEIGHTS, OH

PREP: 15 MIN. + CHILLING
MAKES: 1⅔ CUPS DIP

- 1 pound fresh green or wax beans
- ½ cup mayonnaise
- ½ cup half-and-half cream
- 6 tablespoons canola oil
- 2 tablespoons white vinegar
- 1 tablespoon Dijon mustard
- 1 small onion, quartered
- 1 teaspoon salt
- ¼ teaspoon ground coriander
- ¼ teaspoon dried savory
- ¼ teaspoon pepper
- ⅛ teaspoon dried thyme

1. Place beans in a large saucepan and cover with water; bring to a boil. Cook, uncovered, for 8-10 minutes or until crisp-tender. Drain and rinse with cold water. Chill until serving.
2. In a blender, combine the remaining ingredients. Cover and process until smooth. Cover and refrigerate for at least 1 hour. Serve with the beans for dipping.

Picnic Beans with Dip

IN THE PARK!

Roasted Pepper Salad with Balsamic Vinaigrette

3. In a small bowl, whisk the oil, vinegar, herbs, garlic, garlic powder, cayenne, pepper and salt; pour over pepper mixture and toss to coat. Cover and refrigerate for up to 4 hours.

4. Before serving, allow peppers to come to room temperature. Place on a serving plate; top with tomatoes, cheese and basil leaves.

Marinated Turkey Tenderloins

My turkey tenderloins are fantastic because of the savory teriyaki and soy sauce mixture.

—**LINDA GREGG** SPARTANBURG, SC

PREP: 10 MIN. + MARINATING
GRILL: 15 MIN. • **MAKES:** 8 SERVINGS

- ¼ **cup canola oil**
- ¼ **cup reduced-sodium soy sauce**
- ¼ **cup reduced-sodium teriyaki sauce**
- 2 **tablespoons red wine vinegar**
- 1 **tablespoon lime juice**
- 1 **tablespoon Dijon mustard**
- 2 **garlic cloves, minced**
- 2 **teaspoons coarsely ground pepper**
- 1½ **teaspoons dried parsley flakes**
- 1½ **teaspoons dried basil**
- ½ **teaspoon onion powder**
- 2 **pounds turkey breast tenderloins**

1. In a 2-cup measuring cup, combine the first 11 ingredients. Pour ⅔ cup into a resealable plastic bag; add turkey. Seal bag and turn to coat; refrigerate for 8 hours or overnight. Cover and refrigerate the remaining marinade.

2. Drain and discard marinade from turkey. Moisten a paper towel with cooking oil; using long-handled tongs, rub on grill rack to coat lightly.

3. Grill, covered, over medium heat or broil 4 in. from the heat for 7-9 minutes on each side or until a thermometer reads 165°, basting frequently with reserved marinade.

Roasted Pepper Salad with Balsamic Vinaigrette

I created this colorful salad for a 4-H project and took it all the way to the state competition, where I won first place! Make a day ahead and serve it cold if you'd like. It's a great addition to a grilled picnic.

—**SETH MURDOCH** RED ROCK, TX

PREP: 20 MIN. + MARINATING
BROIL: 20 MIN. + STANDING
MAKES: 5 SERVINGS

- 2 **each large sweet yellow, red and green peppers**
- 1 **small red onion, thinly sliced**
- 6 **tablespoons olive oil**
- 3 **tablespoons balsamic vinegar**
- 1 **tablespoon each minced fresh oregano, rosemary, basil and parsley**
- 1 **garlic clove, minced**
- ½ **teaspoon garlic powder**
- ½ **teaspoon cayenne pepper**
- ½ **teaspoon pepper**
- ¼ **teaspoon salt**
- 1 **cup cherry tomatoes, halved**
- 1 **carton (8 ounces) fresh mozzarella cheese pearls**
- 5 **fresh basil leaves**

1. Broil peppers 4 in. from the heat until skins blister, about 5 minutes. With tongs, rotate peppers a quarter turn. Broil and rotate until all sides are blistered and blackened. Immediately place peppers in a large bowl; cover and let stand for 20 minutes.

2. Peel off and discard charred skin. Remove stems and seeds. Cut peppers into thin strips; place in a large bowl. Add onion.

Dad's Lemony Grilled Chicken

Lemon juice, onions and garlic add tangy flavor to chicken, when firing up the grill.

—**MIKE SCHULZ** TAWAS CITY, MI

PREP: 20 MIN. + MARINATING
GRILL: 30 MIN. • **MAKES:** 8 SERVINGS

- 1 **cup olive oil**
- ⅔ **cup lemon juice**
- 6 **garlic cloves, minced**
- 1 **teaspoon salt**
- ½ **teaspoon pepper**
- 2 **medium onions, chopped**
- 8 **chicken drumsticks (2 pounds)**
- 8 **bone-in chicken thighs (2 pounds)**

1. In a small bowl, whisk the first five ingredients until blended; stir in onions. Pour 1½ cups marinade into a large resealable plastic bag. Add the chicken; seal bag and turn to coat. Refrigerate overnight. Cover and refrigerate remaining marinade.
2. Prepare grill for indirect heat. Drain and discard marinade from chicken. Place chicken on grill rack, skin side up. Grill, covered, over indirect medium heat 15 minutes. Turn; grill 15-20 minutes longer or until a thermometer reads 180°, basting occasionally with reserved marinade.

Let's Talk Turkey

Turkey tenderloins are strips of meat that come from the breast. This white meat is quick-cooking and lean, making it an ideal entree for easy picnics.

Dad's Lemony Grilled Chicken

Mahogany-Glazed
Mushroom Burgers, page 155

IT'S TIME TO BARBECUE...

ON THE
Patio!

Dining alfresco surely has its casual qualities, but when you **want to impress** guests you can still turn to your grill! Here you'll find simply elegant options to dress up a menu and **celebrate the weekend** with good friends, good times and good food!

Tuscan-Style Grilled Trout, page 144

Grilled Vegetables & Goat Cheese Napoleons

My recipe started out as an experiment for vegetarian friends at a small dinner party. It slowly evolved into this savory dish. I find that everyone seems to love it (even non-veggie enthusiasts)!

—JOAN MEYER NEW YORK, NY

PREP: 50 MIN. • **BAKE:** 10 MIN.
MAKES: 4 SERVINGS

- 2 plum tomatoes, halved lengthwise
- ¼ cup olive oil, divided
- ⅛ teaspoon dried oregano
- ⅛ teaspoon dried basil
- ¾ teaspoon salt, divided
- ½ teaspoon pepper, divided
- 1 large zucchini, cut into ½-inch slices
- 1 large yellow summer squash, cut into ½-inch slices
- 4 large portobello mushrooms
- 4 slices eggplant (½ inch thick)
- 1 package (5.3 ounces) fresh goat cheese
- 1 teaspoon minced fresh parsley
- 1 teaspoon minced garlic, divided
- 4 ounces fresh mozzarella cheese, cut into 4 slices
- 1 package (10 ounces) fresh spinach
- ¼ cup balsamic vinaigrette

1. Brush tomatoes with 2 teaspoons oil; sprinkle with oregano, basil and ¼ teaspoon each salt and pepper. Transfer to an ungreased 15-in. x 10-in. x 1-in. baking pan. Bake at 350° for 20-25 minutes or until tender.

2. Brush zucchini and yellow squash with 2 tablespoons oil; sprinkle with ¼ teaspoon salt. Place vegetables in a grill wok or basket. Grill, uncovered, over medium heat for 8-12 minutes or until tender, stirring occasionally.

3. Remove and discard stems and gills from mushrooms. Brush mushrooms and eggplant with 1 tablespoon oil; sprinkle with remaining salt. Grill mushrooms, covered, over medium heat for 12-15 minutes or until tender. Grill eggplant, covered, over medium heat for 4-5 minutes on each side or until tender.

4. In a small bowl, combine the goat cheese, parsley, ½ teaspoon garlic and remaining pepper.

5. Place mushrooms on a greased baking sheet; spread each one with 2 teaspoons cheese mixture. Layer with zucchini, squash, 2 teaspoons cheese mixture, eggplant and remaining cheese mixture. Top with the mozzarella cheese and tomato. Bake at 350° for 8-10 minutes or until cheese is melted.

6. In a large skillet, saute remaining garlic in remaining oil for 1 minute. Add spinach; cook 4-5 minutes or until wilted. Divide among four plates; top with a mushroom stack. Drizzle with vinaigrette.

NOTE *If you do not have a grill wok or basket, use a disposable foil pan. Poke holes in the bottom of the pan with a meat fork to allow liquid to drain.*

Grilled Vegetables & Goat Cheese Napoleons

Did you know?

Goat cheese is a soft, easily spreadable cheese that has a tangy flavor. Feta and chevre are examples of goat cheese.

Carrots on the Grill

Dinner guests and friends are always surprised when I tell them my carrots are prepared on the grill. The soy sauce and ginger flavors complement a wide variety of meaty entrees.

—**CAROL GAUS** ELK GROVE VILLAGE, IL

START TO FINISH: 30 MIN.
MAKES: 4-6 SERVINGS

- ¼ cup soy sauce
- ¼ cup canola oil
- 1 tablespoon minced fresh gingerroot
- 1 tablespoon cider vinegar
- 1 garlic clove, minced
- 1 pound large carrots, halved lengthwise

1. In a large bowl, combine the soy sauce, oil, ginger, vinegar and garlic. Add carrots; toss to coat.

2. With tongs, place carrots on grill rack. Grill, covered, over medium heat for 15-20 minutes or until tender, turning and basting frequently with soy sauce mixture.

Mexican Flank Steak Tacos

Here's a traditional Mexican dish prepared with a twist! The fruity salsa cools down the spicy pesto.

—**STEVE MEREDITH** STREAMWOOD, IL

PREP: 30 MIN. + MARINATING
GRILL: 15 MIN. • **MAKES:** 4 SERVINGS

- 1 medium onion, chopped
- ¼ cup lime juice
- 2 tablespoons lemon-pepper seasoning
- 2 tablespoons minced fresh cilantro
- 2 garlic cloves, minced
- ¼ teaspoon salt
- ¼ teaspoon pepper
- 1 beef flank steak (1 to 2 pounds)

CILANTRO PESTO

- 1 cup fresh cilantro leaves
- 1 habanero pepper
- 1 garlic clove

Mexican Flank Steak Tacos

- ½ teaspoon salt
- ½ teaspoon pepper
- 3 tablespoons olive oil

SALSA

- 1 medium mango, peeled and halved
- ⅔ pound fresh pineapple, cut into 3 spears
- 2 medium ripe avocados, peeled pitted and halved
- 1 medium red onion, chopped
- 8 corn tortillas (6 inches)

1. In a large resealable plastic bag, combine the first seven ingredients. Add the steak; seal bag and turn to coat. Refrigerate for 6 hours or overnight.

2. Place the cilantro, habanero, garlic, salt and pepper in a food processor; cover and pulse until chopped. While processing, gradually add oil.

3. For salsa, grill the mango, pineapple and avocado, covered, over medium heat for 2-3 minutes on each side or until tender; set aside.

4. Drain and discard marinade from steak. Moisten a paper towel with cooking oil; using long-handled tongs, rub on grill rack to lightly coat. Grill steak, covered, over medium heat for 6-8 minutes on each side or until meat reaches desired doneness (for medium-rare, a thermometer should read 145°; medium, 160°; well-done, 170°). Let stand for 10 minutes before slicing.

5. Place onion in a small bowl. Chop the grilled fruit and avocado; add to bowl. Grill tortillas, uncovered, over medium heat for about 1 minute on each side or until warm.

6. Thinly slice beef; place on tortillas. Top with salsa and pesto.
NOTE *Wear disposable gloves when cutting hot peppers; the oils can burn skin. Avoid touching your face.*

ON THE PATIO!

Tuscan-Style
Grilled Trout

Grilled Shrimp Salads with Coconut Vinaigrette

I tried a salad similar to this while visiting a friend in Florida. When I returned, I was determined to re-create the same refreshing combination. The secret is the coconut-milk marinade, which makes the shrimp incredibly tender and flavorful!

—**SARAH VASQUES** MILFORD, NH

PREP: 20 MIN. + MARINATING
GRILL: 10 MIN. • **MAKES:** 4 SERVINGS

- 1 **cup coconut milk**
- ⅓ **cup honey**
- 2 **tablespoons rice vinegar**
- 1 **tablespoon canola oil**
- ¼ **teaspoon salt**
- 1 **pound uncooked large shrimp, peeled and deveined**

SALAD

- 4 **cups spring mix salad greens**
- 1 **cup green grapes**
- ½ **cup flaked coconut**
- ½ **cup dried cranberries**
- ¼ **cup sliced almonds, toasted**

1. In a small bowl, combine the first five ingredients. Pour ¾ cup into a large resealable plastic bag. Add the shrimp; seal bag and turn to coat. Refrigerate for up to 30 minutes. Cover and refrigerate remaining vinaigrette.

2. Drain and discard vinaigrette from shrimp. Thread the shrimp onto four metal or soaked wooden skewers. Moisten a paper towel with cooking oil; using long-handled tongs, rub on grill rack to coat lightly.

3. Grill shrimp, covered, over medium heat or broil 4 in. from the heat for 6-8 minutes or until shrimp turn pink, turning once. Divide salad ingredients among four plates; top with shrimp. Serve with reserved vinaigrette.

Tuscan-Style Grilled Trout

My husband is an avid fisherman, so I am constantly challenged to concoct recipes featuring his catch. The Tuscan accents really shine through in this grilled entree, making it one of our favorites.

—**ROXANNE CHAN** ALBANY, CA

PREP: 25 MIN. • **GRILL:** 15 MIN.
MAKES: 4 SERVINGS (3 CUPS RELISH)

- 4 **pan-dressed trout (about 8 ounces each)**
- 1 **tablespoon olive oil**
- ½ **cup shredded zucchini**
- ¼ **cup chopped roasted sweet red peppers**
- 2 **tablespoons tapenade or ripe olive bruschetta topping**
- 1 **tablespoon minced fresh parsley**
- 1 **garlic clove, minced**
- 1 **teaspoon balsamic vinegar**

RELISH

- 2 **large tomatoes, chopped**
- ½ **cup chopped fennel bulb**
- 1 **green onion, thinly sliced**
- 2 **tablespoons pine nuts, toasted**
- 2 **tablespoons minced fresh basil**
- 1 **teaspoon lemon juice**
- ½ **teaspoon lemon-pepper seasoning**

1. Rub trout with oil. In a small bowl, combine the zucchini, red peppers, tapenade, parsley, garlic and vinegar; spoon into fish cavities.

2. Place fish in a well-greased grill basket. Grill, covered, over medium heat for 8-10 minutes or until fish is browned on the bottom. Turn; grill for 5-7 minutes longer or until fish flakes easily with a fork.

3. In a small bowl, combine the relish ingredients; serve with trout.

FAST FIX ▸ Brown Sugar Grilled Peaches with White Chocolate

When I decided to host a dinner party, I was determined to develop an original dessert that I could serve straight off the grill. This is absolutely divine, especially when topped with whipped cream or a scoop of peach ice cream.

—TONYA BURKHARD DAVIS, IL

START TO FINISH: 20 MIN.
MAKES: 8 SERVINGS

- ¼ cup butter, melted
- 2 tablespoons brown sugar
- ½ teaspoon ground cinnamon
- 4 medium peaches, halved and pitted
- ⅓ cup chopped white baking chocolate
- 3 tablespoons chopped pecans
  Whipped cream, optional

1. In a small bowl, combine the butter, brown sugar and cinnamon. Add the peaches, one half at a time, and toss to coat. Reserve the remaining butter mixture.

2. Moisten a paper towel with cooking oil; using long-handled tongs, rub on grill rack to coat lightly. Place the peaches, cut side down, on the grill rack. Grill, covered, over medium heat for 5 minutes.

3. Turn and fill peaches with white chocolate. Drizzle with reserved butter mixture. Cover and grill 4-5 minutes longer or until peaches are tender and begin to caramelize.

4. Sprinkle peaches with pecans and serve with whipped cream if desired.

Brown Sugar Grilled Peaches with White Chocolate

ON THE PATIO! **145**

ON THE PATIO!

Shrimp-Stuffed Poblano Peppers

Since my mom enjoys shrimp and slightly spicy food, I decided to create these shrimp-stuffed poblanos to surprise her. She was delighted with the results!

—TINA GARCIA-ORTIZ TAMPA, FL

PREP: 35 MIN. • **BAKE:** 10 MIN.
MAKES: 8 SERVINGS

- 4 **large poblano peppers**
- 2 **tablespoons butter, melted, divided**
- 1 **teaspoon coarsely ground pepper**
- ½ **teaspoon kosher salt**
- 1 **small onion, finely chopped**
- 2 **celery ribs, chopped**
- 4 **ounces cream cheese, softened**
- 1 **pound chopped cooked peeled shrimp**
- 1¾ **cups shredded Mexican cheese blend**
- 1½ **cups cooked rice**
- 2 **tablespoons lemon juice**
- 2 **teaspoons dried cilantro flakes**
- ½ **teaspoon onion powder**
- ½ **teaspoon garlic powder**

TOPPING
- 1 **cup panko (Japanese) bread crumbs**
- ¼ **cup grated Parmesan cheese**
- 2 **tablespoons butter, melted**

Shrimp-Stuffed Poblano Peppers

1. Cut peppers in half lengthwise and discard seeds. Place the peppers, cut side down, in an ungreased 15x10x1-in. baking pan. Brush with 1 tablespoon butter; sprinkle with pepper and salt. Bake, uncovered, at 350° for 10-15 minutes or until tender.

2. Meanwhile, in a large skillet, saute onion and celery in remaining butter until tender. Stir in cream cheese until melted. Add the shrimp, cheese blend, rice, lemon juice and seasonings; heat through. Spoon into pepper halves.

3. Place in an ungreased 15x10x1-in. baking pan. Combine all the topping ingredients; sprinkle over peppers. Bake, uncovered, at 350° for 10-15 minutes or until the topping is golden brown.

NOTE *Wear disposable gloves when cutting hot peppers; the oils can burn skin. Avoid touching your face.*

FAST FIX ▸ # Papaya-Avocado Tossed Salad

Fruit makes a terrific addition to green salads in summer. Our salad tosses papaya and avocado into the mix!

—TASTE OF HOME TEST KITCHEN

START TO FINISH: 25 MIN.
MAKES: 8 SERVINGS

- 4 **cups torn red leaf lettuce**
- 4 **cups torn green leaf lettuce**
- 1 **medium papaya, peeled, seeded and sliced**
- 1 **large ripe avocado, peeled and sliced**
- ½ **cup sliced red onion**

DRESSING
- ¼ **cup olive oil**
- 3 **tablespoons lemon juice**
- 1 **tablespoon grated lemon peel**
- 2 **teaspoons white wine vinegar**
- 1 **teaspoon sugar**
- ⅛ **teaspoon salt**

In a large salad bowl, gently toss the lettuce, papaya, avocado and onion. In a jar with a tight-fitting lid, combine the dressing ingredients; shake well. Drizzle over salad; toss to coat.

FAST FIX ▸ Grilled Sesame Orange Tuna Steaks

This recipe was a collaboration between my son and me. He wanted to enter a recipe contest because he aspires to be a chef someday. Although the fish steaks look fancy, they're really easy to make.

—LORNA MCFADDEN
PORT ORCHARD, WA

START TO FINISH: 25 MIN.
MAKES: 4 SERVINGS

- 1½ cups instant brown rice
- 2 cups fresh sugar snap peas
- 2 tablespoons honey
- 1 tablespoon butter
- 1 snack-size cup (4 ounces) mandarin oranges, drained
- ¼ cup unsalted cashews, coarsely chopped
- 4 tuna steaks (6 ounces each)
- 5 tablespoons sesame ginger marinade, divided

1. Cook rice according to the package directions. In a large skillet, saute peas and honey in butter until crisp-tender. Add oranges and cashews; cook and stir 1 minute longer.

2. Brush tuna with 2 tablespoons of marinade. Moisten a paper towel with cooking oil; using long-handled tongs, rub on grill rack to coat lightly. Grill tuna, covered, over high heat or broil 3-4 in. from the heat for 3-4 minutes on each side for medium-rare or until slightly pink in the center.

3. Brush the tuna with the remaining marinade; serve with rice and the snap pea mixture.

Grilled Broccoli

Grilled Broccoli

This is my longtime favorite side dish. With its lemon and Parmesan flavors, it once took second-place in a cooking contest.

—ALICE NULLE WOODSTOCK, IL

PREP: 5 MIN. + STANDING • **GRILL:** 10 MIN.
MAKES: 6 SERVINGS

- 6 cups fresh broccoli spears
- 2 tablespoons plus 1½ teaspoons lemon juice
- 2 tablespoons olive oil
- ¼ teaspoon salt
- ¼ teaspoon pepper
- ¾ cup grated Parmesan cheese
  Shaved Parmesan cheese and purple basil leaves, optional

1. Place broccoli in a large bowl. Combine the lemon juice, oil, salt and pepper; drizzle over broccoli and toss to coat. Let stand for 30 minutes.

2. Toss broccoli, then drain marinade. Place cheese in a large resealable plastic bag. Add broccoli, a few pieces at a time, shake to coat.

3. Moisten a paper towel with cooking oil; using long-handled tongs, rub on grill rack to coat lightly. Prepare grill for indirect heat using a drip pan. Place broccoli over drip pan and grill, covered, over indirect medium heat for 8-10 minutes on each side or until crisp-tender. If desired, garnish with shaved Parmesan and fresh basil.

Grilled Sesame Orange Tuna Steaks

**Apple-Butter
Barbecued Chicken**

Apple-Butter Barbecued Chicken

Cooking is my passion; so much so, that I sometimes think of recipes in my sleep and wake up to write them down! This dream-inspired dish has become my family's most-requested chicken recipe.

—**HOLLY KILBEL** AKRON, OH

PREP: 15 MIN.
GRILL: 1½ HOURS + STANDING
MAKES: 6-8 SERVINGS

- 1 teaspoon salt
- ¾ teaspoon garlic powder
- ¼ teaspoon pepper
- ⅛ teaspoon cayenne pepper
- 1 roasting chicken (6 to 7 pounds)
- 1 can (11½ ounces) unsweetened apple juice
- ½ cup apple butter
- ¼ cup barbecue sauce

1. Combine the salt, garlic powder, pepper and cayenne; sprinkle over the chicken.

2. Prepare grill for indirect heat, using a drip pan. Pour half of the apple juice into another container and save for another use. With a can opener, poke additional holes in the top of the can. Holding the chicken with legs pointed down, lower chicken over the can so it fills the body cavity. Place chicken on grill rack over drip pan.

3. Grill chicken, covered, over indirect medium heat for 1½ to 2 hours or until a thermometer reads 180° in the thigh. Combine apple butter and barbecue sauce; baste chicken occasionally during the last 30 minutes. Remove chicken from grill; cover and let stand for 10 minutes. Remove chicken from can before carving.

Caribbean-Spiced Pork Tenderloin with Peach Salsa

I love this recipe because of its depth of flavors and burst of colors. It's also easy to make and is one of our summertime go-to grill entrees when peaches are in season.

—**HOLLY BAUER** WEST BEND, WI

PREP: 15 MIN. • **GRILL:** 20 MIN.
MAKES: 4 SERVINGS (1⅓ CUPS SALSA)

- ¾ cup chopped peeled fresh peaches
- 1 small sweet red pepper, chopped
- 1 jalapeno pepper, seeded and chopped
- 2 tablespoons finely chopped red onion
- 2 tablespoons minced fresh cilantro
- 1 tablespoon lime juice
- 1 garlic clove, minced
- ⅛ teaspoon salt
- ⅛ teaspoon pepper

- 2 tablespoons olive oil
- 1 tablespoon brown sugar
- 1 tablespoon Caribbean jerk seasoning
- 1 teaspoon dried thyme
- 1 teaspoon dried rosemary, crushed
- ½ teaspoon seasoned salt
- 1 pork tenderloin (1 pound)

1. In a small bowl, combine the first nine ingredients; set aside. In another small bowl, combine the oil, brown sugar, jerk seasoning, thyme, rosemary and seasoned salt. Rub over pork.

2. Grill pork, covered, over medium heat for 9-11 minutes on each side or until a thermometer reads 145°. Let stand for 5 minutes before slicing. Serve with the salsa.

NOTE *Wear disposable gloves when cutting hot peppers; the oils can burn skin. Avoid touching your face.*

Caribbean-Spiced Pork Tenderloin with Peach Salsa

Peppered Steaks with Salsa

We grill all year long, and beef is so good cooked outdoors. The simple marinade makes these steaks very juicy. We enjoy them with the tortillas and refreshing salsa.

—**ROBIN HYDE** LINCOLN, NE

PREP: 25 MIN. + MARINATING
GRILL: 15 MIN. • **MAKES:** 4 SERVINGS

- ½ cup red wine vinegar
- 2 tablespoons lime juice
- 2 tablespoons olive oil
- 2 teaspoons chili powder
- 1 garlic clove, minced
- 1 to 2 teaspoons crushed red pepper flakes
- 1 teaspoon salt
- ½ teaspoon pepper
- 4 beef eye round steaks (6 ounces each)

SALSA
- 1 large tomato, seeded and chopped
- 1 medium ripe avocado, chopped
- 2 green onions, thinly sliced
- 1 tablespoon lime juice
- 1 tablespoon minced fresh cilantro
- 1 garlic clove, minced
- ¼ to ½ teaspoon salt
- ¼ teaspoon pepper

1. In a bowl, combine the first eight ingredients. Pour ½ cup into a large resealable plastic bag; add steaks. Seal bag and turn to coat; refrigerate 8 hours or overnight. Cover and refrigerate remaining marinade for basting.

2. Combine salsa ingredients; cover and chill.

3. Drain and discard marinade from steaks. Grill, covered, over medium heat for 7-8 minutes on each side or until meat reaches desired doneness (for medium-rare, a thermometer should read 145°; medium, 160°; well-done, 170°), basting with reserved marinade. Serve with salsa.

Lemon Vinaigrette Potato Salad

Lemon Vinaigrette Potato Salad

I whipped up this recipe for a friend who needed a potato salad for hot weather. The vinaigrette makes a delicious alternative to traditional mayonnaise-based potato salads. I've also substituted fresh thyme for the basil.

—**MELANIE CLOYD** MULLICA HILL, NJ

PREP: 25 MIN. • **COOK:** 15 MIN.
MAKES: 12 SERVINGS

- 3 pounds red potatoes, cut into 1-inch cubes
- ½ cup olive oil
- 3 tablespoons lemon juice
- 2 tablespoons minced fresh basil
- 2 tablespoons minced fresh parsley
- 1 tablespoon red wine vinegar
- 1 teaspoon grated lemon peel
- ¾ teaspoon salt
- ½ teaspoon pepper
- 1 small onion, finely chopped

1. Place potatoes in a large saucepan and cover with water. Bring to a boil. Reduce heat; cover and simmer for 10-15 minutes or until tender.

2. Meanwhile, in a small bowl, whisk the oil, lemon juice, herbs, vinegar, lemon peel, salt and pepper.

3. Drain potatoes. Place in a large bowl; add onion. Drizzle with the vinaigrette; toss to coat. Serve warm or chill until serving.

Peppered Steaks with Salsa

Tasty 'n' Tangy Baby Back Ribs

For these ribs, I doctor up bottled barbecue sauce with a blend of ingredients, including honey, mustard and red pepper flakes.

—**GLADYS GIBBS** BRUSH CREEK, TN

PREP: 30 MIN. + MARINATING
GRILL: 1¼ HOURS • **MAKES:** 4 SERVINGS

- 1 **bottle (18 ounces) barbecue sauce**
- 1 **cup honey**
- 1 **can (6 ounces) tomato paste**
- ½ **cup white vinegar**
- ½ **cup lemon juice**
- ¼ **cup soy sauce**
- ¼ **cup Dijon mustard**
- 2 **tablespoons Worcestershire sauce**
- 1 **garlic clove, minced**
- 1 **teaspoon crushed red pepper flakes**
- 1 **teaspoon ground allspice**
- 2 **teaspoons coarsely ground pepper, divided**
- 4 **to 5 pounds pork baby back ribs**
- 1 **teaspoon salt**

1. In a large saucepan, combine the first 11 ingredients. Add 1 teaspoon pepper. Bring to a boil. Reduce heat; simmer, uncovered, for 15 minutes. Remove from the heat; set aside 2 cups of sauce for basting.
2. Brush the ribs with the remaining sauce; place in two large resealable plastic bags. Seal bags and turn to coat; refrigerate for 30 minutes.
3. Prepare grill for indirect heat, using a drip pan. Drain and discard marinade from ribs. Sprinkle both sides of ribs with salt and remaining pepper. Place on grill rack over drip pan. Grill, covered, over indirect medium heat for 1 hour, turning occasionally.
4. Baste ribs with some of the reserved sauce. Grill 15 minutes longer or until juices run clear and meat is tender, turning and basting occasionally.

Grilled Fajita Rolled Steak

Grilled Fajita Rolled Steak

My family was tired of eating the same fajitas, so I created this recipe. I like it with chipotle marinade, but black pepper also works well.

—**CRYSTAL BRUNS** ILIFF, CO

PREP: 20 MIN. • **GRILL:** 20 MIN.
MAKES: 4 SERVINGS

- 1 **beef sirloin tip steak (1 inch thick and 1 pound)**
- 1 **cup chipotle marinade**
- 1 **package (14 ounces) frozen pepper strips**
- 1 **tablespoon canola oil**
- 2 **ounces cream cheese, softened**

1. Flatten steak to ¼-in. thickness. Pour marinade into a large resealable plastic bag; add steak. Seal bag and turn to coat; refrigerate for 4 hours or overnight, turning occasionally.
2. In a large skillet, saute pepper strips in oil until tender. Remove from the heat. Drain and discard the marinade from steak. Spread cream cheese over steak to within 1 in. of edges. Top with half of the peppers. Roll up jelly-roll style, starting with a long side; tie with kitchen string.
3. Grill the steak, covered, over medium heat for 20-25 minutes or until meat reaches desired doneness (for medium-rare, a thermometer should read 145°; medium, 160°; well-done, 170°), turning occasionally. Let stand for 10 minutes before slicing. Discard toothpicks. Serve with remaining pepper strips.

ON THE PATIO!

Grilled Sirloin with Chili-Beer Barbecue Sauce

Grilled Sirloin with Chili-Beer Barbecue Sauce

Tender steak is treated to a tangy barbecue sauce that's so tasty! Cayenne pepper and chili powder add a hint of heat that gives this recipe extra pizzazz.
—**TASTE OF HOME TEST KITCHEN**

PREP: 40 MIN. • **GRILL:** 20 MIN.
MAKES: 8 SERVINGS

- 1½ cups beer or nonalcoholic beer
- 1 small onion, chopped
- ¾ cup chili sauce
- 2 tablespoons soy sauce
- 1 tablespoon brown sugar
- 2 teaspoons chili powder
- 2 garlic cloves, minced
- ¼ teaspoon cayenne pepper
- ¼ teaspoon ground mustard
- ⅛ teaspoon ground cumin
- 2 beef top sirloin steaks (1½ pounds each)
- ½ teaspoon salt
- ½ teaspoon pepper

1. In a small saucepan, combine the first 10 ingredients. Bring to a boil. Reduce heat; simmer, uncovered, for 25-30 minutes or until thickened. Set aside ¾ cup and keep warm.

2. Sprinkle steaks with salt and pepper. Grill steaks, covered, over medium heat or broil 4 in. from the heat for 9-13 minutes on each side or until meat reaches desired doneness (for medium-rare, a thermometer should read 145°; medium 160°; well-done 170°), basting occasionally with remaining sauce. Slice meat and serve with reserved sauce.

FAST FIX ▶ Plum Tomatoes with Balsamic Vinaigrette

I like to toss sliced plum tomatoes and red onion with a homemade vinaigrette to create this summery salad. Fresh basil adds the flavorful finishing touch.

—ANN SOBOTKA GLENDALE, AZ

START TO FINISH: 10 MIN.
MAKES: 4 SERVINGS

- 6 medium plum or heirloom tomatoes, sliced
- ½ cup sliced red onion
- 3 tablespoons balsamic vinegar
- 2 tablespoons olive oil
- ½ teaspoon sugar
- ⅛ teaspoon salt
- ⅛ teaspoon garlic powder
- ⅛ teaspoon pepper
- 4 fresh basil leaves, snipped

In a large bowl, gently combine the tomatoes and onion. In a small bowl, whisk the vinegar, oil, sugar, salt, garlic powder and pepper. Pour over tomato mixture; toss gently to coat. Sprinkle with basil. Serve at room temperature with a slotted spoon.

Grilled Asparagus Medley

Plum Tomatoes with Balsamic Vinaigrette

FAST FIX ▶ Grilled Asparagus Medley

This colorful veggie dish happened by accident. One evening, I didn't have room on the grill for all the things I wanted to prepare, so I threw two of the dishes together and came up with this medley! It goes great with any grilled meat.

—PAM GASPERS HASTINGS, NE

START TO FINISH: 25 MIN.
MAKES: 8 SERVINGS

- 1 pound fresh asparagus, trimmed
- 1 each sweet red, yellow and green pepper, julienned
- 1 cup sliced fresh mushrooms
- 1 medium tomato, chopped
- 1 medium onion, sliced
- 1 can (2¼ ounces) sliced ripe olives, drained
- 2 garlic cloves, minced
- 2 tablespoons olive oil
- 1 teaspoon minced fresh parsley
- ½ teaspoon salt
- ½ teaspoon pepper
- ¼ teaspoon lemon-pepper seasoning
- ¼ teaspoon dill weed

1. In a disposable foil pan, combine the vegetables, olives and garlic; drizzle with oil and toss to coat. Sprinkle with parsley, salt, pepper, lemon-pepper and dill; toss to coat.
2. Grill, covered, over indirect medium heat for 20-25 minutes or until the vegetables are crisp-tender, stirring occasionally.

Pineapple Pico Tuna Steaks

Grilled Vegetable Medley

A simple marinade flavors this vegetable blend for a tasty side dish.

—TASTE OF HOME TEST KITCHEN

PREP: 15 MIN. + MARINATING
GRILL: 5 MIN. • **MAKES:** 4 SERVINGS

- 2 tablespoons Worcestershire sauce
- 2 tablespoons olive oil
- 2 tablespoons Dijon mustard
- 1 teaspoon herbes de Provence
- ¼ teaspoon pepper
- 3 baby eggplants or 1 medium eggplant, cut lengthwise into ½-inch slices
- 3 small yellow summer squash, cut lengthwise into ½-inch slices
- 2 cups fresh sugar snap peas

1. In a large resealable plastic bag, combine the first five ingredients; add eggplant, squash and peas. Seal bag and turn to coat; refrigerate for 2 hours, turning once.
2. Drain and discard marinade. Place the vegetables in a grill basket or disposable foil pan with slits cut in the bottom. Grill, covered, over medium heat for 5-7 minutes or until tender, stirring once.
NOTE *Look for herbes de Provence in the spice aisle.*

 **Did you know?**

Herbes de Provence is the essential flavor of Southern France. The blend may contain basil, fennel, lavender, marjoram, rosemary, sage, summer savory and thyme.

Pineapple Pico Tuna Steaks

Bursting with flavor from an easy-to-make marinade, these tuna steaks are topped with a fresh-tasting pico de gallo made from pineapple, tomatoes, lime juice and a nice kick of jalapeno.

—SALLY SIBTHORPE
SHELBY TOWNSHIP, MI

PREP: 10 MIN. + MARINATING
GRILL: 10 MIN. • **MAKES:** 4 SERVINGS

- ½ cup tequila
- 3 tablespoons brown sugar
- 2 tablespoons lime juice
- 1 tablespoon chili powder
- 1 tablespoon olive oil
- 1 teaspoon salt
- 4 tuna steaks (6 ounces each)

PICO DE GALLO
- 1 cup chopped fresh pineapple
- 1 plum tomato, finely chopped
- ⅓ cup finely chopped onion
- ¼ cup minced fresh cilantro
- 2 tablespoons minced seeded jalapeno pepper
- 2 tablespoons lime juice
- 1 tablespoon olive oil
- 2 teaspoons grated lime peel
- ½ teaspoon salt

1. In a large resealable plastic bag, combine the first six ingredients. Add the tuna; seal bag and turn to coat. Refrigerate for 30 minutes.
2. Meanwhile, in a small bowl, combine pico de gallo ingredients. Cover and refrigerate until serving.
3. Drain and discard marinade. Moisten a paper towel with cooking oil; using long-handled tongs, rub on grill rack to lightly coat. For medium-rare, grill tuna, covered, over high heat or broil 3-4 inches from the heat for 3-4 minutes on each side or until slightly pink in the center. Serve with pico de gallo.
NOTE *Wear disposable gloves when cutting hot peppers; the oils can burn skin. Avoid touching your face.*

Mahogany-Glazed Mushroom Burgers

These burgers are covered with a few of my favorite things...portobello mushrooms, goat cheese, basil and mascarpone. They're quite juicy, so serve them with extra napkins!

—**LISA KEYS** KENNET SQUARE, PA

PREP: 30 MIN. • **GRILL:** 10 MIN.
MAKES: 6 SERVINGS

- ¼ cup maple syrup
- ¼ cup Kahlua (coffee liqueur)
- ¼ cup reduced-sodium soy sauce
- 10 ounces sliced baby portobello mushrooms
- ½ cup thinly sliced red onion
- 2 tablespoons olive oil
- ¼ teaspoon kosher salt
- ⅛ teaspoon pepper

CHEESE SPREAD
- ½ cup mascarpone cheese
- ½ cup crumbled goat cheese
- ¼ cup minced fresh parsley
- 2 tablespoons minced fresh basil or 2 teaspoons dried basil
- ⅛ teaspoon pepper

BURGERS
- 1½ pounds ground beef
- 1 teaspoon kosher salt
- ½ teaspoon pepper
- 6 hard rolls, split

1. In a small saucepan, combine the maple syrup, Kahlua and soy sauce. Bring to a boil; cook for 8 minutes or until liquid is reduced by half.

2. In a large skillet, saute mushrooms and onion in oil until tender. Add the salt, pepper and ¼ cup of Kahlua mixture. Cook and stir until liquid is almost evaporated.

3. In a small bowl, combine the cheese spread ingredients; cover and refrigerate until serving.

4. Crumble beef into a large bowl. Sprinkle with salt and pepper; mix well. Shape into six patties.

5. Grill burgers, covered, over medium heat for 6 minutes. Turn; grill 5-8 minutes longer or until a thermometer reads 160° and juices run clear, basting occasionally with remaining Kahlua mixture. Grill rolls, uncovered, for 1-2 minutes or until toasted.

6. Spread rolls with cheese spread; top with burgers and mushroom mixture. Replace tops.

FAST FIX ▶ Grilled Stone Fruits with Balsamic Syrup

Get ready to experience another side of stone fruits. Hot off the grill, this late-summer dessert practically melts in your mouth. The balsamic vinegar adds a lovely dimension to the fruits.

—**SONYA LABBE** WEST HOLLYWOOD, CA

START TO FINISH: 20 MIN.
MAKES: 4 SERVINGS

- ½ cup balsamic vinegar
- 2 tablespoons brown sugar
- 2 medium peaches, peeled and halved
- 2 medium nectarines, peeled and halved
- 2 medium plums, peeled and halved

1. In a small saucepan, combine the vinegar and brown sugar. Bring to a boil; cook until the liquid is reduced by half.

2. Moisten a paper towel with cooking oil; using long-handled tongs, rub on grill rack to coat lightly. Grill peaches, nectarines and plums, covered, over medium heat or broil 4 in. from the heat for 3-4 minutes on each side or until tender.

3. Slice fruits; arrange on a serving plate. Drizzle with sauce.

Mahogany-Glazed Mushroom Burger

ON THE PATIO!

Grilled
Corn Medley

Jazzed-Up
French Bread

Chili-Beer
Glazed Steaks

Grilled Corn Medley

Who knew a store-bought dressing could add so much flavor? This medley tastes delightful made with garden-fresh veggies.

—TASTE OF HOME TEST KITCHEN

START TO FINISH: 20 MIN.
MAKES: 8 SERVINGS

- 3 **medium ears sweet corn, cut into 2-inch pieces**
- 1 **medium sweet red pepper, cut into 1-inch pieces**
- 1 **medium zucchini, sliced**
- 20 **small fresh mushrooms**
- ¼ **cup creamy Caesar salad dressing**
- ¼ **teaspoon salt**
- ¼ **teaspoon pepper**

In a large bowl, combine all the ingredients; toss to coat. Transfer to a disposable foil pan. Grill, covered, over medium-hot heat for 5 minutes; stir. Grill 3-5 minutes longer or until vegetables are tender.

Chili-Beer Glazed Steaks

Bold ingredients give these tender grilled steaks a taste you won't soon forget. We loved the slightly sweet and pleasantly smoky glaze.

—GEORDYTH SULLIVAN CUTLER BAY, FL

PREP: 25 MIN. • **GRILL:** 10 MIN.
MAKES: 4 SERVINGS

- ⅔ **cup chili sauce**
- ⅔ **cup spicy steak sauce**
- ½ **cup chopped shallots**
- ½ **cup beer or nonalcoholic beer**
- 4 **boneless beef top loin steaks (8 ounces each)**
- ½ **teaspoon salt**
- ½ **teaspoon pepper**

1. In a small saucepan, combine the chili sauce, steak sauce, shallots and beer. Bring to a boil. Reduce heat; simmer, uncovered, for 12-15 minutes or until slightly thickened.

Set aside ½ cup for serving and keep warm. Sprinkle steaks with salt and pepper.
2. Moisten a paper towel with cooking oil; using long-handled tongs, rub on grill rack to coat lightly. Grill steaks, covered, over medium heat or broil 4 in. from the heat for 4-6 minutes on each side or until the meat reaches desired doneness (for medium-rare, a thermometer should read 145°; medium, 160°; well-done, 170°), basting occasionally with sauce mixture. Serve with reserved sauce.
NOTE *Top loin steak may be labeled as strip steak, KS City steak, NY strip steak, ambassador steak or boneless club steak in your region.*

Jazzed-Up French Bread

Fire up the grill for this savory French bread. It takes just seconds to prepare.
—LORI LECROY EAST TAWAS, MI

PREP: 10 MIN.
GRILL: 30 MIN. + STANDING
MAKES: 10 SERVINGS

- 2 **cups (8 ounces) shredded Colby-Monterey Jack cheese**
- ⅔ **cup mayonnaise**
- 6 **green onions, chopped**
- 1 **loaf (1 pound) French bread, halved lengthwise**

1. In a small bowl, combine the cheese, mayonnaise and onions. Spread over cut sides of the bread and reassemble loaf. Wrap in a double thickness of heavy-duty foil (about 28 in. x 18 in.); seal tightly.
2. Grill bread, covered, over indirect medium heat for 25-30 minutes or until cheese is melted, turning once. Let stand for 5 minutes before cutting into slices.

Grilled Mahi Mahi

Instead of the usual burgers or chicken breasts when grilling out, prepare this mahi mahi and reel in the raves!
—TASTE OF HOME TEST KITCHEN

PREP: 20 MIN. + MARINATING
GRILL: 10 MIN. • **MAKES:** 8 SERVINGS

- ¾ **cup reduced-sodium teriyaki sauce**
- 2 **tablespoons sherry or pineapple juice**
- 2 **garlic cloves**
- 8 **mahi mahi fillets (6 ounces each)**

TROPICAL FRUIT SALSA

- 1 **medium mango, peeled and diced**
- 1 **cup chopped seeded peeled papaya**
- ¾ **cup chopped green pepper**
- ½ **cup cubed fresh pineapple**
- ½ **medium red onion, chopped**
- ¼ **cup minced fresh cilantro**
- ¼ **cup minced fresh mint**
- 1 **tablespoon chopped seeded jalapeno pepper**
- 1 **tablespoon lime juice**
- 1 **tablespoon lemon juice**
- ½ **teaspoon crushed red pepper flakes**

1. In a large resealable plastic bag, combine the teriyaki sauce, sherry or pineapple juice and garlic; add mahi mahi. Seal the bag and turn to coat; refrigerate for 30 minutes.
2. Meanwhile, in a large bowl, mix the salsa ingredients. Cover and refrigerate until serving.
3. Drain and discard marinade. Moisten a paper towel with cooking oil; using long-handled tongs, rub on grill rack to coat lightly. Grill mahi mahi, covered, over medium heat or broil 4 in. from the heat for 4-5 minutes on each side or until fish flakes easily with a fork. Serve with salsa.
NOTE *Wear disposable gloves when cutting hot peppers; the oils can burn skin. Avoid touching your face.*

ON THE PATIO!

Planked Spicy Strip Steaks

To infuse steaks with a sweet, smoky flavor, cook them on wood grilling planks. Simple seasonings are all you need.

—TASTE OF HOME TEST KITCHEN

PREP: 10 MIN. + SOAKING • **GRILL:** 20 MIN.
MAKES: 4 SERVINGS

- 2 **maple grilling planks**
- 4 **boneless beef top loin steaks (12 ounces each)**
- 1 **tablespoon olive oil**
- ¾ **teaspoon ground coriander**
- ¾ **teaspoon chili powder**
- ½ **teaspoon ground allspice**
- ½ **teaspoon cayenne pepper**

1. Soak grilling planks in water for 1 hour. Drizzle the steaks with oil. Combine the coriander, chili powder, allspice and cayenne; rub over both sides of steaks.

2. Grill, covered, over medium heat for 1-2 minutes on each side or until grill marks appear; remove.

3. Place planks on grill over direct medium heat. Cover and heat until planks create a light to medium smoke and begin to crackle (this indicates planks are ready), about 3 minutes. Turn planks over. Place the steaks on the planks.

4. Grill, covered, for 15-20 minutes or until meat reaches desired doneness (for medium-rare, a thermometer should read 145°; medium, 160°; well-done, 170°).

NOTE *Top loin steak may be labeled as strip steak, KS City steak, NY strip steak, ambassador steak or boneless club steak in your region.*

Chocolate Raspberry Pie

After tasting this pie at my sister-in-law's house, I had to have the recipe. I love the chocolate and raspberry layers separated by a dreamy cream layer. It's a joy to serve this treat to dinner guests!

—RUTH BARTEL MORRIS, MB

PREP: 30 MIN. + CHILLING
BAKE: 15 MIN. + COOLING
MAKES: 6-8 SERVINGS

- **Pastry for single-crust pie (9 inches)**
- 3 **tablespoons sugar**
- 1 **tablespoon cornstarch**
- 2 **cups fresh or frozen unsweetened raspberries, thawed**

FILLING

- 1 **package (8 ounces) cream cheese, softened**
- ⅓ **cup sugar**
- ½ **teaspoon vanilla extract**
- ½ **cup heavy whipping cream, whipped**

TOPPING

- 2 **ounces semisweet chocolate**
- 3 **tablespoons butter**

1. Line unpricked pie shell with a double thickness of heavy-duty foil. Bake at 450° for 8 minutes. Remove foil; bake 5 minutes longer. Cool.

2. In a large saucepan, combine sugar and cornstarch. Stir in the raspberries; bring to a boil over medium heat. Boil and stir for 2 minutes. Remove from the heat; cool for 15 minutes. Spread into shell; refrigerate.

3. In a large bowl, beat the cream cheese, sugar and vanilla until fluffy. Fold in whipped cream. Carefully spread over raspberry layer. Cover and refrigerate for at least 1 hour.

4. In a microwave, melt chocolate and butter; stir until smooth. Cool for 4-5 minutes. Pour over filling. Cover and chill for at least 2 hours. Store in the refrigerator. Top with fresh berries.

Chocolate Raspberry Pie

Summer Vegetable Cobbler

Summer Vegetable Cobbler

Here's a comforting vegetarian main dish that uses up a lot of garden produce. Try different squashes like pattypan and crookneck or zucchini.

—ELISABETH LARSEN
PLEASANT GROVE, UT

PREP: 40 MIN. • **BAKE:** 25 MIN.
MAKES: 4 SERVINGS

- 2 tablespoons butter
- 3 small zucchini, sliced
- 1 small sweet red pepper, finely chopped
- 1 small onion, finely chopped
- 2 garlic cloves, minced
- 2 tablespoons all-purpose flour
- 1 cup 2% milk
- ½ teaspoon salt
- ¼ teaspoon pepper

BISCUIT TOPPING
- 1 cup all-purpose flour
- 1 teaspoon baking powder
- ½ teaspoon salt
- 3 tablespoons cold butter
- ¼ cup shredded Parmesan cheese
- 3 tablespoons minced fresh basil
- ⅔ cup 2% milk

1. Preheat oven to 400°. In a large skillet, heat butter over medium-high heat. Add zucchini, red pepper and onion; cook and stir 10-12 minutes or until zucchini is crisp-tender. Add garlic; cook 1 minute longer.
2. In a small bowl, whisk flour, milk, salt and pepper; stir into vegetables. Bring to a boil, stirring constantly; cook and stir 2-3 minutes or until sauce is thickened. Spoon into a greased 8-in.-square baking dish.
3. For topping, in a small bowl, whisk flour, baking powder and salt. Cut in butter until mixture resembles coarse crumbs. Stir in cheese and basil. Add milk; stir just until moistened. Drop by rounded tablespoonfuls over filling. Bake 25-30 minutes or until filling is bubbly and biscuits are golden brown.

FAST FIX ## Raspberry Lemon Layer Cake

Cooking is my favorite hobby. I just love trying recipes with different flavor combinations—such as this pound cake with lemon curd and raspberries.

—JANICE BAKER LONDON, KY

START TO FINISH: 25 MIN.
MAKES: 6 SERVINGS

- 1½ cups heavy whipping cream
- 3 tablespoons confectioners' sugar
- 3 tablespoons orange juice
- 1 loaf (10¾ ounces) frozen pound cake, thawed
- 1 jar (10 ounces) lemon curd
- 2½ cups fresh raspberries

1. In a bowl, beat cream until it begins to thicken. Add confectioners' sugar and orange juice; beat until stiff peaks form. Using a long serrated knife, cut cake horizontally into three layers.
2. Place bottom cake layer on a serving plate; spread with about ⅓ cup lemon curd. Top with 1 cup raspberries and ⅓ cup cream mixture; repeat layers. Replace cake top; spread with the remaining lemon curd.
3. Frost top and sides of cake with remaining cream mixture. Top with remaining raspberries; refrigerate until serving.

Raspberry Lemon Layer Cake

Backyard Red Potato Salad

The distinctive flavors of tarragon and balsamic vinegar combine to make my potato salad something wonderful...it's definitely not your typical side dish.

—**HOLLY BAUER** WEST BEND, WI

PREP: 25 MIN. • **GRILL:** 10 MIN.
MAKES: 9 SERVINGS

- 2½ **pounds small red potatoes**
- 1 **medium onion, cut into ½-inch slices**
- ½ **cup olive oil, divided**
- 1 **teaspoon salt, divided**
- ½ **teaspoon pepper, divided**
- 3 **tablespoons balsamic vinegar**
- 2 **tablespoons lemon juice**
- 1 **tablespoon Dijon mustard**
- 2 **teaspoons sugar**
- 2 **garlic cloves, minced**
- ¼ **cup minced fresh tarragon**

1. Place potatoes in a saucepan and cover with water. Bring to a boil. Reduce heat; cover and cook for 10 minutes. Drain; cool slightly. Cut each in half.

2. In a large bowl, combine potatoes, onion, ¼ cup oil, ½ teaspoon salt and ¼ teaspoon pepper; toss to coat. Arrange, cut sides down, on a grilling grid; place on a grill rack. Grill, covered, over medium heat for 8-10 minutes or until the vegetables are tender and lightly browned, turning occasionally. Chop onion. Place the onion and potatoes in a bowl.

3. In a small bowl, whisk the vinegar, lemon juice, mustard, sugar, garlic and remaining oil, salt and pepper. Add to potato mixture; toss to coat. Sprinkle with tarragon. Serve warm or at room temperature. Refrigerate leftovers.

NOTE *If you do not have a grilling grid, use a disposable foil pan. Poke holes in the bottom of the pan with a meat fork to allow any liquid to drain.*

Steaks with Mushroom Sauce

FAST FIX Steaks with Mushroom Sauce

A versatile sauce tops these sirloin steaks and enhances their beefy flavor. Try the sauce over grilled chicken, too.

—**LADONNA REED** PONCA CITY, OK

START TO FINISH: 25 MIN.
MAKES: 4 SERVINGS

- 4 **beef top sirloin steaks (6 ounces each)**
- ¼ **teaspoon salt**
- ¼ **teaspoon pepper**

SAUCE

- 1 **jar (4½ ounces) sliced mushrooms, drained**
- 1 **teaspoon minced garlic**
- 1 **teaspoon canola oil**
- ½ **cup French onion dip**
- 2 **tablespoons half-and-half cream**
- ½ **teaspoon minced chives**
- ¼ **teaspoon pepper**

1. Sprinkle steaks with salt and pepper. Grill steaks, covered, over medium heat or broil 4 in. from heat for 5-7 minutes on each side or until the meat reaches desired doneness (for medium-rare, a thermometer should read 145°; medium, 160°; well-done, 170°).

2. In a large skillet, saute mushrooms and garlic in oil for 3 minutes. Stir in onion dip, cream, chives and pepper. Bring to a gentle boil. Reduce heat; simmer, uncovered, for 2-3 minutes or until heated through. Serve with steaks.

FAST FIX ▶ Swordfish with Fennel and Tomatoes

Step aside, marinara—there's a new sauce in town! Best of all, it's blissfully fresh with fennel and basil. Television-inspired and husband-adored, this is one recipe too good not to share.

—LAUREL DALZELL MANTECA, CA

START TO FINISH: 25 MIN.
MAKES: 4 SERVINGS

- 1 medium onion, halved and thinly sliced
- 1 fennel bulb, halved and thinly sliced
- 3 tablespoons olive oil
- 1 garlic clove, minced
- 1 can (28 ounces) whole tomatoes, drained
- 2 tablespoons chicken broth
- 2 tablespoons white wine
- ¾ teaspoon pepper
- ½ teaspoon kosher salt
- ½ cup loosely packed basil leaves, thinly sliced
- 1 tablespoon butter

FISH

- 4 swordfish steaks (8 ounces each)
- 2 tablespoons olive oil
- ½ teaspoon kosher salt
- ¼ teaspoon pepper

1. In a large skillet, saute onion and fennel in oil until tender. Add garlic; cook 1 minute longer. Stir in the tomatoes, broth, wine, pepper and salt. Bring to a boil. Reduce heat; simmer, uncovered, for 5 minutes. Stir in basil and butter. Remove from the heat and set aside.

2. Brush swordfish steaks with oil; sprinkle with salt and pepper. Moisten a paper towel with cooking oil; using long-handled tongs, rub on grill rack to coat lightly. Grill swordfish, covered, over medium-hot heat or broil 4 in. from the heat for 5-7 minutes on each side or just until fish turns opaque. Serve with tomato mixture.

Mediterranean Grilled Chicken & Greens

Any chicken entree that's this easy and yummy is a win-win for me. And, it's healthful as well!

—DIANE HALFERTY CORPUS CHRISTI, TX

PREP: 15 MIN. + MARINATING
GRILL: 10 MIN. **•** **MAKES:** 4 SERVINGS

- ¼ cup orange juice
- 6 garlic cloves, minced
- 1 tablespoon balsamic vinegar
- 1½ teaspoons dried thyme
- ½ teaspoon salt
- 4 boneless skinless chicken breast halves (5 ounces each)
- 2 packages (5 ounces each) spring mix salad greens
- 2 cups cherry tomatoes, halved
- ½ cup crumbled feta cheese
- ¼ cup pitted Greek olives, halved
- ¼ cup prepared vinaigrette

1. In a large resealable plastic bag, combine the first five ingredients. Add the chicken; seal bag and turn to coat. Refrigerate 8 hours or overnight.

2. Drain and discard marinade. Moisten a paper towel with cooking oil; using long-handled tongs, rub on grill rack to coat lightly. Grill chicken, covered, over medium heat or broil 4 in. from heat 5-6 minutes on each side or until a thermometer reads 165°.

3. In a large bowl, combine greens, tomatoes, feta cheese and olives. Drizzle with vinaigrette; toss to coat. Slice chicken; serve with salad.

Swordfish with Fennel and Tomatoes

ON THE PATIO!

**Grilled Shrimp
with Spicy-Sweet Sauce**

FAST FIX ▶ Grilled Shrimp
with Spicy-Sweet Sauce

Just the right amount of spice adds zip
to the plump and juicy shrimp in this
five-ingredient appetizer.

—SUSAN HARRISON LAUREL, MD

START TO FINISH: 30 MIN.
MAKES: 15 SERVINGS (⅓ CUP SAUCE)

- 3 tablespoons reduced-fat mayonnaise
- 2 tablespoons sweet chili sauce
- 1 green onion, thinly sliced
- ¾ teaspoon Sriracha Asian hot chili sauce or ½ teaspoon hot pepper sauce
- 45 uncooked large shrimp, peeled and deveined
- ¼ teaspoon salt
- ¼ teaspoon pepper

1. In a small bowl, mix mayonnaise, chili sauce, green onion and Sriracha. Sprinkle shrimp with salt and pepper. Thread three shrimp onto each of 15 metal or soaked wooden skewers.

2. Moisten a paper towel with cooking oil; using long-handled tongs, rub on grill rack to coat lightly. Grill shrimp, covered, over medium heat or broil 4 in. from heat 3-4 minutes on each side or until shrimp turn pink. Serve with sauce.

**Shrimp
Strategy**

Shrimp are sold by size. The bigger the shrimp, the fewer there are per pound. On average, there are 26 to 30 large shrimp in a pound.

Bacon-Wrapped Corn

FAST FIX ▶

Blackened Chicken

This spicy standout packs a one-two punch of flavor. The grilled chicken is basted with a peppery white sauce, and there's always plenty of extra sauce left for dipping.

—**STEPHANIE KENNEY** FALKVILLE, AL

START TO FINISH: 25 MIN.
MAKES: 4 SERVINGS

- 1 tablespoon paprika
- 4 teaspoons sugar, divided
- 1½ teaspoons salt, divided
- 1 teaspoon garlic powder
- 1 teaspoon dried thyme
- 1 teaspoon lemon-pepper seasoning
- 1 teaspoon cayenne pepper
- 1½ to 2 teaspoons pepper, divided
- 4 boneless skinless chicken breast halves (4 ounces each)
- 1⅓ cups mayonnaise
- 2 tablespoons water
- 2 tablespoons cider vinegar

1. In a small bowl, combine the paprika, 1 teaspoon sugar, 1 teaspoon salt, garlic powder, thyme, lemon-pepper, cayenne and ½ to 1 teaspoon pepper; sprinkle over both sides of chicken. Set aside.

2. In another bowl, combine the mayonnaise, water, vinegar and remaining sugar, salt and pepper; cover and refrigerate 1 cup for serving. Save remaining sauce for basting.

3. Grill chicken, covered, over indirect medium heat for 4-6 minutes on each side or until a thermometer reads 165°, basting frequently with remaining sauce. Serve with reserved sauce.

FAST FIX ▶

Bacon-Wrapped Corn

After one bite of this grilled corn on the cob, you'll never go back to your old way of preparing it. The incredible flavor of roasted corn combined with bacon and chili powder is sure to please your palate and bring raves at your next barbecue.

—**LORI BRAMBLE** OMAHA, NE

START TO FINISH: 30 MIN.
MAKES: 8 SERVINGS

- 8 large ears sweet corn, husks removed
- 8 bacon strips
- 2 tablespoons chili powder

Wrap each ear of corn with a bacon strip; place each on a piece of heavy-duty foil. Sprinkle with chili powder. Wrap securely, twisting foil ends to make handles for turning. Grill, uncovered, over medium-hot heat for 20 minutes or until corn is tender and bacon is cooked, turning once.

Blackened Chicken

Creamy Dilled Cucumber Salad

This crunchy, savory side dish, a traditional Norwegian favorite, was a staple at all of our family holidays.
—**PATTY LANOUE STEARNS**
TRAVERSE CITY, MI

PREP: 20 MIN. + CHILLING
MAKES: 6 SERVINGS

- 2 English cucumbers, thinly sliced
- 1 teaspoon salt
- 1½ cups (12 ounces) sour cream
- ¼ cup thinly sliced red onion
- ¼ cup snipped fresh dill
- 2 tablespoons white wine vinegar
- 2 garlic cloves, minced
- 1 teaspoon sugar
- 1 teaspoon coarsely ground pepper

1. Place cucumbers in a colander over a bowl; sprinkle with salt and toss. Let stand 15 minutes. Squeeze and blot dry with paper towels.
2. In a large bowl, combine the remaining ingredients; stir in the cucumbers. Refrigerate, covered, at least 1 hour.

Crispy Grilled Zucchini with Marinara

Creamy Dilled Cucumber Salad

Crispy Grilled Zucchini with Marinara

You don't need a deep-fat fryer for the crispiest little snacks around; let the indoor grill do the work! Try the marinara over ziti or bow-tie pasta for a delicious side dish.
—**STEVE FOY** KIRKWOOD, MO

PREP: 15 MIN. • **COOK:** 5 MIN./BATCH
MAKES: 2 DOZEN (2⅓ CUPS SAUCE)

- 1 can (14½ ounces) diced tomatoes with basil, oregano and garlic, undrained
- 1 can (6 ounces) tomato paste
- ½ cup water
- 2 teaspoons sugar
- ¼ teaspoon salt
- ¼ teaspoon dried basil
- ¼ teaspoon dried oregano
- 1 egg
- ⅓ cup prepared Italian salad dressing
- 1 cup Italian-style panko (Japanese) bread crumbs
- 2 medium zucchini, cut diagonally into ¼-inch slices

1. In a large saucepan, combine the first seven ingredients. Bring to a boil. Reduce heat; simmer, uncovered, for 5-10 minutes or until thickened, stirring occasionally.
2. Meanwhile, in a shallow bowl, whisk egg and salad dressing. Place bread crumbs in another shallow bowl. Dip zucchini slices in egg mixture, then coat with bread crumbs. Cook on an indoor grill for 2-3 minutes or until golden brown. Serve with marinara.

Chipotle Sliders

Here's a recipe that has to be the ultimate in a mini burger. It's simply fabulous! Creamy mayo, cheese and change-of-pace Hawaiian rolls help tame the spicy heat of the chipotle peppers.

—SHAWN SINGLETON VIDOR, TX

START TO FINISH: 30 MIN.
MAKES: 10 SLIDERS

- 1 package (12 ounces) Hawaiian sweet rolls, divided
- 1 teaspoon salt
- ½ teaspoon pepper
- 8 teaspoons minced chipotle peppers in adobo sauce, divided
- 1½ pounds ground beef
- 10 slices pepper Jack cheese
- ½ cup mayonnaise

1. Place 2 rolls in a food processor; process until crumbly. Transfer to a large bowl; add the salt, pepper and 6 teaspoons chipotle peppers. Crumble beef over mixture and mix well. Shape into 10 patties.

2. Grill burgers, covered, over medium heat for 3-4 minutes on each side or until a thermometer reads 160° and juices run clear. Top with the cheese. Grill 1 minute longer or until the cheese is melted.

3. Split remaining rolls and grill, cut side down, over medium heat for 30-60 seconds or until toasted. Combine the mayonnaise and remaining chipotle peppers; spread over roll bottoms. Top each with a burger. Replace roll tops.

FAST FIX
Bacon Garlic Bread

Once they've tasted it, your dinner guests will request this grilled garlic bread all summer long! Serve it as an appetizer or as a quick side dish.

—TASTE OF HOME TEST KITCHEN

START TO FINISH: 30 MIN.
MAKES: 10-12 SERVINGS

- ⅓ cup butter, softened
- ⅓ cup mayonnaise
- 4 bacon strips, cooked and crumbled
- 5 garlic cloves, minced
- 1 loaf (1 pound) French bread, halved lengthwise
- 1 cup (4 ounces) shredded Italian cheese blend

1. In a bowl, mix butter, mayonnaise, bacon and garlic. Spread over cut sides of bread; reassemble loaf. Wrap in a large piece of heavy-duty foil (about 36 in. x 18 in.); seal tightly.

2. Grill, covered, over medium heat for 4-5 minutes on each side. Unwrap and separate bread halves. Sprinkle with cheese. Grill 5 minutes longer or until cheese is melted.

Grilled Pineapple & Maple Sundaes

This is one of our all-time favorite summer desserts. It's easy, elegant and makes a nice light treat after a big meal. You've gotta try it at your next cookout!

—SHERALYN FRIESEN WINNIPEG, MB

PREP: 10 MIN. + MARINATING
GRILL: 10 MIN. • **MAKES:** 8 SERVINGS

- ¾ cup maple syrup
- 2 tablespoons brown sugar
- ¾ teaspoon ground cinnamon
- 1 fresh pineapple, peeled, cut into 8 wedges
- 8 scoops vanilla ice cream

1. In a large resealable bag, combine the syrup, brown sugar and cinnamon; add pineapple. Seal bag and turn to coat. Refrigerate for 10-20 minutes. Drain, reserving syrup mixture.

2. Moisten a paper towel with cooking oil; using long-handled tongs, rub on grill rack to coat lightly. Grill pineapple, covered, over medium heat or broil 4 in. from the heat for 8-10 minutes or until lightly browned, turning once.

3. Serve pineapple with ice cream and drizzle with reserved syrup mixture.

Chipotle Sliders

ON THE PATIO!

Grilled Pineapple with Lime Dip

Curried Salmon

Grilled Pineapple with Lime Dip

This fruity dessert is sure to be a hit with kids. If desired, roll the pineapple wedges in flaked coconut before grilling.

—TASTE OF HOME TEST KITCHEN

PREP: 20 MIN. + MARINATING
GRILL: 10 MIN. • **MAKES:** 8 SERVINGS

- 1 fresh pineapple
- ¼ cup packed brown sugar
- 3 tablespoons honey
- 2 tablespoons lime juice

LIME DIP

- 1 package (3 ounces) cream cheese, softened
- ¼ cup plain yogurt
- 2 tablespoons honey
- 1 tablespoon brown sugar
- 1 tablespoon lime juice
- 1 teaspoon grated lime peel

1. Peel and core the pineapple; cut into eight wedges. Cut each wedge into two spears. In a large resealable plastic bag, combine the brown sugar, honey and lime juice; add pineapple. Seal bag and turn to coat; refrigerate for 1 hour.
2. In a bowl, beat cream cheese until smooth. Beat in the yogurt, honey, brown sugar, lime juice and peel. Cover and refrigerate.
3. Coat grill rack with cooking spray before starting the grill. Drain and discard marinade. Grill pineapple, covered, over medium heat for 3-4 minutes on each side or until golden brown. Serve with lime dip.

Curried Salmon

Until our daughter shared this recipe, my husband and I swore we didn't like salmon. But after one taste of this grilled version, we were converts!

—CARMA BLOSSER LIVERMORE, CO

PREP: 10 MIN. + MARINATING
GRILL: 10 MIN. • **MAKES:** 6 SERVINGS

- ⅓ cup soy sauce
- ⅓ cup canola oil
- 1 teaspoon garlic powder
- 1 teaspoon curry powder
- 1 teaspoon lemon-pepper seasoning
- 1 teaspoon Worcestershire sauce
- ¼ teaspoon liquid smoke, optional
- 6 salmon fillets (8 ounces each)

1. In a large resealable plastic bag, combine the soy sauce, oil, garlic powder, curry powder, lemon-pepper, Worcestershire sauce and liquid smoke if desired; add the salmon. Seal bag and turn to coat. Refrigerate for 1 hour.
2. Drain and discard marinade. Moisten a paper towel with cooking oil; using long-handled tongs, rub on grill rack to coat lightly. Place salmon, skin side down, on rack. Grill, covered, over medium heat or broil 4 in. from the heat for 10-12 minutes or until fish flakes easily with a fork.

FAST FIX

Feta Romaine Salad

My friend Cathy, who is of Greek heritage, prepared this simple salad for me. She served it with lamb chops.

—MICHAEL VOLPATT SAN FRANCISCO, CA

START TO FINISH: 15 MIN.
MAKES: 6 SERVINGS

- 1 bunch romaine, chopped
- 3 plum tomatoes, seeded and chopped
- 1 cup (4 ounces) crumbled feta cheese
- 1 cup chopped seeded cucumber
- ½ cup Greek olives, chopped
- 2 tablespoons minced fresh parsley
- 2 tablespoons minced fresh cilantro
- 3 tablespoons lemon juice
- 2 tablespoons olive oil
- ¼ teaspoon pepper

In a large bowl, combine the first seven ingredients. In a small bowl, whisk the remaining ingredients. Drizzle over salad; toss to coat. Serve immediately.

Feta Romaine Salad

ON THE PATIO!

Honey-Mustard Chicken

If my family had their wish, I'd serve this chicken on the grill every night. A sweet and tangy glaze makes a nice alternative to traditional tomato-based sauces.

—**HEIDI HOLMES** RENTON, WA

PREP: 10 MIN. • **GRILL:** 50 MIN.
MAKES: 4 SERVINGS

- 1 **cup pineapple juice**
- ¾ **cup honey**
- ½ **cup Dijon mustard**
- 1 **teaspoon ground ginger**
- 2 **tablespoons cornstarch**
- ¼ **cup cold water**
- 1 **broiler/fryer chicken
  (3½ to 4 pounds), cut up**

1. In a saucepan, combine pineapple juice, honey, mustard and ginger; bring to a boil. Combine cornstarch and water; gradually whisk into honey mixture. Cook and stir for 2-3 minutes or until thickened. Reserve ¾ cup to serve with chicken if desired.

2. Baste chicken with remaining glaze. Grill, covered, over medium-low heat for 30 minutes. Turn chicken; brush again with glaze. Grill, uncovered, for 20 minutes or until juices run clear. Serve with reserved glaze if desired.

**Saucy Grilled
Baby Back Ribs**

Honey-Mustard Chicken

Saucy Grilled Baby Back Ribs

Don't worry about the beer in this sauce—it's just root beer, which adds a subtle undertone to the yummy flavors.

—**TERRI KANDELL** ADDISON, MI

PREP: 2 HOURS • **GRILL:** 15 MIN.
MAKES: 8 SERVINGS

- 2 **cups ketchup**
- 2 **cups cider vinegar**
- 1 **cup corn syrup**
- ¼ **cup packed brown sugar**
- ¼ **cup root beer**
- ½ **teaspoon salt**
- ½ **teaspoon garlic powder**
- ½ **teaspoon onion powder**
- ½ **teaspoon hot pepper sauce**
- 4 **pounds pork baby back ribs**

1. In a large saucepan, combine the first nine ingredients. Bring to a boil. Reduce heat; simmer, uncovered, for 20-25 minutes or until slightly thickened, stirring occasionally. Set aside 3 cups for basting and serving.

2. Brush remaining sauce over ribs. Place bone side down on a rack in a large shallow roasting pan. Cover tightly with foil and bake at 325° for 1½ to 2 hours or until tender.

3. Moisten a paper towel with cooking oil; using long-handled tongs, rub on grill rack to coat lightly. Grill ribs, covered, over medium heat for 15-25 minutes or until browned, turning and brushing occasionally with some of the reserved sauce. Cut into serving-size pieces; serve with remaining sauce.

Garden Vegetable Pasta Salad

My family has been grilling vegetables for side dishes for a long time. To make the veggies more substantial, I added pasta.

—TINA REPAK MIRILOVICH

JOHNSTOWN, PA

PREP: 40 MIN. • **GRILL:** 10 MIN.
MAKES: 26 SERVINGS (¾ CUP EACH)

- 1 pound fusilli or pasta of your choice
- 2 medium eggplant
- 2 medium zucchini
- 2 medium yellow summer squash
- 1 large red onion, cut into ½-inch slices
- 1 medium sweet red pepper, cut in half and seeds removed
- ¼ cup olive oil
- ½ teaspoon salt
- ¼ teaspoon pepper
- 3 plum tomatoes, chopped
- 1½ cups (6 ounces) crumbled feta cheese
- 2 cans (2¼ ounces each) sliced ripe olives, drained
- 2 tablespoons minced fresh parsley

PARMESAN VINAIGRETTE

- ¾ cup olive oil
- ⅓ cup grated Parmesan cheese
- ⅓ cup white wine vinegar
- 3 tablespoons lemon juice
- 1 teaspoon sugar
- 1 garlic clove, minced
- 1 teaspoon salt
- ½ teaspoon dried oregano
- ½ teaspoon pepper

1. Cook pasta according to package directions; drain and rinse. Place pasta in a bowl and set aside.

2. Meanwhile, cut the eggplant, zucchini and summer squash lengthwise into ¾-in.-thick slices. Brush the eggplant, zucchini, summer squash, red onion and red pepper with oil; sprinkle with salt and pepper. Grill vegetables, covered, over medium heat for 4-6 minutes on each side or until crisp-tender. When cool enough to handle, cut into cubes.

3. Add tomatoes, feta cheese, olives, parsley and grilled vegetables to the pasta. In a small bowl, whisk the vinaigrette ingredients. Pour over the salad; toss to coat. Cover and refrigerate until serving.

Garden Vegetable Pasta Salad

FAST FIX ▶ Molasses-Glazed Pork Chops

It's hard to believe this flavorful and easy dish calls for just four simple ingredients. And the pork chops are so juicy!

—ANGELA SPENGLER CLOVIS, NM

START TO FINISH: 30 MIN.
MAKES: 4 SERVINGS

- ¼ cup molasses
- 1 tablespoon Worcestershire sauce
- 1½ teaspoons brown sugar
- 4 boneless pork loin chops (¾ inch thick and 5 ounces each)

1. In a bowl, combine the molasses, Worcestershire sauce and brown sugar. Reserve 3 tablespoons sauce for serving.

2. Grill the pork, covered, over medium heat or broil 4 in. from heat 4-5 minutes on each side or until a thermometer reads 145°, brushing with remaining sauce during the last 3 minutes of cooking. Let stand 5 minutes before serving. Serve with the reserved sauce.

ON THE PATIO!

FAST FIX ▸ Tuna with Tuscan White Bean Salad

Here's a recipe for medium-rare tuna that is still pink in the middle. Increase the cooking time if you'd like to have tuna that is cooked through a bit more. Once the tuna hits the grill, do not move it around or you may tear it. I enjoy the dish with a glass of chilled sauvignon blanc.

—VANCE WERNER JR. FRANKLIN, WI

START TO FINISH: 30 MIN.
MAKES: 4 SERVINGS

- 1 can (15 ounces) white kidney or cannellini beans, rinsed and drained
- 3 celery ribs, finely chopped
- 1 medium sweet red pepper, finely chopped
- 1 plum tomato, seeded and finely chopped
- ½ cup fresh basil leaves, thinly sliced
- ¼ cup finely chopped red onion
- 3 tablespoons olive oil
- 2 tablespoons red wine vinegar
- 1 tablespoon lemon juice
- ¼ teaspoon salt
- ¼ teaspoon pepper

TUNA
- 4 tuna steaks (6 ounces each)
- 1 tablespoon olive oil
- ¼ teaspoon salt
- ¼ teaspoon pepper

1. In a large bowl, combine the first six ingredients. In a small bowl, whisk the oil, vinegar, lemon juice, salt and pepper. Pour over bean mixture; toss to coat. Refrigerate until serving.

2. Brush tuna with oil. Sprinkle with salt and pepper. Moisten a paper towel with cooking oil; using long-handled tongs, rub on grill rack to coat lightly. Grill tuna, covered, over high heat or broil 3-4 in. from the heat for 3-4 minutes on each side for medium-rare or until slightly pink in the center. Serve with salad.

Smoky Garlic and Spice Chicken

A soy sauce-based marinade gives this moist, crispy chicken rich flavor. To make chicken satay, I vary the ingredients a bit and marinate the meat a little longer.

—TINA REPAK MIRILOVICH
JOHNSTOWN, PA

PREP: 20 MIN. + MARINATING
GRILL: 1 HOUR + STANDING
MAKES: 4 SERVINGS

- ⅓ cup reduced-sodium soy sauce
- 3 tablespoons lime juice
- 6 garlic cloves, minced
- 1 tablespoon olive oil
- 1 tablespoon ground cumin
- 1 teaspoon paprika
- ½ teaspoon dried oregano
- ½ teaspoon pepper
- 1 broiler/fryer chicken (3 to 4 pounds), split in half lengthwise

1. In a large resealable plastic bag, combine the first eight ingredients. Add chicken; seal bag and turn to coat. Refrigerate for 8 hours or overnight.

2. Drain and discard marinade. Prepare grill for indirect heat, using a drip pan. Moisten a paper towel with cooking oil; using long-handled tongs, rub on grill rack to coat lightly.

3. Place chicken, cut side down, over drip pan and grill, covered, over indirect medium heat for 1 to 1¼ hours or until a thermometer in thigh reads 180°, turning occasionally. Let stand for 10 minutes before carving.

Tuna with Tuscan White Bean Salad

FAST FIX Balsamic-Glazed Beef Skewers

With only four ingredients, which can easily be doubled, these mouthwatering kabobs are a favorite to make and eat. To prevent wooden skewers from burning, soak them in water for 30 minutes before threading the meat on them.

—CAROLE FRASER TORONTO, ON

START TO FINISH: 25 MIN.
MAKES: 4 SERVINGS

- ¼ **cup balsamic vinaigrette**
- ¼ **cup barbecue sauce**
- 1 **teaspoon Dijon mustard**
- 1 **beef top sirloin steak (1 pound), cut into 1-inch cubes**
- 2 **cups cherry tomatoes**

1. In a large bowl, whisk vinaigrette, barbecue sauce and mustard until blended. Reserve ¼ cup marinade for basting. Add beef to the remaining marinade; toss to coat.

2. Alternately thread the beef and tomatoes on four metal or soaked wooden skewers. Moisten a paper towel with cooking oil; using long-handled tongs, rub on grill rack to coat lightly.

3. Grill skewers, covered, over medium heat or broil 4 in. from heat 6-9 minutes or until beef reaches desired doneness, turning occasionally and basting frequently with reserved marinade during the last 3 minutes.

Did you know?

The type of barbecue sauce you use in a marinade will affect the overall flavor. The basic choices are smoky, sweet, tangy or spicy.

Balsamic-Glazed Beef Skewers

Flank Steak Crostini

Perfect for gatherings, holidays or as a Sunday football snack, this recipe is a favorite with friends and family. You can also substitute butter for the olive oil and use any kind of steak.

—DONNA EVARO CASPER, WY

PREP: 25 MIN. • **GRILL:** 15 MIN.
MAKES: 3 DOZEN

- 1 beef flank steak (1½ pounds)
- ½ teaspoon salt
- ½ teaspoon pepper
- 3 tablespoons olive oil
- 3 garlic cloves, minced
- 1 teaspoon dried basil
- 1 French bread baguette (10½ ounces), cut into 36 slices
- ½ cup finely chopped fresh portobello mushrooms
- ¼ cup shredded part-skim mozzarella cheese
- 2 tablespoons grated Parmesan cheese
- 1 tablespoon minced chives

Mango-Lime Pork Chops

1. Sprinkle beef with salt and pepper. Grill the beef, covered, over medium heat or broil 4 in. from the heat for 6-8 minutes on each side or until the meat reaches desired doneness (for medium-rare, a thermometer should read 145°; medium, 160°; well-done, 170°). Let stand for 5 minutes. Thinly slice across the grain.

2. Meanwhile, in a small bowl, combine the oil, garlic and basil; brush over baguette slices. Place on baking sheets. Bake at 400° for 5 minutes. Top with mushrooms and mozzarella cheese. Bake 2-3 minutes longer or until the cheese is melted.

3. Top with sliced steak, Parmesan cheese and chives. Serve immediately.

Mango-Lime Pork Chops

Marinated pork chops are topped with a beautiful fruity salsa of emerald kiwifruit, golden mango and red peppers for an eye-catching presentation. This one's pretty enough to serve to guests!

—TASTE OF HOME TEST KITCHEN

PREP: 20 MIN. + MARINATING
GRILL: 15 MIN. • **MAKES:** 6 SERVINGS

- ½ cup lime juice
- ½ cup reduced-sodium soy sauce
- 2 tablespoons honey
- 2 garlic cloves, minced
- 6 boneless pork loin chops (4 ounces each)

SALSA

- 2 medium mangoes, peeled and cubed (about 1⅓ cups)
- 4 medium kiwifruit, peeled and cubed (about 1 cup)
- ½ cup chopped sweet red pepper
- ½ cup chopped onion
- 1 jalapeno pepper, seeded and minced

- 1 tablespoon lemon juice
- 1 tablespoon lime juice
- 2 teaspoons minced fresh mint or ¾ teaspoon dried mint
- 1 teaspoon honey
- ¼ teaspoon salt

1. In a large resealable plastic bag, combine the lime juice, soy sauce, honey and garlic. Add pork chops. Seal bag and turn to coat; refrigerate for 8 hours or overnight.

2. Drain and discard marinade. Grill chops, covered, over medium heat or broil 4-5 in. from the heat for 4-5 minutes on each side or until a thermometer reads 145°. Let meat stand for 5 minutes before serving.

3. In a small bowl, combine the salsa ingredients. Cover and refrigerate until serving. Serve with pork.

NOTE *Wear disposable gloves when cutting hot peppers; the oils can burn skin. Avoid touching your face.*

Grilled Vegetable Orzo Salad

Vegetables that are in season make great additions to this orzo salad. It's the perfect side dish for a picnic, can easily be doubled for a crowd, or you can add grilled chicken to make it a filling entree.
—**DANIELLE MILLER** WESTFIELD, IN

PREP: 35 MIN. • **GRILL:** 10 MIN.
MAKES: 8 SERVINGS

- 1¼ cups uncooked orzo pasta
- ½ pound fresh asparagus, trimmed
- 1 medium zucchini, cut lengthwise into ½-inch slices
- 1 medium sweet yellow or red pepper, halved
- 1 large portobello mushroom, stem removed
- ½ medium red onion, halved

DRESSING

- ⅓ cup olive oil
- ¼ cup balsamic vinegar
- 3 tablespoons lemon juice
- 4 garlic cloves, minced
- 1 teaspoon lemon-pepper seasoning

SALAD

- 1 cup grape tomatoes, halved
- 1 tablespoon minced fresh parsley
- 1 tablespoon minced fresh basil
- ½ teaspoon salt
- ¼ teaspoon pepper
- 1 cup (4 ounces) crumbled feta cheese

1. Cook orzo according to the package directions. Place vegetables in a large bowl. In a small bowl, whisk dressing ingredients. Add to vegetables and toss to coat.
2. Remove vegetables, reserving dressing. Grill mushroom, pepper and onion, covered, over medium heat for 5-10 minutes or until tender, turning occasionally. Grill asparagus and zucchini, uncovered, 3-4 minutes or until desired doneness is reached, turning occasionally.
3. When cool enough to handle, cut vegetables into bite-size pieces. In a bowl, combine cooked orzo, grilled vegetables, tomatoes, parsley, basil, salt, pepper and reserved dressing; toss to combine. Serve at room temperature or refrigerate until cold. Just before serving, stir in cheese.

Sizzling Beef Kabobs

A mild soy sauce marinade lends an appealing flavor to these tender beef-and-veggie kabobs. With colorful chunks of yellow squash and sweet red and green peppers, they're great for parties!
—**KATHY SPANG** MANHEIM, PA

PREP: 20 MIN. + MARINATING
GRILL: 10 MIN. • **MAKES:** 8 SERVINGS

- ⅓ cup canola oil
- ¼ cup soy sauce
- 2 tablespoons red wine vinegar
- 2 teaspoons garlic powder
- 2 pounds beef top sirloin steak, cut into 1-inch pieces
- 2 medium yellow summer squash, cut into ½-inch slices
- 1 large onion, cut into 1-inch chunks
- 1 large green pepper, cut into 1-inch pieces
- 1 large sweet red pepper, cut into 1-inch pieces

1. In a large resealable plastic bag, mix the oil, soy sauce, vinegar and garlic powder; add beef. Seal bag and turn to coat; refrigerate for at least 1 hour.
2. Drain and discard marinade. On eight metal or soaked wooden skewers, alternately thread beef and vegetables. Grill, covered, over medium-hot heat or broil 4-6 in. from the heat for 8-10 minutes or until meat reaches desired doneness, turning occasionally.

Grilled Vegetable Orzo Salad

Raspberry Turkey Tenderloins

Raspberry Turkey Tenderloins

Fast to prepare, even quicker to grill, this dish is always a winner at my house. We love the raspberry-Dijon sauce. And you can substitute chicken breasts for the turkey if you wish.

—JOANN HANDLEY MOUNT DORA, FL

PREP: 20 MIN. • **GRILL:** 15 MIN.
MAKES: 6 SERVINGS

- ½ cup seedless raspberry jam
- ⅓ cup cider vinegar
- ¼ cup Dijon mustard
- 1 teaspoon grated orange peel
- ½ teaspoon minced fresh thyme or ⅛ teaspoon dried thyme
- 4 turkey breast tenderloins (6 ounces each)
- ⅛ teaspoon salt

1. In a small saucepan, combine the first five ingredients. Cook and stir for 2-3 minutes or until heated through. Set aside ¼ cup for serving.
2. Sprinkle turkey with salt. Moisten a paper towel with cooking oil; using long-handled tongs, rub on grill rack to coat lightly. Grill turkey, covered, over medium heat or broil 4 in. from the heat for 13-18 minutes or until a meat thermometer reads 165°, turning occasionally. Baste with remaining sauce during last 5 minutes of cooking.
3. Let stand for 5 minutes before slicing. Serve with reserved sauce.

Grilled Ribeyes with Blue Cheese Butter

FAST FIX ▶ Grilled Ribeyes with Blue Cheese Butter

Fire up the grill for my steaks that just melt in your mouth. They're garlic-infused, and the char-broiled flavor is off the charts. With this recipe on hand, weeknight menus can really sizzle!

—JIM MOODY WICHITA, KS

START TO FINISH: 25 MIN.
MAKES: 8 SERVINGS

- 8 beef ribeye steaks (10 ounces each)
- 12 garlic cloves, sliced
- ¼ cup olive oil
- 1 teaspoon salt
- ¾ teaspoon cayenne pepper
- ½ teaspoon pepper
- ½ cup crumbled blue cheese
- ¼ cup butter, softened

1. Cut slits into each steak; insert garlic slices. Brush with oil and sprinkle with salt, cayenne and pepper.
2. Grill the steaks, covered, over medium heat or broil 4 in. from the heat for 4-6 minutes on each side or until the meat reaches desired doneness (for medium-rare, a thermometer should read 145°; medium, 160°; well-done, 170°).
3. Combine blue cheese and butter. Serve with steaks.

A Perfect Steak

Trim steaks to avoid flare-ups, leaving a thin layer of fat, if desired, to help maintain juiciness. Pat dry with paper towels before grilling—a dry steak will brown better than a moist one.

Chicken Salad with Blueberry Vinaigrette

A scrumptious combo of colors and textures come together easily in this impressive main-dish salad.

—**SUSAN GAUTHIER** FALMOUTH, ME

PREP: 20 MIN. + MARINATING
GRILL: 10 MIN. • **MAKES:** 4 SERVINGS

- 3 **tablespoons olive oil**
- 1 **garlic clove, minced**
- 1 **teaspoon salt**
- 1 **teaspoon pepper**
- 2 **boneless skinless chicken breast halves (6 ounces each)**

VINAIGRETTE
- ¼ **cup olive oil**
- ¼ **cup blueberry preserves**
- 2 **tablespoons maple syrup**
- 2 **tablespoons balsamic vinegar**
- ¼ **teaspoon ground mustard**
- ⅛ **teaspoon salt**
  Dash pepper

SALADS
- 1 **package (10 ounces) ready-to-serve salad greens**
- 1 **cup fresh blueberries**
- 1 **snack-size cup (4 ounces) mandarin oranges, drained**
- 1 **cup crumbled goat cheese**

1. In a large resealable plastic bag, combine the oil, garlic, salt and pepper; add the chicken. Seal bag and turn to coat; refrigerate for 30 minutes.

2. In a small bowl, whisk vinaigrette ingredients. Chill until ready to use.

3. Drain and discard marinade. Grill chicken, covered, over medium heat for 5-7 minutes on each side or until a thermometer reads 165°. When cool enough to handle, slice chicken.

4. Divide salad greens among four serving plates. Top each with chicken, blueberries and oranges. Whisk vinaigrette and drizzle over salads; sprinkle with cheese.

Chicken Salad with Blueberry Vinaigrette

Steak and Blue Cheese Bruschetta with Onion and Roasted Tomato Jam

An appetizer bursting with flavor from blue cheese, caramelized onion, jam and balsamic vinegar, these hefty bites always disappear in a hurry.

—**DEBBIE REID** CLEARWATER, FL

PREP: 45 MIN. • **GRILL:** 10 MIN.
MAKES: 16 APPETIZERS
(¾ CUP TOMATO JAM)

- 1 **large sweet onion, halved and thinly sliced**
- 5 **tablespoons olive oil, divided**
- 1 **cup grape tomatoes, halved**
- ½ **teaspoon kosher salt, divided**
- ¼ **teaspoon freshly ground pepper, divided**
- 6 **ounces cream cheese, softened**
- 3 **ounces crumbled blue cheese**
- 3 **garlic cloves, minced**
- 16 **slices French bread baguette (½ inch thick)**
- 2 **beef ribeye steaks (¾ inch thick and 8 ounces each)**
- 1½ **teaspoons Montreal steak seasoning**
- 2 **tablespoons balsamic vinegar**

1. In large skillet, cook and stir onion in 2 tablespoons oil over medium-high heat until softened. Reduce heat to medium-low; cook 30 minutes or until golden brown, stirring occasionally.

2. Place tomatoes in a shallow baking pan. Add 1 tablespoon oil, ¼ teaspoon salt and ⅛ teaspoon pepper; toss to coat. Bake at 400° for 10-15 minutes or until softened. Lightly mash tomatoes; stir into onion.

3. In small bowl, mix cream cheese, blue cheese, garlic and remaining salt and pepper until blended.

4. Brush both sides of baguette slices with the remaining oil. Grill over medium heat 1-2 minutes on each side or until toasted.

5. Sprinkle both sides of the steaks with steak seasoning. Grill, covered, over medium heat for 3-5 minutes on each side or until the meat reaches desired doneness (for medium-rare, a thermometer should read 145°; medium, 160°; well-done, 170°). Let stand 5 minutes before slicing.

6. Spread cheese mixture on toasts; top with steak and onion mixture. Drizzle with vinegar.

Steak and Blue Cheese Bruschetta with Onion and Roasted Tomato Jam

Did you know?

In the beginning, bruschetta was a toasted bread rubbed with cut garlic and drizzled with extra-virgin olive oil. As cooks became more inventive, the toasted bread became the serving platform for all sorts of toppings.

ON THE PATIO!

Ribeyes with Chili Butter

Frozen Strawberry Delight

Simple, pretty and refreshing, this cool dessert will become a family favorite.

—BARBARA CHRISTENSEN
JACKSONVILLE, FL

PREP: 20 MIN. + FREEZING
MAKES: 10 SERVINGS

- 1 can (14 ounces) sweetened condensed milk
- ¼ cup lemon juice
- 4 cups sliced fresh strawberries, divided
- 1 carton (8 ounces) frozen whipped topping, thawed and divided
- 8 Oreo cookies, crushed

1. Line an 8-in. x 4-in. loaf pan with foil, letting edges hang over the sides; set aside.
2. In a large bowl, combine milk and lemon juice; fold in 2 cups strawberries and 2 cups whipped topping. Transfer half of the mixture to prepared pan. Sprinkle with cookie crumbs; top with remaining strawberry mixture. Cover and freeze for 6 hours or overnight.
3. To serve, using foil, lift dessert out of pan. Invert onto a serving plate; discard foil. Spread remaining whipped topping over top and sides of dessert; garnish with remaining strawberries. Cut into slices.

Frozen Strawberry Delight

FAST FIX Ribeyes with Chili Butter

A couple spoonfuls of spicy butter instantly give this steak a terrific Southwestern slant. Meat lovers will be delighted by the combination of chili and mustard flavors.

—ALLAN STACKHOUSE JR.
JENNINGS, LA

START TO FINISH: 20 MIN.
MAKES: 2 SERVINGS

- ¼ cup butter, softened
- 1 teaspoon chili powder
- ½ teaspoon Dijon mustard
  Dash cayenne pepper
- 2 beef ribeye steaks (8 ounces each)
- ½ to 1 teaspoon coarsely ground pepper
- ¼ teaspoon sugar

1. In a small bowl, beat the butter, chili powder, mustard and cayenne until smooth. Refrigerate until serving.
2. Rub the steaks with pepper and sugar. Grill, covered, over medium heat for 5-6 minutes on each side or until meat reaches desired doneness (for medium-rare, a thermometer should read 145°; medium, 160°; well-done, 170°). Spoon chili butter over steak.

Steak House Burgers

When I asked my brothers to come over for barbecue, they laughed. So I came up with this. They don't laugh anymore.

—BONNIE GEAVARAS-BOOTZ
SCOTTSDALE, AZ

PREP: 25 MIN. • **GRILL:** 15 MIN.
MAKES: 4 SERVINGS

- 5 tablespoons mayonnaise
- 4½ teaspoons prepared horseradish
- ¼ cup shredded Parmesan cheese
- 3 tablespoons butter, softened, divided
- ½ teaspoon garlic powder
- 4 hamburger buns, split
- 1½ pounds ground beef
- ¼ cup steak sauce
- 4½ teaspoons onion soup mix
- 4 slices Swiss cheese
- 1½ pounds sliced fresh mushrooms
- 2 green onions, chopped
- ¼ cup French-fried onions
  Sliced tomato and lettuce, optional

1. In a bowl, combine mayonnaise and horseradish; cover and refrigerate until serving. In another small bowl, combine the Parmesan cheese with 1 tablespoon butter and garlic powder; spread over bun tops. Set aside.

2. In a large bowl, combine the beef, steak sauce and onion soup mix. Shape into four patties.

3. Moisten a paper towel with cooking oil; using long-handled tongs, rub on grill rack to coat lightly. Grill burgers, covered, over medium heat or broil 4 in. from the heat for 4-5 minutes on each side or until a thermometer reads 160° and juices run clear.

4. Top with Swiss cheese; cover and grill 1-2 minutes longer or until cheese is melted. Place buns, cut side down, on grill for 1-2 minutes or until toasted.

5. Meanwhile, in a large skillet, saute mushrooms and green onions in the remaining butter until tender. Serve the burgers on buns; top with French-fried onions, mushroom mixture and tomato and lettuce if desired.

Grilled Steak Appetizers with Stilton Sauce

Grilled Steak Appetizers with Stilton Sauce

Here's a hefty appetizer that gets any dinner party off to a delicious start. The rich, creamy cheese sauce complements the grilled steak to perfection.

—RADELLE KNAPPENBERGER
OVIEDO, FL

PREP: 25 MIN. • **GRILL:** 10 MIN.
MAKES: 20 APPETIZERS (¾ CUP SAUCE)

- 2 boneless beef top loin steaks (8 ounces each)
- ¼ teaspoon salt
- ¼ teaspoon pepper
- ½ cup white wine or chicken broth
- ⅓ cup heavy whipping cream
- 3 tablespoons sour cream
- 2 ounces Stilton cheese, cubed

1. Sprinkle steaks with salt and pepper. Grill steaks, covered, over medium heat for 4-6 minutes on each side or until meat reaches desired doneness (for medium-rare, a thermometer should read 145°; medium, 160°; well-done, 170°). Remove meat to a cutting board and keep warm.

2. In a small saucepan, bring the wine to a boil; cook until reduced by half. Add the cream. Bring to a gentle boil. Reduce heat; simmer, uncovered, until thickened, stirring occasionally. Remove from the heat. Add sour cream and cheese; stir until cheese is melted.

3. Cut steaks into 1-in. cubes; skewer with toothpicks. Serve with sauce.

NOTE *Top loin steak may be labeled as strip steak, KS City steak, NY strip steak, ambassador steak or boneless club steak in your region. You may substitute ⅓ cup crumbled blue cheese for the Stilton cheese.*

ON THE PATIO!

Hickory Turkey

This grilled turkey has become a tradition at our house. Our guests love its hickory-smoked flavor. Conveniently, it makes the oven available for the many side dishes I like to prepare to go with it.
—**KIM RUSSELL** NORTH WALES, PA

PREP: 45 MIN. + MARINATING
GRILL: 2 HOURS + STANDING
MAKES: 12 SERVINGS

- 2 **cups packed brown sugar**
- ¾ **cup salt**
- 1 **jar (6 ounces) pickled ginger slices, drained**
- 4 **bay leaves**
- 2 **whole garlic bulbs, halved**
- 2 **tablespoons minced fresh marjoram or 2 teaspoons dried marjoram**
- 2 **tablespoons minced fresh thyme or 2 teaspoons dried thyme**
- 2 **tablespoons minced fresh sage**
- 2 **teaspoons crushed red pepper flakes**
- 3 **quarts water**
- 1½ **cups reduced-sodium soy sauce**
- 1 **cup maple syrup**
- 1 **turkey (12 to 14 pounds)**
- 4 **cups soaked hickory wood chips**
- 1 **large onion, cut into wedges**
- 1 **large navel orange, cut into wedges**
- 6 **garlic cloves, peeled**
- ¼ **cup canola oil**
- 2 **tablespoons sesame oil**

Hickory Turkey

1. In a stockpot, bring the first 12 ingredients to a boil. Cook and stir until sugar and salt are dissolved. Remove from the heat; cool to room temperature.

2. Remove giblets from turkey; discard. Place a turkey-size oven roasting bag inside a second roasting bag; add turkey. Carefully pour cooled marinade into bag. Squeeze out as much air as possible; seal bags and turn to coat. Place in a roasting pan. Refrigerate for 18-24 hours, turning occasionally.

3. Prepare grill for indirect heat, using a drip pan. Add wood chips to grill according to the manufacturer's directions. Drain turkey and discard brine. Rinse turkey under cold water; pat dry. Place the onion, orange and garlic inside cavity. Tuck wings under turkey; tie drumsticks together. Combine oils; rub over skin.

4. Place turkey over the drip pan. Grill, covered, over indirect medium heat for 1 hour. Tent the turkey with foil; grill 1-2 hours longer or until a thermometer in thigh reads 180°. Cover and let stand 15 minutes before carving.

NOTE *It is best not to use a prebasted turkey for this recipe.*

Grilled Steaks with Cilantro Sauce

Fresh herbs in the sauce help give these steaks top billing on our grilling menu.

—LYNNE KEAST MONTE SERENO, CA

PREP: 25 MIN. • **GRILL:** 15 MIN.
MAKES: 8 SERVINGS (3 CUPS SAUCE)

- 2 **cups fresh parsley leaves**
- 2 **cups fresh cilantro leaves**
- 1 **cup fresh mint leaves**
- 8 **garlic cloves, chopped**
- 1¾ **teaspoons kosher salt, divided**
- ½ **teaspoon plus ¾ teaspoon freshly ground pepper, divided**
- 2 **cups olive oil**
- ⅔ **cup red wine vinegar**
- 2 **tablespoons lemon juice**
- ½ **teaspoon crushed red pepper flakes**

- 4 **pounds beef flat iron steaks or top sirloin steaks (1 inch thick)**

1. Place herbs, garlic, 1 teaspoon salt and ½ teaspoon pepper in a food processor; pulse until herbs are chopped. While processing, gradually add the oil, vinegar, lemon juice and pepper flakes, processing just until all are blended.

2. Sprinkle steaks with remaining salt and pepper. Grill, covered, over medium heat or broil 4 in. from heat 6-8 minutes on each side or until the meat reaches desired doneness (for medium-rare, a thermometer should read 145°; medium, 160°; well-done, 170°). Let stand 5 minutes. Cut steaks into ¼-in. slices; serve with sauce.

Grilled Steaks with Cilantro Sauce

Peppered T-Bone Steaks with Salsa

Keep steaks juicy with this easy marinade.

—ROBIN HYDE LINCOLN, NE

PREP: 25 MIN. + MARINATING
GRILL: 15 MIN.
MAKES: 4 SERVINGS (3 CUPS SALSA)

- 1 **cup red wine vinegar**
- ¼ **cup lime juice**
- ¼ **cup olive oil**
- 4 **teaspoons chili powder**
- 2 **garlic cloves, minced**
- 2 **to 4 teaspoons crushed red pepper flakes**
- 2 **teaspoons salt**
- 1 **teaspoon pepper**
- 4 **beef T-bone steaks (1 inch thick and 1 pound each)**

SALSA

- 2 **large tomatoes, seeded and chopped**
- 2 **medium ripe avocados, peeled and chopped**
- 4 **green onions, thinly sliced**
- 2 **tablespoons minced fresh cilantro**
- 2 **tablespoons lime juice**
- ½ **jalapeno pepper, seeded and finely chopped, optional**
- 2 **garlic cloves, minced**
- ½ **teaspoon salt**
- ½ **teaspoon pepper**

1. In a small bowl, whisk the first eight ingredients. Divide steaks between two large resealable plastic bags. Add ½ cup marinade to each; seal bags and turn to coat. Refrigerate steaks and remaining marinade 1 to 2 hours.

2. Combine salsa ingredients; chill.

3. Drain and discard marinade. Grill steaks, covered, over medium heat 6-8 minutes on each side or until meat reaches desired doneness (for medium-rare, a thermometer should read 145°; medium, 160°; well-done, 170°). Brush with reserved marinade during last 5 minutes of cooking. Serve with salsa.

Chopped Garden Salad, page 194; Chocolate Chip Molasses Cookies, page 195; Three-Bean Baked Beans, page 194; Spinach Feta Burgers, page 192; Best Italian Sausage Sandwiches, page 194; Deluxe Marshmallow Brownies, page 193

BBQ Chicken Sliders,
page 199

IT'S TIME TO BARBECUE...

AT THE
Block Party!

Hot dogs, pasta salads, brats, brownies and bars...these are the makings of a **neighborly get-together!** The next time you're attending a block party, church picnic or warm-weather potluck, consider these **high-yield recipes** perfect for large groups.

Cookout Potato Salad

Instead of using all mayonnaise in the dressing, I used some plain yogurt. It really lightens up the dish and gives it a nice tang.

—**ANN GROVE** GREENWOOD, MS

PREP: 10 MIN.
COOK: 20 MIN. + CHILLING
MAKES: 6 SERVINGS

- 2 pounds medium Yukon Gold potatoes, cut into ½-inch cubes
- 1 garlic clove, chopped
- ½ cup plain yogurt
- 3 tablespoons mayonnaise
- 1 tablespoon olive oil
- 2 teaspoons white wine vinegar
- ¾ teaspoon salt
- ¼ teaspoon pepper
- 1 tablespoon minced fresh parsley
  Optional toppings: chopped hard-cooked eggs, blanched green beans and salad croutons

Cookout Potato Salad

Honey Chipotle Ribs

1. Place potatoes and garlic in a large saucepan and cover with water. Bring to a boil. Reduce heat; cover and simmer for 13-18 minutes or until potatoes are tender. Drain potatoes; cool completely.
2. Place potatoes in a large bowl. In a small bowl, whisk yogurt, mayonnaise, oil, vinegar, salt and pepper; pour over potatoes and toss to coat. Refrigerate, covered, until chilled. Sprinkle with parsley; serve with toppings if desired.

top tip Sticking to Ribs

Baby back ribs are smaller, leaner and meatier than spareribs. They also carry a higher price tag. So, stock up when they are on sale.

Honey Chipotle Ribs

Nothing's better for ribs than a sauce with a perfect slathering consistency. Here's one that will ensure a lip-smacking feast for a crowd. Go ahead and mix up the sauce a week ahead of time, if that's convenient.

—**CAITLIN HAWES** WESTWOOD, MA

PREP: 5 MIN. • **COOK:** 1½ HOURS
MAKES: 12 SERVINGS

- 6 pounds pork baby back ribs
BARBECUE SAUCE
- 3 cups ketchup
- 2 bottles (11.2 ounces each) Guinness beer
- 2 cups barbecue sauce
- ⅔ cup honey
- 1 small onion, chopped
- ¼ cup Worcestershire sauce
- 2 tablespoons Dijon mustard
- 2 tablespoons chopped chipotle peppers in adobo sauce
- 4 teaspoons ground chipotle pepper
- 1 teaspoon salt
- 1 teaspoon garlic powder
- ½ teaspoon pepper

1. Wrap ribs in large pieces of heavy-duty foil; seal edges of foil. Grill ribs, covered, over indirect medium heat for 1 to 1½ hours or until tender.
2. In a large saucepan, combine sauce ingredients; bring to a boil. Reduce heat; simmer, uncovered, for about 45 minutes or until thickened, stirring occasionally.
3. Carefully remove ribs from foil. Place over direct heat; baste with some of the sauce. Grill, covered, over medium heat for about 30 minutes or until browned, turning once and basting occasionally with additional sauce. Serve with remaining sauce.

FAST FIX ▸ Cannellini Bean Hummus

My version of hummus features a delightful nuttiness from tahini, a peanut-butter-like paste made from ground sesame seeds. The beans pack a lot of protein so it's a healthy snack for kids.

—MARINA CASTLE CANYON COUNTRY, CA

START TO FINISH: 5 MIN.
MAKES: 1¼ CUPS

- 2 garlic cloves, peeled
- 1 can (15 ounces) white kidney or cannellini beans, rinsed and drained
- ¼ cup tahini
- 3 tablespoons lemon juice
- 1½ teaspoons ground cumin
- ¼ teaspoon salt
- ¼ teaspoon crushed red pepper flakes
- 2 tablespoons minced fresh parsley
  Pita breads, cut into wedges

1. Place garlic in a food processor; cover and process until minced. Add the beans, tahini, lemon juice, cumin, salt and pepper flakes; cover and process until smooth.
2. Transfer to a small bowl; stir in parsley. Refrigerate until serving. Serve with pita wedges.

Sweet & Hot
Baked Beans

Cannellini Bean
Hummus

Sweet & Hot Baked Beans

Baked beans belong at a barbecue. They're sweet with just a little heat when you add pineapple and jalapenos!

—ROBIN HAAS CRANSTON, RI

PREP: 20 MIN. • **COOK:** 5 HOURS
MAKES: 12 SERVINGS (½ CUP EACH)

- 4 cans (15 ounces each) white kidney or cannellini beans, rinsed and drained
- 2 cans (8 ounces each) crushed pineapple, undrained
- 2 large onions, finely chopped
- 1 cup packed brown sugar
- 1 cup ketchup
- 10 bacon strips, cooked and crumbled
- ½ cup molasses
- ¼ cup canned diced jalapeno peppers
- 2 tablespoons white vinegar
- 4 garlic cloves, minced
- 4 teaspoons ground mustard
- ¼ teaspoon ground cloves

In a 3- or 4-qt. slow cooker, combine all ingredients. Cook, covered, on low for 5-6 hours.

AT THE BLOCK PARTY!

Minted Fresh Fruit Salad

Minted Fresh Fruit Salad

Here's a colorful, tasty fruit salad that allows for substitutions such as peaches, plums, watermelon, oranges or grapefruit, depending on availability.
—**ANNE KEEDY** LEBANON, CT

START TO FINISH: 25 MIN.
MAKES: 24 SERVINGS (¾ CUP EACH)

- 1 **medium cantaloupe, peeled, seeded and cubed**
- 1 **pound fresh strawberries, halved**
- 1 **fresh pineapple, peeled and cubed**
- 2 **large Granny Smith apples, cubed**
- 2 **cups seedless red or green grapes**
- ½ **cup dried cranberries**
- ¾ **cup orange juice**
- ⅓ **cup lemon juice**
- 2 **tablespoons minced fresh mint**
- 1 **teaspoon ground cinnamon**
- ½ **cup flaked coconut, optional**

In a large bowl, combine the first six ingredients. In a small bowl, whisk orange juice, lemon juice, mint and cinnamon. Drizzle over fruit; toss lightly to coat. If desired, top with coconut before serving.

top tip

Pineapple Pointers

It's easy to prepare a pineapple. Simply cut off the crown of the fruit. Cut off the base. Follow the pattern of the eyes to cut diagonal wedge-shaped grooves in pineapple. Remove the wedges. Stand pineapple upright and cut off fruit next to, but not through, the core. Cut pieces into chunks or spears.

Italian Meatball Kabobs

When the temperature's high, and so is your craving for Italian fare, turn to these deliciously different kabobs. A green salad and rustic bread are all you'll need to complete this easy entree.

—**MARIE RIZZIO** INTERLOCHEN, MI

PREP: 30 MIN. • **GRILL:** 10 MIN.
MAKES: 12 KABOBS

- 2 eggs, lightly beaten
- ⅔ cup seasoned bread crumbs
- ½ cup grated Parmesan cheese
- ¼ cup minced fresh parsley
- 4 teaspoons Italian seasoning
- ½ teaspoon salt
- ½ teaspoon garlic powder
- 2½ pounds ground beef
- 1 medium onion, cut into 1-inch pieces
- 1 medium sweet red pepper, cut into 1-inch pieces
- 1 medium zucchini, cut into 1-inch pieces
- ½ small eggplant, cut into 1-inch pieces
- ½ cup balsamic vinegar
- ½ cup olive oil

1. In a large bowl, combine the first seven ingredients. Crumble beef over mixture and mix well. Shape into 1½-in. balls.
2. On 12 metal or soaked wooden skewers, alternately thread meatballs and vegetables. In a small bowl, mix the vinegar and oil.
3. Grill the kabobs, covered, over medium heat for 8-10 minutes or until the meatballs are no longer pink and the vegetables are tender, basting frequently with vinegar mixture and turning occasionally.

FAST FIX ▶ Bacon Caprese Salad

In summer, I am always looking for ways to use the tomatoes and fresh basil that grow in my garden. This recipe combines the two flavors in a wonderful salad that you and your guests will enjoy with any meal!

—**MARY ANN TURK** JOPLIN, MO

START TO FINISH: 15 MIN.
MAKES: 12 SERVINGS

- 1 pound fresh mozzarella cheese, cut into ¼-inch slices
- 3 plum tomatoes, cut into ¼-inch slices
- 1½ cups fresh baby spinach
- 8 bacon strips, cooked and crumbled
- ½ cup minced fresh basil
- 2 green onions, chopped
- ¼ cup balsamic vinaigrette
- ½ teaspoon salt
- ¼ teaspoon coarsely ground pepper

Arrange cheese, tomatoes and spinach on a large serving platter; top with bacon, basil and green onions. Just before serving, drizzle with vinaigrette; sprinkle with salt and pepper.

Bacon Caprese Salad

Homemade Potato Chips

You can make these potato chips at home. They're perfect alongside any grilled food!

—TASTE OF HOME TEST KITCHEN

PREP: 30 MIN. + SOAKING
COOK: 5 MIN./BATCH • **MAKES:** 8½ CUPS

- 7 unpeeled medium potatoes (about 2 pounds)
- 2 quarts ice water
- 5 teaspoons salt
- 2 teaspoons garlic powder
- 1½ teaspoons celery salt
- 1½ teaspoons pepper
  Oil for deep-fat frying

1. Using a vegetable peeler or metal cheese slicer, cut potatoes into very thin slices. Place in a large bowl; add ice water and salt. Soak for 30 minutes.

2. Drain potatoes; place on paper towels and pat dry. In a small bowl, combine the garlic powder, celery salt and pepper; set aside.

3. In an electric skillet, heat 1½ in. of oil to 375°. Fry potatoes in batches for 3-4 minutes or until golden brown, stirring frequently.

4. Remove with a slotted spoon; drain on paper towels. Immediately sprinkle with seasoning mixture. Store in an airtight container.

Scrumptious Scrambled Salad

Scrumptious Scrambled Salad

Try my delicious supersize salad! It always disappears as fast as it comes together.

—BECKY MULDROW HIGHLANDS, TX

PREP: 45 MIN. + CHILLING
MAKES: 24 SERVINGS

- 2 large bunches romaine, torn
- 12 green onions, thinly sliced
- 1½ cups sliced water chestnuts, coarsely chopped
- 1 package (16 ounces) frozen peas, thawed
- 2¼ cups mayonnaise
- ½ cup plus 1 tablespoon evaporated milk
- ¼ cup plus 1½ teaspoons cider vinegar
- ¾ teaspoon garlic powder
- 2 cups (8 ounces) shredded cheddar cheese
- 3 medium tomatoes, chopped
- 1 pound sliced bacon, cooked, crumbled and drained
- 3 hard-cooked eggs, sliced

1. In a very large salad bowl, layer the romaine, onions, water chestnuts and peas. Combine the mayonnaise, milk, vinegar and garlic powder; spread over peas. Sprinkle with cheese. Cover and refrigerate for 8 hours or overnight.

2. Just before serving, add tomatoes, bacon and eggs; toss gently.

Best Barbecue Wings

My husband always calls this recipe "finger lickin' good!" The sweet-and-spicy flavor really is to die for. The sauce is also great on chicken breasts.

—**LINDA GARDNER** RICHMOND, VA

PREP: 20 MIN. • **GRILL:** 20 MIN.
MAKES: 2½ DOZEN

- ½ cup finely chopped onion
- ¼ cup canola oil
- 3 teaspoons minced garlic
- 1½ cups ketchup
- ½ cup cider vinegar
- ⅓ cup packed brown sugar
- ⅓ cup Worcestershire sauce
- 2 teaspoons chili powder
- ½ teaspoon cayenne pepper
- ½ teaspoon ground cumin
- ⅛ teaspoon hot pepper sauce

WINGS

- ¼ cup cider vinegar
- ¼ cup olive oil
- ⅛ teaspoon salt
- ⅛ teaspoon pepper
- 30 frozen chicken wingettes, thawed

1. For barbecue sauce, in a large saucepan, saute onion in oil until tender. Add the garlic; cook 1 minute longer. Stir in the ketchup, vinegar, brown sugar, Worcestershire sauce, chili powder, cayenne and cumin. Simmer, uncovered, for 8-10 minutes, stirring often. Remove from the heat; stir in pepper sauce. Set aside ⅔ cup for serving.

2. In a large resealable plastic bag, combine the vinegar, olive oil, salt and pepper; add chicken wings in batches and turn to coat.

3. Moisten a paper towel with cooking oil; using long-handled tongs, rub on grill rack to coat lightly. Grill wings, covered, over medium heat or broil 4 in. from the heat for 12-16 minutes, turning occasionally. Brush with some of the barbecue sauce.

4. Grill, uncovered, 8-10 minutes longer or until juices run clear, basting and turning several times. Serve with reserved barbecue sauce.

Pineapple Apricot Bars

A buttery crust holds an apricot-and-pineapple filling in this fruity dessert. Also great, these bars feed a crowd and there are rarely ever any left!

—**JANE BRICKER** SCOTTDALE, PA

PREP: 30 MIN. • **BAKE:** 30 MIN. + COOLING
MAKES: 2 DOZEN

- 1 can (20 ounces) crushed pineapple, undrained
- 1 cup diced dried apricots
- 1½ cups sugar, divided
- ¾ cup butter, softened
- 2 cups all-purpose flour
- ½ teaspoon baking soda
- ½ teaspoon salt
- 1¾ cups flaked coconut
- ¾ cup finely chopped walnuts

1. In a large saucepan, bring the pineapple and apricots to a boil. Reduce heat; cover and simmer for 20 minutes, stirring occasionally. Stir in ½ cup sugar. Simmer, uncovered, for 5 minutes.

2. Meanwhile, in a large bowl, cream butter and remaining sugar until light and fluffy. Combine the flour, baking soda and salt; gradually add to creamed mixture. Stir in coconut and nuts.

3. Press 4 cups of the mixture into a greased 13-in. x 9-in. baking pan. Bake at 375° for 10 minutes. Spread hot pineapple mixture over crust; sprinkle with the remaining coconut mixture.

4. Bake 20-25 minutes longer or until lightly browned. Cool on a wire rack. Cut into squares.

Best Barbecue Wings

AT THE BLOCK PARTY!

Freezer Slaw

**Grilled Beer
Brats with Kraut**

Grilled Beer Brats with Kraut

I made this for my son's 21st birthday bonfire for about a dozen buddies. The kraut topping flavors are fabulous!
—**KEELEY WEBER** STERLING HEIGHTS, MI

PREP: 45 MIN. • **GRILL:** 35 MIN.
MAKES: 12 SERVINGS

- 6 bacon strips, chopped
- 1 large onion, chopped
- 1 medium apple, peeled and thinly sliced
- 2 garlic cloves, minced
- 1 can (14 ounces) sauerkraut, rinsed and well drained
- 3 tablespoons spicy brown mustard
- 1 tablespoon brown sugar
- 12 uncooked bratwurst links
- 1 bottle (12 ounces) dark beer
- 12 hoagie buns, split

1. In a large skillet, cook bacon over medium heat until crisp, stirring occasionally. Remove with a slotted spoon; drain on paper towels.
2. Cook and stir the onion in bacon drippings until softened. Reduce heat to medium-low; cook 15-20 minutes or until deep golden brown, stirring occasionally. Add the apple and garlic; cook 2 minutes longer. Stir in the sauerkraut, mustard, brown sugar and cooked bacon.
3. Transfer to a 13x9-in. disposable foil pan. Arrange bratwurst over top. Pour beer over bratwurst. Place pan on grill rack over medium heat; cook, covered, 30-35 minutes or until sausages are no longer pink. Remove pan from heat.
4. Remove bratwurst and return to grill. Grill, covered, 2-3 minutes on each side or until browned. Serve on buns with sauerkraut mixture.

Freezer Slaw

This unusual and handy slaw recipe from my mother combines all the ingredients, then stores in the freezer. Just thaw before serving. For extra convenience, you can use a packaged cole slaw mix.
—**ALICE CAMPBELL** DICKINSON, ND

PREP: 30 MIN. + FREEZING
COOK: 10 MIN. + COOLING
MAKES: 18 SERVINGS (¾ CUP EACH)

- 2 medium heads cabbage, shredded (about 16 cups)
- 2 teaspoons salt
- 2 cups sugar
- 2 cups water
- 2 cups cider vinegar
- 2 teaspoons celery seed
- 2 teaspoons mustard seed
- 2 medium sweet red peppers, chopped
- 2 medium carrots, shredded

1. Place cabbage in a very large bowl; toss with salt. Let stand 1 hour.
2. Meanwhile, in a saucepan, combine sugar, water, vinegar, celery seed and mustard seed. Bring to a boil, stirring to dissolve sugar. Cook 1 minute. Remove from heat; cool slightly.
3. Drain excess liquid from cabbage, if necessary. Add red peppers and carrots to cabbage. Add dressing; toss to coat. Cool completely. Transfer to freezer containers. Freeze, covered, for up to 3 months.
4. To serve, thaw coleslaw overnight in refrigerator. Stir before serving.

FAST FIX ▸ Chunky Veggie Slaw

Classic coleslaw with cabbage gets a fresh and tasty new take when you add broccoli, cucumbers, snap peas and walnuts.

—**NICHOLAS KING** DULUTH, MN

START TO FINISH: 25 MIN.
MAKES: 14 SERVINGS (1 CUP EACH)

- 1 small head cabbage, chopped
- 6 cups (1½ pounds) fresh broccoli florets
- 1 medium cucumber, chopped
- 2 celery ribs, sliced
- 12 fresh sugar snap peas, halved
- 1 small green pepper, chopped
- ¾ cup buttermilk
- ½ cup reduced-fat mayonnaise
- 3 tablespoons cider vinegar
- 2 tablespoons sugar
- ½ teaspoon salt
- 1 cup chopped walnuts, toasted
- 2 green onions, thinly sliced

In a large bowl, combine the first six ingredients. In a small bowl, whisk buttermilk, mayonnaise, vinegar, sugar and salt. Pour over salad; toss to coat. Top with walnuts and green onions. Refrigerate leftovers.

NOTE *To toast nuts, spread in a 15x10x1-in. baking pan. Bake at 350° for 5-10 minutes or until lightly browned; stir occasionally. Or, in a dry nonstick skillet, heat over low heat until lightly browned; stir occasionally.*

FAST FIX ▸ Spinach Feta Burgers

My husband is Greek, and these burgers are a compliment to his heritage. We like to serve them with a tomato-and-cucumber salad on the side.

—**SUZANNE KERN** LOUISVILLE, KY

START TO FINISH: 20 MIN.
MAKES: 8 SERVINGS

- 1 cup torn fresh spinach
- ½ cup crumbled feta cheese
- ½ cup chopped seeded plum tomatoes
- 2 green onions, chopped
- 1½ teaspoons dill weed
- 1 teaspoon salt
- 1 teaspoon pepper
- 2 pounds ground beef
- 8 hamburger buns, split

1. In a large bowl, combine the first seven ingredients. Crumble beef over mixture and mix well. Shape into eight 4-in. patties.

2. Grill, covered, over medium heat or broil 4 in. from the heat for 4-5 minutes on each side or until a thermometer reads 160° and juices run clear. Serve on buns.

? Did you know?

Feta is a salty, semi-firm cheese. Traditionally, it was made from sheep or goat's milk but is now also made with cow's milk. After feta is formed in a mold, it's sliced, salted and soaked in brine. Although feta is associated with Greek cooking, "feta" comes from the Italian word "fette," meaning "slice of food."

Chunky Veggie Slaw

Deluxe Marshmallow Brownies

I found this recipe in a garden club cookbook many years ago. I always bring these to church suppers and potlucks.

—MARTHA STINE JOHNSTOWN, PA

PREP: 25 MIN. • **BAKE:** 25 MIN. + COOLING
MAKES: ABOUT 3 DOZEN

- 1 cup butter, cubed
- 4 ounces unsweetened chocolate, coarsely chopped
- 2 cups sugar
- 4 eggs
- 2 teaspoons vanilla extract
- 1½ cups all-purpose flour
- 1½ teaspoons baking powder
- 1 cup chopped walnuts or pecans

TOPPING

- ½ cup butter, cubed
- 4 ounces unsweetened chocolate, coarsely chopped
- 1 cup sugar
- 1 can (5 ounces) evaporated milk
- 3¾ cups confectioners' sugar
- 3 teaspoons vanilla extract
- 4 cups miniature marshmallows

1. In a microwave, melt butter and chocolate; stir until smooth. Cool. In a large bowl, combine sugar, eggs, vanilla and melted chocolate. Combine flour and baking powder; add to chocolate mixture and beat just until blended. Fold in nuts.

2. Spread into a greased 15-in. x 10-in. x 1-in. baking pan. Bake at 325° for 25-30 minutes or until a toothpick inserted near the center comes out clean.

3. Meanwhile, in a large heavy saucepan, melt butter and chocolate. Stir in the sugar and milk. Cook over low heat for 20 minutes, stirring frequently. Gradually whisk in the confectioners' sugar until smooth. Remove from the heat; stir in vanilla.

4. Place marshmallows over warm brownies; pour warm topping over marshmallows. Cool on a wire rack for at least 2 hours before cutting.

Grilled Sausage & Pepper Heroes

Grilled Sausage & Pepper Heroes

Chicken sausage lightens up this recipe yet preserves all the great, grilled flavor. I promise that you'll be a hero if you make this for your next cookout!

—MARLA CLARK MORIARTY, NM

PREP: 20 MIN. • **GRILL:** 30 MIN.
MAKES: 12 SERVINGS

- 2 jars (24 ounces each) roasted garlic Parmesan spaghetti sauce
- ⅛ teaspoon crushed red pepper flakes
- 2 medium green peppers
- 2 medium sweet red peppers
- 2 medium sweet yellow peppers
- 1 large sweet onion, cut crosswise into ¼-inch slices
- 3 packages (12 ounces each) fully cooked Italian chicken sausage links
- 12 brat or hoagie buns, split
- 12 slices provolone cheese, halved

1. In a Dutch oven, mix spaghetti sauce and pepper flakes. Heat over medium heat; stir occasionally. Keep warm.

2. Cut peppers in half. Remove and discard stems and seeds. Grill peppers and onion, covered, over medium heat 8-10 minutes on each side or until tender. Slice peppers. Stir onion and peppers into sauce; heat through.

3. Grill sausages, covered, over medium heat until heated through; turn occasionally. Place buns on baking sheets, cut side up. Top with cheese. Broil 3-4 in. from the heat 2-3 minutes or until cheese is melted. Top with sausages and pepper mixture.

Chopped Garden Salad

My children always request this salad for their birthday meal and many other get-togethers. The flavor combination is so yummy, and it's really easy to make.

—ANNA SUTHERLAND CAMP, AR

PREP: 30 MIN. + CHILLING
MAKES: 16 SERVINGS

6	medium tomatoes
2	medium green peppers
2	large cucumbers
2	medium red onions
1¼	cups water
¾	cup cider vinegar
4½	teaspoons sugar
1½	teaspoons mustard seed
1½	teaspoons celery salt
½	teaspoon salt
⅛	teaspoon pepper

1. Dice the tomatoes, green peppers, cucumbers and onions; place in a 3-qt. salad bowl.
2. In a small saucepan, combine the remaining ingredients. Bring to a boil. Reduce heat; simmer, uncovered, for 1 minute, stirring occasionally. Cool slightly. Pour over the vegetables and toss to coat. Cover and refrigerate overnight. Serve with a slotted spoon.

Three-Bean Baked Beans

Here's a side dish that's perfect for large get-togethers because it's so delicious and can be easily doubled for a big crowd!

—DARLENE BRENDEN SALEM, OR

PREP: 10 MIN. • **BAKE:** 1¼ HOURS
MAKES: 8 SERVINGS

1	can (16 ounces) maple-cured bacon baked beans
1	can (16 ounces) hot chili beans, undrained
1	can (15 ounces) black beans, rinsed and drained
1	can (10 ounces) diced tomatoes and green chilies, undrained

1½	teaspoons minced chipotle peppers in adobo sauce

In a large bowl, combine all ingredients. Transfer to a greased 11-in. x 7-in. baking dish. Cover and bake at 350° for 1 hour. Uncover; bake 15-20 minutes longer or until bubbly.

Best Italian Sausage Sandwiches

Looking for a different type of sandwich for your party? You'll be the talk of the town with these great-tasting sausages smothered in rich tomato sauce.

—TASTE OF HOME TEST KITCHEN

PREP: 10 MIN. • **COOK:** 4 HOURS
MAKES: 10 SERVINGS

2	jars (24 ounces each) meatless spaghetti sauce
2	medium green peppers, cut into strips
2	medium onions, thinly sliced
½	teaspoon garlic powder
½	teaspoon fennel seed, crushed
2	packages (20 ounces each) Italian turkey sausage links
10	sandwich buns, split

1. In a 3-qt. slow cooker, combine the spaghetti sauce, green peppers, onions, garlic powder and fennel seed. Cover and cook on low for 4 hours or until vegetables are tender.
2. Grill sausages according to package directions. Serve on buns with sauce.

Best Italian Sausage Sandwiches

FAST FIX Speedy Salsa

In only minutes you can make a fabulous, fresh-tasting salsa for the gang. If it's more than you need, just cut the recipe in half.

—**DANA SAPP** SCOTTSVILLE, KY

START TO FINISH: 20 MIN.
MAKES: 7 CUPS

- 4 cans (14½ ounces each) diced tomatoes, drained
- 2 medium onions, chopped
- ½ cup minced fresh cilantro
- 2 jalapeno peppers, seeded and minced
- 2 tablespoons sugar
- 1 teaspoon salt
  Tortilla chips

In a large bowl, combine the first six ingredients. Cover and chill until serving. Serve with tortilla chips.
NOTE *Wear disposable gloves when cutting hot peppers; the oils can burn skin. Avoid touching your face.*

Speedy Salsa

Chocolate Chip Molasses Cookies

I altered my grandmother's cookie a bit to add my favorite ingredient: chocolate chips. This isn't a traditional molasses cookie so even people who don't enjoy molasses will like these treats!

—**MELLOWDEE JAE BROOKS** MOSCOW, ID

PREP: 25 MIN. • **BAKE:** 10 MIN./BATCH
MAKES: 7½ DOZEN

- 1 cup shortening
- 1½ cups sugar
- ½ cup molasses
- 2 eggs
- 3 cups all-purpose flour
- 1½ teaspoons baking soda
- 1 teaspoon salt
- 2 cups (12 ounces) semisweet chocolate chips

1. In a large bowl, beat the shortening, sugar and molasses. Add eggs, one at a time, beating well after each addition. Combine the flour, baking soda and salt; gradually add to creamed mixture. Stir in chocolate chips.
2. Roll into 1-in. balls. Place 2 in. apart on ungreased baking sheets. Bake at 375° for 8-10 minutes or until edges are firm. Remove to wire racks.

FAST FIX Pesto Pasta Medley

When I worked at a prep school, I'd bring this dish in for potlucks. Co-workers always emptied the bowl and gave me a lot of compliments. Many asked for a copy of the recipe so they could make it at home.

—**BETH LEPORE** WINCHESTER, MA

START TO FINISH: 25 MIN.
MAKES: 16 SERVINGS

- 3 packages (7 ounces each) dried cheese tortellini
- 1 package (12 ounces) tricolor spiral pasta
- 1 can (14 ounces) water-packed artichoke hearts, rinsed, drained and quartered
- 2 jars (3½ ounces each) prepared pesto
- 1 jar (6 ounces) oil-packed sun-dried tomatoes, drained and chopped
- ½ teaspoon salt
  Grated Parmesan cheese, optional

1. Cook the tortellini and spiral pasta according to package directions; drain and place in a large serving bowl.
2. Add the artichokes, pesto, tomatoes and salt. Sprinkle with the Parmesan cheese if desired. Serve warm or at room temperature. Refrigerate any leftovers.

Fresh Blueberry Pie

In my mind, nothing says summer like a piece of fresh blueberry pie! And I've been making this easy one for decades. It's the perfect addition to a buffet and makes a great contribution to any summer party.

—**LINDA KERNAN** MASON, MI

PREP: 15 MIN. + COOLING
MAKES: 8 SERVINGS

- ¾ cup sugar
- 3 tablespoons cornstarch
- ⅛ teaspoon salt
- ¼ cup cold water
- 5 cups fresh blueberries, divided
- 1 tablespoon butter
- 1 tablespoon lemon juice
- 1 pastry shell (9 inches), baked

In a saucepan over medium heat, combine sugar, cornstarch, salt and water until smooth. Add 3 cups blueberries. Bring to a boil; cook and stir for 2 minutes or until thickened and bubbly. Remove from the heat. Add butter, lemon juice and remaining berries; stir until butter is melted. Cool. Pour into the pastry shell. Store in the refrigerator.

Creamy Herb Deviled Eggs

Fresh Blueberry Pie

FAST FIX ▸ Creamy Herb Deviled Eggs

This variation on deviled eggs incorporates ranch dressing and Greek-style yogurt. The eggs "fly" off the serving dish at my work!

—**JENNI DISE** PHOENIX, AZ

START TO FINISH: 20 MIN.
MAKES: 2 DOZEN

- 12 hard-cooked eggs
- ¼ cup prepared ranch salad dressing
- 3 tablespoons plain Greek yogurt
- 2 teaspoons Dijon mustard
- ¼ teaspoon pepper
- ⅛ teaspoon paprika

Cut eggs lengthwise in half. Remove yolks, reserving whites. In a small bowl, mash yolks. Stir in salad dressing, yogurt, mustard and pepper. Spoon or pipe into egg whites. Refrigerate, covered, until serving. Sprinkle with the paprika.

Garden Bow Tie Salad

Originally a vegetable dish, I added pasta for family gatherings and church potlucks. I also like to toss in sliced mushrooms and diced tomatoes just before serving.

—BARBARA BURKS HUNTSVILLE, AL

PREP: 30 MIN. + CHILLING
COOK: 10 MIN.
MAKES: 24 SERVINGS (¾ CUP EACH)

- 1 medium cucumber
- 1 medium yellow summer squash
- 1 medium zucchini
- 1 medium sweet red pepper
- 1 medium green pepper
- 4 cups fresh broccoli florets
- 3 cups fresh cauliflowerets
- 1 small red onion, finely chopped
- 2 packages Italian salad dressing mix
- 4½ cups uncooked bow tie pasta
- ¼ cup olive oil
- ¼ cup red wine vinegar
- ¾ teaspoon salt
- ½ teaspoon pepper

1. Wash the first five ingredients but do not dry; chop and transfer to a large bowl. Add the remaining vegetables. Sprinkle with dry dressing mix; toss to coat. Refrigerate, covered, 4-6 hours or overnight.

2. Cook pasta according to the package directions. Drain; rinse with cold water. Add to the vegetable mixture. In a small bowl, whisk the remaining ingredients. Add to salad; toss to coat.

Garden Bow Tie Salad

S'mores on a Stick

My kids love to take these treats everywhere. That's lucky for me since they are so easy to make. Beside the sprinkles, try mini candies for toppings.

—**RONDA WEIRICH** PLAINS, KS

PREP: 15 MIN. + STANDING
MAKES: 2 DOZEN

- 1 can (14 ounces) sweetened condensed milk, divided
- 1 cup miniature marshmallows
- 1½ cups miniature semisweet chocolate chips, divided
- 24 whole graham crackers, broken in half
  Assorted sprinkles
- 24 Popsicle sticks

1. In a small microwave-safe bowl, microwave ⅔ cup milk on high for 1½ minutes. Add marshmallows and 1 cup chips; stir until smooth. Drop by tablespoonfuls onto 24 graham cracker halves; spread evenly. Top with remaining graham cracker halves; press down gently.
2. Microwave remaining milk for 1½ minutes. Add remaining chips; stir until smooth. Drizzle over cookies; decorate with sprinkles. Let stand for 2 hours before inserting a Popsicle stick into the center of each.

Red, White and Blue Cheesecake

I made this creamy cheesecake for a patriotic get-together with friends. Everyone raved about it! It looks so festive and tastes delicious.

—**CONNIE LAFOND** TROY, NY

PREP: 40 MIN.
BAKE: 1¼ HOURS + CHILLING
MAKES: 16 SERVINGS

- 1½ cups all-purpose flour
- ⅓ cup sugar
- 1 teaspoon grated lemon peel
- ¾ cup cold butter, cubed
- 2 egg yolks
- ½ teaspoon vanilla extract

FILLING

- 5 packages (8 ounces each) cream cheese, softened
- 1 cup sugar
- ¼ cup half-and-half cream
- 3 tablespoons all-purpose flour
- ½ teaspoon grated lemon peel
- ¼ teaspoon salt
- ¼ teaspoon vanilla extract
- 2 eggs, lightly beaten
- 1 egg yolk
- 1 cup crushed strawberries
- 1 cup crushed blueberries
  Fresh mixed berries, optional

1. Preheat oven to 400°. In a large bowl, combine flour, sugar and lemon peel. Cut in the butter until crumbly. Whisk egg yolks and vanilla; add to the flour mixture, tossing with a fork until dough forms a ball.
2. Press onto bottom and 3 in. up the sides of a greased 9-in. springform pan. Place pan on a baking sheet. Bake for 12-15 minutes or until golden brown. Cool on a wire rack.
3. For filling, in a large bowl, beat the cream cheese and sugar until smooth. Beat in cream, flour, lemon peel, salt and vanilla. Add eggs and yolk; beat on low speed just until combined.
4. Divide batter in half. Fold crushed strawberries and crushed blueberries into half of the batter. Pour into crust. Top with remaining batter. Return pan to baking sheet.
5. Bake at 400° for 10 minutes. Reduce heat to 300°; bake 60-70 minutes longer or until the center is almost set. Cool on a wire rack 10 minutes. Carefully run a knife around edge of pan to loosen; cool 1 hour. Refrigerate overnight. Remove sides of pan.
6. Garnish with fresh mixed berries, if desired.

S'mores on a Stick

Easy Pasta Salad for a Crowd

Spinach, peppers and onions mingle with tangy feta cheese in this simple pasta salad. Make it ahead of time for covenience.

—JACQUELYN SAINT JOHN
CAMBRIDGE, MA

START TO FINISH: 30 MIN.
MAKES: 13 SERVINGS (¾ CUP EACH)

- 1 package (14½ ounces) multigrain penne pasta
- 1 jar (12 ounces) roasted sweet red peppers, drained and chopped
- 1 package (10 ounces) frozen chopped spinach, thawed and squeezed dry
- 1 bottle (8 ounces) Italian salad dressing
- 1 bottle (8 ounces) ranch salad dressing
- 6 green onions, chopped
- 1 small red onion, chopped
- 1 cup (4 ounces) crumbled feta cheese

1. Cook pasta according to package directions. In a large bowl, combine the remaining ingredients.
2. Drain pasta and rinse in cold water; add to the spinach mixture. Toss to coat. Refrigerate until serving.

Easy Pasta Salad for a Crowd

BBQ Chicken Sliders

BBQ Chicken Sliders

Brining the chicken overnight helps to make these sliders exceptionally good. The meat literally melts in your mouth!

—RACHEL KUNKEL SCHELL CITY, MO

PREP: 25 MIN. + BRINING
COOK: 4 HOURS
MAKES: 8 SERVINGS (2 SLIDERS EACH)

BRINE
- 1½ quarts water
- ¼ cup packed brown sugar
- 2 tablespoons salt
- 1 tablespoon liquid smoke
- 2 garlic cloves, minced
- ½ teaspoon dried thyme

CHICKEN
- 2 pounds boneless skinless chicken breast halves
- ⅓ cup liquid smoke
- 1½ cups hickory smoke-flavored barbecue sauce
- 16 slider buns or dinner rolls, split and warmed
  Prepared coleslaw

1. In a large bowl, mix the brine ingredients, stirring to dissolve brown sugar. Reserve 1 cup brine for cooking chicken; cover and refrigerate.
2. Place chicken in a large resealable bag; add remaining brine. Seal bag, pressing out as much air as possible; turn to coat chicken. Place in a large bowl; refrigerate 18-24 hours, turning occasionally.
3. Remove chicken from brine and transfer to a 3-qt. slow cooker; discard brine in bag. Add reserved 1 cup brine and ⅓ cup liquid smoke to chicken. Cook, covered, on low 4-5 hours or until chicken is tender.
4. Remove chicken; cool slightly. Discard cooking juices. Shred chicken with two forks and return to slow cooker. Stir in barbecue sauce; heat through. Serve on buns with coleslaw.

Summertime Fruit Trifles

Eye-catching trifles are easy to prepare when you use purchased pound cake, instant pudding and frozen whipped topping. Letting guests assemble their own makes it fun—and saves you time!

—DARLENE BRENDEN SALEM, OR

PREP: 45 MIN. + CHILLING
MAKES: 12 SERVINGS

- ⅓ cup sugar
- ¼ cup all-purpose flour
- 1½ cups whole milk
- 1 egg, lightly beaten
- ½ cup orange juice
- 1 tablespoon butter
- 1 teaspoon grated orange peel
- 1 can (20 ounces) crushed pineapple, undrained
- 1 package (3.4 ounces) instant vanilla pudding mix
- 1 cup whipped topping
- 2 cups sliced peeled fresh or frozen peaches, thawed
- 1 cup sliced fresh strawberries
- 1 cup fresh raspberries
- ½ cup fresh blueberries
- 2 loaves (10¾ ounces each) frozen pound cake, thawed and cut into ½-inch cubes

1. In a large saucepan, combine sugar and flour; stir in milk until smooth. Cook and stir over medium-high heat until thickened and bubbly. Reduce heat to low; cook and stir 2 minutes longer. Remove from the heat.

2. Stir a small amount of hot mixture into egg; return all to pan. Bring to a gentle boil, stirring constantly; cook and stir for 2 minutes. Remove from the heat. Gently stir in the orange juice, butter and orange peel. Transfer to a small bowl; refrigerate until chilled.

3. In a large bowl, combine pineapple and pudding mix; fold in whipped topping. In another bowl, combine peaches and berries.

4. In individual parfait glasses, layer cake cubes, pineapple mixture and berry mixture; top with custard. Refrigerate until serving.

Marshmallow Monkey Business

Marshmallow Monkey Business

Just like my kids, I love fun treats, and these really fit the bill. And they couldn't be easier to make and package! I wrap these in cellophane bags with twist ties.

—SUSAN SCARBOROUGH
FERNANDINA BEACH, FL

PREP: 30 MIN. • **COOK:** 10 MIN.
MAKES: 20 SERVINGS

- 1 package (10 ounces) large marshmallows
- 3 tablespoons butter
- 6 cups Rice Krispies
- ½ cup chopped dried banana chips
- 20 Popsicle sticks

TOPPING

- 2 cups (12 ounces) semisweet chocolate chips
- 2 tablespoons shortening
- ½ cup chopped salted peanuts
- ½ cup chopped dried banana chips

1. In a saucepan, heat marshmallows and butter until melted. Remove from the heat. Stir in cereal and banana chips; mix well. Cool for 3 minutes.

2. Transfer mixture to waxed paper; divide into 20 portions. With buttered hands, shape each portion around a Popsicle stick to resemble a banana.

3. In a microwave, melt chocolate chips and shortening; stir until smooth. Dip ends of "bananas" in chocolate; allow excess to drip off. Sprinkle with peanuts and banana chips. Place on waxed paper; let stand until set. Store in an airtight container.

Barbecued Chicken

Every summer, we have a neighborhood cookout. I always take this chicken and watch it disappear! My family loves the dish because of its zesty seasoning blend and I love the no-fuss barbecue sauce.

—LINDA SCOTT HAHIRA, GA

PREP: 10 MIN. • **GRILL:** 40 MIN.
MAKES: 8 SERVINGS

- 2 broiler/fryer chickens (3 to 4 pounds each), cut up

SPICE RUB
- 2 tablespoons onion powder
- 4 teaspoons salt or salt substitute
- 1 tablespoon paprika
- 2 teaspoons garlic powder
- 1½ teaspoons chili powder
- 1½ teaspoons pepper
- ¼ teaspoon ground turmeric
  Pinch cayenne pepper

SAUCE
- 2 cups ketchup
- 3 tablespoons brown sugar
- 2 tablespoons dried minced onion
- 2 tablespoons thawed orange juice concentrate
- ½ teaspoon liquid smoke, optional

1. Pat chickens dry. In a small bowl, mix the spice rub ingredients; reserve 1 tablespoon spice rub for sauce. Rub the remaining spice rub on all sides of the chicken.

2. Grill chicken, uncovered, over medium heat 20 minutes, skin side down. Meanwhile, combine all sauce ingredients; stir in reserved spice rub. Turn chicken; grill 20-30 minutes longer or until juices run clear, basting frequently with sauce.

Barbecued Chicken

FAST FIX ▶ Leah's Party Popcorn

Popcorn is good just about any way, but spicing it up makes it all the more special. I love this recipe because so many people enjoy it! Pile it in bowls for parties or spoon individual portions into sealed bags for take-home treats after the barbecue!

—LEAH STEENBERG CIRCLE PINES, MN

START TO FINISH: 30 MIN.
MAKES: ABOUT 4 QUARTS

- 4 quarts popped popcorn
- 2 cups miniature sesame breadsticks or sesame sticks
- 2 cups mixed nuts
- 1 cup sunflower kernels
- 1 cup salted pumpkin seeds or pepitas
- 1 cup potato sticks, optional
- ¼ cup olive oil
- 2 tablespoons lemon juice
- 1 tablespoon Worcestershire sauce
- 1 teaspoon salt
- 1 teaspoon dill weed
- 1 teaspoon coarsely ground pepper
- ½ teaspoon onion powder
- ½ teaspoon garlic powder
- ½ teaspoon hot pepper sauce

1. Preheat oven to 325°. In a large bowl, combine first five ingredients. If desired, stir in potato sticks. In a small bowl, whisk the remaining ingredients. Drizzle over the popcorn mixture; toss to coat.

2. Transfer to two greased 15x10x 1-in. baking pans. Bake 10-15 minutes or until toasted, stirring every 5 minutes. Cool completely on wire racks. Store in airtight containers.

AT THE BLOCK PARTY!

Chocolate
Delight Dessert

Cool Watermelon Pops

The kids are going to flip for these picture-perfect pops!

—TASTE OF HOME TEST KITCHEN

PREP: 20 MIN. + FREEZING
MAKES: 28 POPS

- 2 **cups boiling water**
- 1 **cup sugar**
- 1 **package (3 ounces) watermelon gelatin**
- 1 **envelope unsweetened watermelon cherry Kool-Aid mix**
- 2 **cups refrigerated watermelon juice blend**
- ⅓ **cup miniature semisweet chocolate chips**
- 2 **cups prepared limeade**
- 2 **to 3 teaspoons green food coloring, optional**
- 28 **freezer pop molds or 28 paper cups (3 ounces each) and wooden pop sticks**

1. In a bowl, Combine water, sugar, gelatin and Kool-Aid mix; stir until sugar is dissolved. Add watermelon juice. Fill each mold or cup with 3 tablespoons watermelon mixture. Freeze until almost slushy, about 1 hour. Sprinkle with chocolate chips. Top with holders or insert sticks into cups. Freeze.
2. In a small bowl, combine limeade and food coloring if desired. If using freezer molds, remove holders. Pour limeade mixture over tops. Return holders. Freeze completely.

Cool Watermelon Pops

Chocolate Delight Dessert

My children loved this dessert so much. Preparing it ahead can free up your time!
—**RUTH DYCK** FOREST, ON

PREP: 30 MIN. + FREEZING
MAKES: 12 SERVINGS

- 1 **cup crushed saltines**
- ½ **cup graham cracker crumbs**
- ⅓ **cup butter, melted**
- 2 **cups milk**
- 1 **package (3.9 ounces) instant chocolate pudding mix**
- 1 **package (3.4 ounces) instant vanilla pudding mix**
- 1½ **quarts cookies and cream ice cream, softened**
- 1 **carton (12 ounces) frozen whipped topping, thawed**
- 3 **Heath candy bars (1.4 ounces each), crushed**

1. In a small bowl, combine saltine and graham cracker crumbs; stir in butter. Press onto the bottom of a greased 13x9-in. baking pan. Refrigerate for 15 minutes.
2. Meanwhile, in a large bowl, whisk milk and pudding mixes for 2 minutes. Fold in ice cream. Spread over crust. Top with whipped topping; sprinkle with crushed candy bars. Freeze, covered, until firm. Remove from the freezer 30 minutes before serving.

Jersey-Style Hot Dogs

I grew up in northern New Jersey, where this way of eating hot dogs was created. My husband never had them as a kid but has come to love them even more than I do. The combination of ingredients and flavors is so easy, but just right!

—SUZANNE BANFIELD

BASKING RIDGE, NJ

PREP: 20 MIN. • **GRILL:** 40 MIN.
MAKES: 12 SERVINGS
(10 CUPS POTATO MIXTURE)

- 6 medium Yukon Gold potatoes (about 3 pounds), halved and thinly sliced
- 3 large sweet red peppers, thinly sliced
- 3 large onions, peeled, halved and thinly sliced
- ⅓ cup olive oil
- 6 garlic cloves, minced
- 3 teaspoons salt
- 1½ teaspoons pepper
- 12 bun-length beef hot dogs
- 12 hot dog buns, split

1. In a large bowl, combine potatoes, red peppers and onions. In a small bowl, mix oil, garlic, salt and pepper; add to potato mixture and toss to coat.

2. Transfer to two 13x9-in. disposable foil pans; cover with foil. Place pans on grill rack over medium heat; cook, covered, 30-35 minutes or until potatoes are tender. Remove from heat.

3. Grill the hot dogs, covered, over medium heat 7-9 minutes or until heated through, turning occasionally. Place buns on grill, cut side down; grill until lightly toasted. Place hot dogs and potato mixture in buns. Serve with remaining potato mixture.

Jersey-Style
Hot Dogs

Fireside Cheese
Spread, page 224

IT'S TIME TO BARBECUE...

AT THE
Game!

Catch the tailgate spirit with
food so good, friends and
family will cheer you into the
stadium. Whether celebrating
baseball season, gearing up
for a football championship
or simply enjoying the kids'
soccer game, **win over** your
hungry bunch with this lineup.

Sweet and Spicy Peanuts, page 225; Cantina
Beer-Cheese Dip, page 223; Smokin' Spiced
Corn, page 223; Grilled Italian Sandwiches,
page 224; Baja Bean Salad, page 213

AT THE GAME!

FAST FIX ▶ Corn 'n' Pepper Packets

Grilling foods in foil packets lets steam cook the vegetables to perfection. It also means little mess and cleanup for you. Try experimenting with different seasonings.
—**TASTE OF HOME TEST KITCHEN**

START TO FINISH: 15 MIN.
MAKES: 4 SERVINGS

- 4 **medium ears sweet corn, cut into 2-inch chunks**
- 1 **medium green pepper, cut into 2-inch strips**
- 1 **medium sweet red pepper, cut into 2-inch strips**
- 2 **tablespoons minced fresh parsley**
- ¾ **teaspoon garlic salt**
- ¼ **teaspoon celery seed**
- ¼ **teaspoon pepper**
- ¼ **cup butter, melted**

1. In a large bowl, combine vegetables, parsley and seasonings. Place on a piece of heavy-duty foil (about 18 in. x 12 in.). Drizzle with butter. Fold foil around vegetables and seal tightly.

2. Grill, covered, over medium-hot heat for 5-6 minutes on each side. Open the foil carefully to allow the steam to escape.

Grilled Seasoned Bratwurst

Corn 'n' Pepper Packets

FAST FIX ▶ Grilled Seasoned Bratwurst

Whether you're hosting a picnic at home or at a park, cook your bratwurst on the stovetop first. Then you can quickly brown them on the grill later.
—**TASTE OF HOME TEST KITCHEN**

START TO FINISH: 25 MIN.
MAKES: 8 SERVINGS

- 8 **uncooked bratwurst links**
- 3 **cans (12 ounces each) beer or nonalcoholic beer**
- 1 **large onion, halved and sliced**
- 2 **tablespoons fennel seed**
- 8 **bratwurst sandwich buns, split**

1. Place the bratwurst in a large saucepan or Dutch oven; add the beer, onion and fennel. Bring to a boil. Reduce heat; cover and simmer for 8-10 minutes or until meat is no longer pink. Drain and discard beer mixture.

2. Grill bratwurst, covered, over indirect medium heat for 4-6 minutes on each side or until a thermometer reads 160°, turning occasionally. Serve on buns.

Cream Cheese Cutouts

Decorating cookies always puts me in a happy mood. These cookies don't rise a lot or lose their shape, so they're very easy to decorate.

—JULIE DAWSON GALENA, OH

PREP: 15 MIN. + CHILLING
BAKE: 10 MIN./BATCH + COOLING
MAKES: ABOUT 7 DOZEN

- 1 cup butter, softened
- 1 package (3 ounces) cream cheese, softened
- 1 cup sugar
- ¼ teaspoon salt
- 1 egg
- 1 teaspoon vanilla extract
- 2½ cups all-purpose flour

FROSTING

- 3 cups confectioners' sugar
- ⅓ cup butter, softened
- 1½ teaspoons vanilla extract
- 2 to 3 tablespoons 2% milk
  Food coloring, optional
  Assorted sprinkles or candies

1. In a large bowl, cream butter, cream cheese, sugar and salt until light and fluffy. Beat in the egg and vanilla. Gradually beat in flour. Refrigerate, covered, 1-2 hours or until firm enough to roll.
2. Preheat oven to 375°. On a lightly floured surface, roll dough to ⅛-in. thickness. Cut with floured cookie cutters. Place 1 in. apart on ungreased baking sheets.
3. Bake 7-8 minutes or until edges are lightly browned. Cool on pans 1 minute. Remove the cookies to wire racks to cool completely.
4. In a small bowl, beat confectioners' sugar, butter, vanilla and enough milk to reach desired consistency. If desired, add food coloring. Decorate cookies with frosting and sprinkles.

Picnic Salad Skewers

Try these make-ahead kabobs for a fun way to serve a chilled salad. A homemade vinaigrette complements the potatoes, peppers, cherry tomatoes and zucchini.

—IOLA EGLE BELLA VISTA, AR

PREP: 15 MIN. + MARINATING
COOK: 15 MIN. • **MAKES:** 8 SERVINGS

- 8 unpeeled small red potatoes
- 8 fresh pearl onions
- 1 tablespoon water
- 1 medium sweet red pepper, cut into 1-inch pieces
- 1 medium green pepper, cut into 1-inch pieces
- 16 cherry tomatoes
- 1 small zucchini, cut into ¼-inch slices

VINAIGRETTE

- ⅔ cup olive oil
- ⅓ cup red wine vinegar
- 2 garlic cloves, minced
- 1 tablespoon dried oregano
- 1 teaspoon salt
- ¼ teaspoon pepper
- 4 ounces crumbled feta cheese, optional

1. Place potatoes in a saucepan and cover with water; bring to a boil. Cook for 10-13 minutes or until tender; drain. Place onions and water in a microwave-safe bowl. Cover and microwave on high for 1 to 1½ minutes or until crisp-tender; drain.
2. On metal or wooden skewers, alternately thread potatoes, onions, peppers, tomatoes and zucchini. Place in a large shallow plastic container or large resealable plastic bag.
3. Whisk together the oil, vinegar, garlic, oregano, salt and pepper. Pour over vegetable skewers. Marinate for at least 1 hour, turning frequently. Sprinkle with feta cheese if desired.
NOTE *This recipe was tested in a 1,100-watt microwave.*

Cream Cheese Cutouts

**Bacon-Wrapped
Stuffed Hot Dogs**

Bacon-Wrapped Stuffed Hot Dogs

Here's a juicy, delicious and savory meal in a bun! I make these dogs for picnics, barbecues and tailgate parties, and they always gets compliments. To transport, wrap the hot dogs in foil, then in paper.

—**PETER HALFERTY** CORPUS CHRISTI, TX

PREP: 25 MIN. • **GRILL:** 10 MIN.
MAKES: 8 SERVINGS

- 12 bacon strips
- 8 cheese beef hot dogs
- 8 bakery hot dog buns, split and toasted
- ¼ cup chopped red onion
- 2 cups sauerkraut, rinsed and well drained
  Optional condiments: mayonnaise, ketchup or Dijon mustard

1. In a large skillet, cook bacon over medium heat until partially cooked but not crisp. Remove to paper towels to drain; cool slightly. Wrap 1½ strips of bacon around each hot dog, securing with toothpicks as needed (do not wrap tightly or the bacon may tear during grilling).
2. Grill, covered, over medium heat or broil 4 in. from heat 6-8 minutes or until bacon is crisp and hot dog is heated through, turning frequently. Discard toothpicks. Serve hot dogs in buns with onion and sauerkraut; top with condiments of your choice.

Buttery Potato Chip Cookies

Can't decide whether to bring chips or cookies to the tailgate? These crisp and buttery cookies make plenty for a crowd, and they'll keep people guessing what the secret ingredient might be.

—**RACHEL ROBERTS** LEMOORE, CA

PREP: 15 MIN. • **BAKE:** 10 MIN./BATCH
MAKES: 4½ DOZEN

- 2 cups butter, softened
- 1 cup sugar
- 1 teaspoon vanilla extract
- 3½ cups all-purpose flour
- 2 cups crushed potato chips
- ¾ cup chopped walnuts

1. In a large bowl, cream butter and sugar until light and fluffy. Beat in vanilla. Gradually add flour to creamed mixture and mix well. Stir in potato chips and walnuts.
2. Drop by rounded tablespoonfuls 2 in. apart onto ungreased baking sheets. Bake at 350° for 10-12 minutes or until lightly browned. Cool for 2 minutes before removing from the pans to wire racks.

Truffle Football Cupcakes

Peanut butter and chocolate never tasted better together than in these luscious truffles! Shape them into balls for a holiday treat tray or make into snappy footballs to top cupcakes for a tailgate party or any gathering to cheer on your favorite team.

—**KIM BARKER** RICHMOND, TX

PREP: 25 MIN. + STANDING
MAKES: 3 DOZEN

- 3 ounces white candy coating, coarsely chopped, divided
- ⅔ cup creamy peanut butter
- ½ cup confectioners' sugar
- 3 teaspoons vanilla extract
- ⅔ cup crushed granola cereal with oats and honey
- 6 ounces semisweet chocolate, chopped
- 2 tablespoons shortening
- 2 cans (16 ounces each) vanilla frosting, divided
  Green paste food coloring
- 36 cupcakes of your choice

1. In a microwave, melt white candy coating at 70% power for 1 minute; stir. Microwave at additional 10- to 20-second intervals, stirring until smooth. Stir in peanut butter until smooth. Add the confectioners' sugar, vanilla and cereal. Chill for 2-3 hours or until easy to handle.
2. Shape into 1-in. balls; form each ball into a football shape and set aside. In a microwave, melt the chocolate and shortening; stir until smooth. Dip footballs in chocolate; allow excess to drip off. Place on a wire rack over waxed paper; let stand until set, about 30 minutes.
3. Pipe frosting laces onto footballs. Tint the remaining frosting green. Using a #233 or #234 tip, pipe grass over cupcakes. Just before serving, insert a toothpick into each football. Insert toothpick into cupcake to position the football.

Truffle Football Cupcakes

Melt-in-Your-Mouth Sausages

Family-Friendly Stuffed Cheeseburgers

We were experimenting one night and came up with these tasty cheeseburgers. Our kids and neighbors fell in love with them. They're so good that we often don't add any condiments.

—**ALETHEA OSBORNE** FLORENCE, KY

PREP: 30 MIN. • **GRILL:** 10 MIN.
MAKES: 6 SERVINGS

- 1 cup chopped sweet onion
- ½ cup crushed saltines (about 15 crackers)
- 1 egg
- 1 jalapeno pepper, seeded and minced
- 1 envelope ranch salad dressing mix
- 1 tablespoon Worcestershire sauce
- 1 garlic clove, minced
- 1 teaspoon pepper
- 2 pounds ground beef
- 1½ cups (6 ounces) shredded cheddar cheese
- 1 jar (4½ ounces) sliced mushrooms, drained
- 3 tablespoons cream cheese, softened
- 6 kaiser rolls, split

1. In a large bowl, combine the first eight ingredients. Crumble beef over mixture and mix well. Shape into twelve thin patties.

2. Combine the cheddar cheese, mushrooms and cream cheese; spoon onto centers of six patties. Top with remaining patties; press edges firmly to seal.

3. Grill the burgers, covered, over medium heat or broil 4 in. from heat for 5-7 minutes on each side or until a thermometer reads 160° and juices run clear. Serve on rolls.

Melt-in-Your-Mouth Sausages

My family's crazy for this recipe! It's such a good all-around dish, either in sandwiches like these or served with hot spaghetti.

—**ILEAN SCHULTHEISS** COHOCTON, NY

PREP: 10 MIN. • **COOK:** 4 HOURS
MAKES: 8 SERVINGS

- 8 Italian sausage links (2 pounds)
- 1 jar (26 ounces) meatless spaghetti sauce
- ½ cup water
- 1 can (6 ounces) tomato paste
- 1 large green pepper, thinly sliced
- 1 large onion, thinly sliced
- 1 tablespoon grated Parmesan cheese
- 1 teaspoon dried parsley flakes
- 8 brat buns, split
  Additional Parmesan cheese, optional

1. Place sausages in a large skillet; cover with water. Bring to a boil. Reduce heat; cover and simmer for 10-15 minutes or until a thermometer reads 160°; drain well.

2. Meanwhile, in a 3-qt. slow cooker, combine the spaghetti sauce, water, tomato paste, green pepper, onion, cheese and parsley. Add the sausages. Cover and cook on low for 4-5 hours or until vegetables are tender. Serve in the buns. Sprinkle with the additional cheese if desired.

Fired-Up Polenta Shrimp Rounds

Do more on the grill than just sear burgers. Here's a great way to expand your horizons!

—JENNIFER RODRIGUEZ
WEST JORDAN, UT

PREP: 25 MIN. + MARINATING
GRILL: 10 MIN. • **MAKES:** 1 DOZEN

- ¼ cup olive oil
- 3 garlic cloves, minced
- 2 teaspoons lime juice
- 1 teaspoon chopped seeded jalapeno pepper
- ½ teaspoon cayenne pepper
- ¼ teaspoon pepper
- 1 pound uncooked medium shrimp, peeled and deveined

SAUCE
- ½ cup mayonnaise
- 1 green onion, finely chopped
- 1 teaspoon chopped seeded jalapeno pepper
- 1 teaspoon hot pepper sauce
- ½ teaspoon cayenne pepper

POLENTA
- 1 tube (1 pound) polenta, cut into 12 slices
- 2 tablespoons seafood seasoning

1. In a resealable plastic bag, mix first six ingredients. Add shrimp. Seal bag; turn to coat. Chill up to 2 hours. Mix sauce ingredients; chill until serving.

2. Sprinkle polenta with seafood seasoning. Drain shrimp; discard marinade. Thread shrimp onto metal or soaked wooden skewers.

3. Moisten a paper towel with oil; using long-handled tongs, rub on grill rack to coat. Grill polenta and shrimp, covered, over medium heat 5-8 minutes or until polenta is lightly browned and shrimp turn pink; turn once. Spoon sauce over polenta; top with shrimp.

NOTE *Wear disposable gloves when cutting hot peppers; the oils can burn skin. Avoid touching your face.*

Fired-Up Polenta Shrimp Rounds

Baja Chicken & Slaw Sliders

Between the flavorful sauce and colorful, crunchy slaw, these hand-held sandwiches demand attention from partygoers.

—JANET HYNES MT. PLEASANT, WI

PREP: 30 MIN. • **GRILL:** 10 MIN.
MAKES: 8 SERVINGS

- ¼ cup reduced-fat sour cream
- ½ teaspoon grated lime peel
- ¼ teaspoon lime juice

SLAW

- 1 cup broccoli coleslaw mix
- 2 tablespoons finely chopped sweet red pepper
- 2 tablespoons finely chopped sweet onion
- 2 tablespoons minced fresh cilantro
- 2 teaspoons finely chopped seeded jalapeno pepper
- 2 teaspoons lime juice
- 1 teaspoon sugar

SLIDERS

- 4 boneless skinless chicken breast halves (4 ounces each)
- ½ teaspoon ground cumin
- ½ teaspoon chili powder
- ¼ teaspoon salt
- ¼ teaspoon coarsely ground pepper
- 8 Hawaiian sweet rolls, split
- 8 small lettuce leaves
- 8 slices tomato

1. In a bowl, combine the sour cream, lime peel and lime juice. In another bowl, combine the slaw ingredients. Chill the sauce and slaw until serving.

2. Cut each chicken breast in half widthwise; flatten to ½-in. thickness. Sprinkle with seasonings.

3. Moisten a paper towel with cooking oil; using long-handled tongs, rub on grill rack to coat lightly. Grill chicken, covered, over medium heat or broil 4 in. from the heat for 4 to 7 minutes on each side or until no longer pink.

Baja Chicken & Slaw Sliders

4. Grill rolls, cut sides down, for just 30-60 seconds or until toasted. Serve chicken on rolls with the lettuce, tomato, sauce and slaw.
NOTE *Wear disposable gloves when cutting hot peppers; the oils can burn skin. Avoid touching your face.*

FAST FIX Tailgate Sausages

You'll need just a handful of ingredients to fix these tasty sandwiches. Fully cooked sausages are stuffed with cheese and a homemade relish, then wrapped in foil so they're so easy to transport and a breeze to grill at the game!

—TASTE OF HOME TEST KITCHEN

START TO FINISH: 20 MIN.
MAKES: 4 SERVINGS

- ½ cup giardiniera
- ½ teaspoon sugar
- 4 cooked Italian sausage links
- 4 slices provolone cheese, cut into strips
- 4 brat buns or hot dog buns, split

1. In a small food processor, combine giardiniera and sugar; cover and process until blended. Make a lengthwise slit three-fourths of the way through each sausage to within ½ in. of each end. Fill with giardiniera mixture and cheese.

2. Place sausages in buns; wrap individually in a double thickness of heavy-duty foil (about 12 in. x 10 in.). Grill, uncovered, over medium-hot heat for 8-10 minutes or until heated through and cheese is melted. Open foil carefully to allow steam to escape.
NOTE *Giardiniera, a pickled vegetable mixture, is available in mild and hot varieties and can be found in the Italian or pickle section of your grocery store.*

Tijuana Tidbits

I love how salty and sweet Tex-Mex flavors come together in this mix, and a kick of heat just sneaks up on you at the end. It's great for tailgating, road-trip snacking and gift giving.

—**BEVERLY PHILLIPS** DUNCANVILLE, TX

PREP: 20 MIN. • **BAKE:** 1 HOUR + COOLING
MAKES: 4¾ QUARTS

- 12 cups popped popcorn
- 4 cups bite-size tortilla chips
- 3 cups Crispix
- 1 can (11½ ounces) mixed nuts
- ½ cup butter, cubed
- ½ cup light corn syrup
- ½ cup packed brown sugar
- 3 teaspoons chili powder
- ¼ teaspoon salt
- ⅛ to ¼ teaspoon cayenne pepper
- ⅛ teaspoon ground cinnamon

1. In a large greased roasting pan, combine the popcorn, tortilla chips, cereal and nuts.

2. In a small saucepan, combine the remaining ingredients. Bring to a boil, stirring constantly. Pour over popcorn mixture and toss to coat.

3. Bake, uncovered, at 250° for 1 hour; stir every 20 minutes. Cool on waxed paper. Store in an airtight container.

Baja Bean Salad

My mayo-free Baja Bean Salad uses bright, fresh flavors of lime, jalapeno and cilantro to really bring this colorful bean-medley salad to life!

—**JEANNE HOLT** MENDOTA HEIGHTS, MN

PREP: 30 MIN. + CHILLING
MAKES: 12 SERVINGS (¾ CUP EACH)

- 1 pound cut fresh green beans
- 1 can (15 ounces) black beans, rinsed and drained
- 1 can (15 ounces) garbanzo beans or chickpeas, rinsed and drained
- 1 can (14½ ounces) cut wax beans, drained
- 1 cup julienned peeled jicama
- 1 medium sweet red pepper, finely chopped
- 4 green onions, thinly sliced
- 2 tablespoons finely chopped seeded jalapeno pepper
- ⅓ cup sugar
- ⅓ cup cider vinegar
- ¼ cup canola oil
- 2 tablespoons lime juice
- 2 tablespoons minced fresh cilantro
- ½ teaspoon salt
- ¼ teaspoon pepper

1. In a saucepan, bring 5 cups water to a boil. Add green beans; cover and cook for 4-6 minutes or until crisp-tender. Drain and immediately place beans in ice water. Drain and pat dry.

2. In a large bowl, combine the black beans, garbanzo beans, wax beans, jicama, red pepper, onions, jalapeno and green beans.

3. In a bowl, whisk the sugar, vinegar, oil, lime juice, cilantro, salt and pepper. Pour over salad; toss to coat. Cover and refrigerate for at least 1 hour before serving. Serve with a slotted spoon.

NOTE *Wear disposable gloves when cutting hot peppers; the oils can burn skin. Avoid touching your face.*

Tijuana Tidbits

Summer Sausage Hobo Packets

We love to grill, especially when we go camping in our RV. This is a family-favorite recipe and the foil packet makes for fast and easy cleanup.

—TONIA ANNE CARRIER
ELIZABETHTON, TN

PREP: 25 MIN. • **GRILL:** 20 MIN.
MAKES: 8 SERVINGS

- 1 **pound summer sausage, cut into 1-inch pieces**
- 4 **medium potatoes, peeled and cut into ½-inch cubes**
- 3 **cups shredded cabbage**
- 1 **large sweet onion, halved and sliced**
- 1 **medium green pepper, cut into strips**
- 1 **medium sweet red pepper, cut into strips**
- 1 **small zucchini, sliced**
- 1 **small yellow summer squash, sliced**
- 1 **pound chicken tenderloins, cut into 1-inch pieces**
- 2 **medium tomatoes, cut into wedges**
- ½ **cup butter, cut into eight cubes**
- ¼ **cup prepared Italian salad dressing**

1. In a large bowl, combine the first eight ingredients. Gently stir in the chicken and tomatoes. Divide mixture among eight double thicknesses of heavy-duty foil (about 12 in. square). Top each with a butter cube.

2. Fold foil around mixture and seal tightly. Grill, covered, over medium heat for 20-25 minutes or until the chicken is no longer pink and the vegetables are tender. Carefully open foil to allow steam to escape; drizzle with dressing.

Picnic Sweet Potato Salad

FAST FIX ▶ ## Picnic Sweet Potato Salad

A homemade vinaigrette coats this colorful salad chock-full of sweet potato cubes. It's ideal for warm-weather picnics, tailgates and patio parties, but my family loves it year-round!

—MARY MARLOWE LEVERETTE
COLUMBIA, SC

START TO FINISH: 30 MIN.
MAKES: 13 SERVINGS (¾ CUP EACH)

- 4 **medium sweet potatoes, peeled and cubed**
- 3 **medium apples, chopped**
- 6 **bacon strips, cooked and crumbled**
- ¼ **cup chopped onion**
- 3 **tablespoons minced fresh parsley**
- ½ **teaspoon salt**
- ¼ **teaspoon pepper**
- ⅔ **cup canola oil**
- 2 **tablespoons red wine vinegar**

1. Place sweet potatoes in a Dutch oven and cover with water. Bring to a boil. Reduce heat; cover and cook for 10-15 minutes or just until tender. Drain.

2. Transfer to a large bowl; cool to room temperature. Add the apples, bacon, onion, parsley, salt and pepper to the potatoes. In a small bowl, whisk oil and vinegar. Pour over salad; toss gently to coat. Chill until serving.

Summer Sausage Hobo Packets

Teriyaki Grilled Chicken

Here's a super recipe you can use with any chicken pieces you like, with or without skin. Plan ahead to marinate the chicken overnight for wonderful flavor. Leftovers are fabulous the next day in a salad as well.

—JENNIFER NICHOLS TUCSON, AZ

PREP: 10 MIN. + MARINATING
GRILL: 40 MIN. • **MAKES:** 6 SERVINGS

- ⅓ cup reduced-sodium soy sauce
- ¼ cup canola oil
- 2 green onions, thinly sliced
- 2 tablespoons plus 1½ teaspoons honey
- 2 tablespoons sherry or chicken broth
- 2 garlic cloves, minced
- 1 teaspoon minced fresh gingerroot
- 6 bone-in chicken breast halves (8 ounces each)

1. In a large resealable plastic bag, combine the first seven ingredients; add chicken. Seal bag and turn to coat; refrigerate at least 5 hours.
2. Drain and discard marinade from chicken. Prepare grill for indirect heat, using a drip pan. Place chicken, skin side down, on grill rack. Grill, covered, over indirect medium heat 20 minutes. Turn; grill 20-30 minutes more or until the juices run clear.

Picnic Fruit Punch

This pink cooler is deliciously thirst-quenching on a warm day. The bubbly blend includes cranberry, pineapple, orange and lemon juices.

—MARION LOWERY MEDFORD, OR

PREP: 10 MIN. + CHILLING
MAKES: 5 QUARTS

- 8 cups cranberry juice
- 3 cups pineapple juice
- 3 cups orange juice
- ¼ cup lemon juice
- 1 liter ginger ale, chilled
- 1 medium navel orange, sliced

In a large container, combine juices; refrigerate. Just before serving, transfer to a punch bowl; stir in ginger ale and orange slices.

Deli-Style Pasta Salad

Pasta provides the base for this make-ahead salad. It has lots of fresh and satisfying ingredients topped with a flavorful dressing.

—JOYCE MCLENNAN ALGONAC, MI

PREP: 20 MIN. + CHILLING
MAKES: 10-12 SERVINGS

- 1 package (7 ounces) tricolor spiral pasta
- 6 ounces thinly sliced hard salami, julienned
- 6 ounces provolone cheese, cubed
- 1 can (2¼ ounces) sliced ripe olives, drained
- 1 small red onion, thinly sliced
- 1 small zucchini, halved and thinly sliced
- ½ cup chopped green pepper
- ½ cup chopped sweet red pepper
- ¼ cup minced fresh parsley
- ¼ cup grated Parmesan cheese
- ½ cup olive oil
- ¼ cup red wine vinegar
- 1 garlic clove, minced
- 1½ teaspoons ground mustard
- 1 teaspoon dried basil
- 1 teaspoon dried oregano
- ¼ teaspoon salt
    Dash pepper
- 2 medium tomatoes, cut into wedges

1. Cook the pasta according to package directions; rinse in cold water and drain. Place in a large bowl; add the next nine ingredients.
2. In a jar with tight-fitting lid, combine oil, vinegar, garlic, mustard, basil, oregano, salt and pepper; shake well.
3. Pour over salad; toss to coat. Cover and chill for 8 hours or overnight. Toss before serving. Garnish with tomatoes.

Deli-Style
Pasta Salad

Tailgate Apple Pies

Made as single servings, this dessert is ideal for football games or other events. When I serve a platter of my pies, they disappear quickly. While these pies are shaped into footballs, you can cut out the pastry with large cookie cutters into holiday shapes, too. For Valentine's Day, I use heart-shape cutters and cut out a small heart in the top crust...it's a special treat for my family.

—**JENNIFER STOLTZ** SPRING GREEN, WI

PREP: 35 MIN. + CHILLING
BAKE: 15 MIN./BATCH • **MAKES:** 1 DOZEN

- 3¾ **cups all-purpose flour**
- ¾ **teaspoon salt**
- 1 **cup cold butter, cubed**
- ¾ **cup shortening**
- 9 **to 10 tablespoons cold water**

FILLING
- 2 **tablespoons butter**
- 5 **cups finely chopped peeled tart apples (about 3 medium)**
- ⅓ **cup packed brown sugar**
- ½ **teaspoon cornstarch**
- ⅛ **teaspoon ground cinnamon**
- 1 **teaspoon lemon juice**
- ½ **teaspoon vanilla extract**
- 1 **egg, lightly beaten**
  Coarse sugar

Tailgate Apple Pies

1. In a large bowl, combine flour and salt; cut in butter and shortening until crumbly. Gradually add water, tossing with a fork until dough holds together when pressed. Divide dough in half; form each half into a disk. Wrap separately in plastic wrap; refrigerate 1 hour or until easy to handle.

2. In a skillet, heat butter over medium heat. Add the apples; cook and stir for 5 minutes. Mix brown sugar, cornstarch and cinnamon; add to apples. Cook and stir 7-8 minutes longer or until the apples begin to soften and caramelize. Remove from heat; stir in lemon juice and vanilla. Cool completely.

3. Preheat oven to 400°. On a lightly floured surface, roll one portion of dough to ⅛-in. thickness. Cut out 12 footballs with a floured 4-in. football-shaped cookie cutter.

4. Transfer half of the footballs to a parchment-lined baking sheet. Spoon about 2 tablespoons filling onto center of each. Brush edges of pastry with egg. Top with remaining footballs; press edges with a fork to seal. Cut three slits in top of pastry and score a curved line on each end of the footballs. Brush tops with egg; sprinkle with coarse sugar.

5. Bake 15-20 minutes or until golden brown. While pies are baking, repeat with remaining dough and filling.

6. Let pies stand 5 minutes before removing to wire racks. Serve warm or at room temperature.

FAST FIX ▶ ## Homemade Guacamole

My daughters sometimes call this "five-finger" guacamole to acknowledge that it is made with only five ingredients.

—**NANETTE HILTON** LAS VEGAS, NV

START TO FINISH: 10 MIN.
MAKES: 2 CUPS

- 3 **medium ripe avocados, peeled and cubed**
- ¼ **cup finely chopped onion**
- ¼ **cup minced fresh cilantro**
- 2 **tablespoons lime juice**
- ⅛ **teaspoon salt**
  Tortilla chips

In a small bowl, mash avocados with a fork. Stir in onion, cilantro, lime juice and salt. Serve with chips.

Bourbon Brat Skewers

Once the executive decision was made to marinate veggies in a tasty bourbon sauce and serve with grilled bratwurst, this recipe was promoted to our VIP tailgate party list!

—MARY MARLOWE LEVERETTE
COLUMBIA, SC

PREP: 20 MIN. + MARINATING
GRILL: 15 MIN. • **MAKES:** 6 SKEWERS

- ½ cup reduced-sodium soy sauce
- ½ cup bourbon
- 3 tablespoons brown sugar
- 1 teaspoon seasoned salt
- ¼ teaspoon cayenne pepper
- 2 cups whole mushrooms
- 2 medium sweet red peppers, cut into 1-inch pieces
- 1 medium green pepper, cut into 1-inch pieces
- 1 medium onion, cut into wedges
- 1 package (16 ounces) uncooked bratwurst links, cut into 1-inch slices

1. In a large resealable plastic bag, combine the first five ingredients. Add the vegetables; seal bag and turn to coat. Refrigerate for at least 1 hour.

2. Drain and reserve marinade. On six metal or soaked wooden skewers, alternately thread the vegetables and bratwurst. Brush with the reserved marinade. Grill, covered, over medium heat for 15-20 minutes or until the bratwurst is no longer pink and the vegetables are tender; turn and baste frequently with reserved marinade.

Game Day Brats

FAST FIX Game Day Brats

Looking for a twist on the usual pregame fare? With French dressing and Monterey Jack cheese, these brats make a tasty sandwich. Instead of bratwurst, you can also make the recipe with cooked Italian sausage links if you prefer.

—LAURA MCDOWELL LAKE VILLA, IL

START TO FINISH: 25 MIN.
MAKES: 6 SERVINGS

- 6 fully cooked bratwurst links
- ¾ cup sauerkraut, rinsed and well drained
- 6 tablespoons French salad dressing
- 6 tablespoons shredded Monterey Jack cheese
- 6 brat buns, split

1. Make a lengthwise slit three-fourths of the way through each bratwurst to within ½ in. of each end. Fill with sauerkraut; top with dressing and cheese.

2. Place bratwurst in buns; wrap individually in a double thickness of heavy-duty foil (about 12 in. x 10 in.). Grill, covered, over medium-hot heat for 10-15 minutes or until heated through and the cheese is melted.

Bourbon Brat Skewers

Basic Chicken Barbecue

As far as I'm concerned, there's no better way to spend a summer night than sitting outdoors with the family and enjoying a hot-off-the-grill meal like this one.

—**SHERRY SCHMIDT** FRANKLIN, VA

PREP: 10 MIN. + MARINATING
GRILL: 35 MIN. • **MAKES:** 4 SERVINGS

- 1 cup white vinegar
- 3 tablespoons sugar
- 2 tablespoons salt
- 1 cup water
- ½ cup canola oil
- 1 tablespoon poultry seasoning
- 1 tablespoon pepper
- 1 broiler/fryer chicken (3 to 3½ pounds), cut up

1. In a small bowl, whisk the vinegar, sugar and salt. Whisk in the water, oil, poultry seasoning and pepper. Reserve ½ cup for basting; cover and refrigerate. Pour remaining marinade into a large resealable plastic bag; add the chicken. Seal bag and turn to coat. Refrigerate for 2-4 hours.

2. Drain chicken and discard the marinade. Grill, covered, over medium heat for 35-45 minutes or until juices run clear, turning and basting occasionally with reserved marinade.

Reuben Rolls

Basic Chicken Barbecue

Reuben Rolls

I wanted the flavor of a classic Reuben in a fun-to-eat appetizer. And the empty plate at my party signaled these rolls were a hit!

—**DARLENE ABNEY** MUENSTER, TX

PREP: 30 MIN. + CHILLING
MAKES: ABOUT 8 DOZEN

- 1 package (8 ounces) cream cheese, softened
- 3 tablespoons spicy brown mustard
- ¼ teaspoon prepared horseradish
- 5 flour tortillas (10 inches), room temperature
- 7 packages (2 ounces each) thinly sliced deli corned beef
- 15 thin slices Swiss cheese
- 1 can (14 ounces) sauerkraut, rinsed and well drained

1. In a small bowl, beat the cream cheese, mustard and horseradish until blended. Spread a heaping tablespoonful of cream cheese mixture over each tortilla.

2. Layer each tortilla with 8 slices of corned beef, 3 slices of cheese, another heaping tablespoonful of cream cheese mixture and ½ cup sauerkraut. Roll up tightly. Refrigerate for 1 hour. Cut each roll-up into ½-in. slices.

Connie's
Tortellini Salad

Whenever my family spends a long weekend at the lake, I bring this salad with us so they can just grab a bowl if hungry.

—**CONNIE EATON** PITTSBURGH, PA

START TO FINISH: 30 MIN.
MAKES: 16 SERVINGS (¾ CUP EACH)

- 1 **package (13 ounces) dried cheese tortellini**
- 1 **medium zucchini, halved and sliced**
- 1 **cup Italian salad dressing**
- 1 **pint grape tomatoes**
- 1 **can (14 ounces) water-packed artichoke hearts, rinsed, drained and quartered**
- 1 **jar (11.1 ounces) pitted Greek olives, drained**
- 1 **carton (8 ounces) miniature fresh mozzarella cheese balls, drained**

In a saucepan, cook tortellini according to package directions. Drain; transfer to a large bowl. Immediately add zucchini and dressing; toss to coat. Stir in the remaining ingredients. Serve warm or refrigerate and serve cold.

Connie's
Tortellini Salad

Baseball Cupcakes

Here's a simple recipe that can be mixed up by hand. I worked and reworked it until I was finally was successful in coming up with just the right measurements to yield four to six cupcakes, which is the perfect amount for my family.

—**JANE PEARSON** DAYTON, OH

PREP: 15 MIN. • **BAKE:** 20 MIN. + COOLING
MAKES: 4 CUPCAKES

- 2 **tablespoons shortening**
- ¼ **cup sugar**
- ¼ **cup 2% milk**
- 1 **egg white**
- ¼ **teaspoon vanilla extract**
- ⅔ **cup cake flour**
- ¾ **teaspoon baking powder**
- ¼ **teaspoon salt**

FROSTING

- 2 **tablespoons butter**
- ½ **cup confectioners' sugar**
- 2 **teaspoons 2% milk**
  Red shoestring licorice

1. In a small bowl, cream shortening and sugar until crumbly, about 2 minutes. Beat in milk, egg white and vanilla. Combine flour, baking powder and salt; gradually add to creamed mixture and mix well.

2. Fill paper-lined muffin cups two-thirds full. Bake at 350° for 16-20 minutes or until a toothpick inserted near the center comes out clean. Cool for 10 minutes before removing from pan to a wire rack to cool completely.

3. In a small bowl, beat the butter, confectioners' sugar and milk until smooth. Frost cupcakes. Decorate with licorice pieces to form lacing.

AT THE GAME!

Brats with Corn
Maze Relish

FAST FIX ## Brats with Corn Maze Relish

Sweet corn stars in this amazing relish that kicks basic brats and hot dogs up a notch!

—**TASTE OF HOME TEST KITCHEN**

START TO FINISH: 25 MIN.
MAKES: 4 SERVINGS

- 3 **tablespoons Dijon mustard**
- 3 **tablespoons balsamic vinaigrette, divided**
- 4 **uncooked bratwurst links**
- 2 **medium ears sweet corn, husks removed**
- ¼ **cup chopped roasted sweet red peppers**
- 1 **green onion, thinly sliced**
- 4 **brat buns**

1. Combine mustard and 2 of the tablespoons of vinaigrette. Grill bratwurst and corn, covered, over medium heat for 15-20 minutes or until meat is no longer pink and corn is tender, turning frequently and basting with mustard mixture.

2. Cut corn from cobs. In a small bowl, combine the corn, peppers, green onion and remaining vinaigrette. Serve brats in buns with corn relish.

top tip

Balsamic Vinegar is Like A Fine Wine

Balsamic vinegar is made from sweet white grapes and aged in wooden barrels for at least 10 years (that explains the hefty price!). You can substitute cider vinegar or a mild red wine vinegar.

Cajun Beef Burgers

Flavor abounds in these hefty Cajun Beef Burgers, spiked with bits of veggies and Cajun seasoning. A creamy mayonnaise and Creole mustard spread adds even more Louisiana-style flair.

—**REBECCA BAIRD** SALT LAKE CITY, UT

PREP: 30 MIN. • **GRILL:** 10 MIN.
MAKES: 4 SERVINGS

- ¼ cup mayonnaise
- 1 green onion, thinly sliced
- 1½ teaspoons Creole mustard
- ½ teaspoon minced garlic
- ½ teaspoon grated lime peel
- ½ teaspoon lime juice
- ¼ teaspoon pepper
- ⅛ teaspoon salt
- Dash hot pepper sauce
- Dash Worcestershire sauce

BURGERS
- ¼ cup each finely chopped onion, celery and carrot
- 2 tablespoons minced fresh parsley
- 1 tablespoon butter
- 1 tablespoon Cajun seasoning
- ¼ teaspoon salt
- ¼ teaspoon hot pepper sauce
- 1 pound lean ground beef (90% lean)
- 4 onion rolls, split

1. In a small bowl, combine the first 10 ingredients until blended; chill until serving.

2. In a skillet, saute the onion, celery, carrot and parsley in butter for 6-8 minutes or until tender; cool slightly.

3. In a large bowl, combine the vegetable mixture, Cajun seasoning, salt and pepper sauce. Crumble beef over mixture and mix well. Shape into four patties.

4. Grill burgers, covered, over medium heat or broil 4 in. from the heat for 5-7 minutes on each side or until a thermometer reads 160° and juices run clear. Grill rolls, cut side down, over medium heat for 30-60 seconds or until toasted. Serve burgers on rolls with the sauce.

Honey Granola Bars

Honey Granola Bars

I make these at least once a week for my husband, David. He takes one in his lunch every day and never gets tired of them. I love being able to provide him with something so healthy to snack on—that doesn't taste low-fat!

—**JESSICA VANLANINGHAM**
COCKEYSVILLE, MD

PREP: 15 MIN. • **BAKE:** 15 MIN. + COOLING
MAKES: 1 DOZEN

- ¼ cup butter, softened
- 1 cup packed brown sugar
- 1 egg
- 2 tablespoons ground flaxseed
- 2 tablespoons honey
- 2 cups old-fashioned oats
- 1 cup all-purpose flour
- 1 teaspoon ground cinnamon
- ½ teaspoon baking soda
- ½ cup raisins

1. In a large bowl, beat butter and brown sugar until crumbly, about 2 minutes. Add egg; beat well. Stir in flaxseed and honey.

2. In a small bowl, combine the oats, flour, cinnamon and baking soda; stir into creamed mixture just until blended. Gently stir in the raisins.

3. Press into an 11-in. x 7-in. baking dish coated with cooking spray. Bake at 350° for 14-18 minutes or until set and edges are lightly browned. Cool on a wire rack. Cut into bars.

Lime-Honey
Fruit Salad

Lime-Honey Fruit Salad

Nothing is more refreshing to me than a seasonal fruit salad enhanced with this simple lime-honey dressing. Nothing!

—VICTORIA SHEVLIN CAPE CORAL, FL

PREP: 20 MIN. + CHILLING
MAKES: 12 SERVINGS (¾ CUP EACH)

- 1 teaspoon cornstarch
- ¼ cup lime juice
- ¼ cup honey
- ½ teaspoon poppy seeds
- 3 medium Gala or Red Delicious apples, cubed
- 2 medium pears, cubed
- 2 cups seedless red grapes
- 2 cups green grapes

1. In a small microwave-safe bowl, combine cornstarch and lime juice until smooth. Microwave, uncovered, on high for 20 seconds; stir. Cook for 15 seconds longer; stir. Stir in honey and poppy seeds.

2. In a large bowl, combine the apples, pears and grapes. Pour dressing over fruit; toss to coat. Cover and refrigerate overnight. **NOTE** *This recipe was tested in a 1,100-watt microwave.*

FAST FIX Cantina Beer-Cheese Dip

Ever since I found a recipe for beer cheese dip, which my husband loves, I've made it often. Being adventurous, I wanted to try a Mexican-style version for variety. It's ideal for tailgating—even in your living room!

—PATRICIA HARMON BADEN, PA

START TO FINISH: 20 MIN.
MAKES: ABOUT 3 CUPS

- 2 cups (8 ounces) shredded cheddar cheese
- ½ cup sour cream
- ¼ cup butter, softened
- ¼ cup beer
- 1 envelope onion soup mix
- 1 garlic clove, minced
- 1 teaspoon ground mustard
- 1 teaspoon Worcestershire sauce
- ¾ cup chunky salsa
- 2 tablespoons apricot preserves
- 4 bacon strips, cooked and crumbled
  Blue corn tortilla chips

1. In a food processor, combine the cheese, sour cream, butter, beer, onion soup mix, garlic, mustard and Worcestershire sauce. Cover and process until smooth. Spread onto a serving plate.

2. Mix salsa and apricot preserves. Spoon over cheese mixture. Sprinkle with bacon. Serve with tortilla chips.

FAST FIX Smokin' Spiced Corn

My dad, the family gardener, grew corn in abundance, so it graced our table A LOT. This is one of the ways my grandmother spiced it up on the grill.

—SHIRLEY HODGE BANGOR, PA

START TO FINISH: 25 MIN.
MAKES: 6 SERVINGS

- 3 tablespoons butter
- ½ cup honey
- 1 to 2 tablespoons hot pepper sauce
- 2 garlic cloves, minced
- ½ teaspoon salt
- ¼ teaspoon smoked paprika
- ¼ teaspoon ground cumin
- ¼ teaspoon pepper
- 6 medium ears sweet corn, husks removed

1. In a small saucepan, melt butter. Stir in the honey, pepper sauce, garlic and seasonings until blended; heat through. Brush some over corn.

2. Moisten a paper towel with cooking oil; using long-handled tongs, rub on grill rack to coat lightly. Grill corn, covered, over medium heat for 10-15 minutes or until corn is tender, turning and basting occasionally with the remaining sauce.

FAST FIX Spicy Olive Relish

I was looking for a zippy relish to take my plain hot dogs up a notch. Not wishing to make a run to the store, I rummaged through my refrigerator and found these items and thought they might be good together—and I was right! This relish also goes well on toasted bagel bites.

—JAMES MACGILLIVRAY
SAN MARCOS, CA

START TO FINISH: 10 MIN.
MAKES: 2 CUPS

- 1 jar (16 ounces) pickled hot cherry peppers, drained
- 1 jar (7 ounces) pimiento-stuffed olives, drained
- 1 small onion, quartered
- 1 tablespoon yellow mustard

Place peppers, olives and onion in a food processor; cover and process until finely chopped. Transfer to a bowl; stir in mustard.

Spicy Olive Relish

Grilled Italian Sandwiches

I made this for a family gathering, and they all raved about it! It's a fun recipe to grill for a crowd and can be adjusted according to everyone's favorite sandwich fillings.

—TAMMY KRIZ MARSHALL, MN

PREP: 30 MIN. • **GRILL:** 10 MIN.
MAKES: 12 SERVINGS

- 1 small sweet yellow pepper, julienned
- 1 small sweet red pepper, julienned
- 1 small green pepper, julienned
- 1 tablespoon olive oil
- ⅛ teaspoon salt
   Dash pepper
- ½ cup butter, softened
- 1 tablespoon prepared mustard
- 2 teaspoons minced chives
- 1 garlic clove, minced
- ¼ teaspoon crushed red pepper flakes
- 1 loaf (18 ounces) unsliced Italian bread
- 6 ounces sliced provolone cheese
- ⅓ pound thinly sliced hard salami
- 6 ounces sliced cheddar cheese
- ⅓ pound sliced deli roast beef

Fireside Cheese Spread

1. In a large skillet, saute peppers in oil just until tender. Sprinkle with salt and pepper. Meanwhile, in a small bowl, combine the butter, mustard, chives, garlic and pepper flakes.

2. Cut bread into ½-in. slices, leaving slices attached at the bottom. Cut loaf through the two center slices, separating loaf into two halves. Cut off and discard end slices. Place each loaf on heavy-duty foil coated with cooking spray. Spread butter mixture between every other slice. Alongside buttered slices, insert cheese, meat and peppers, using provolone cheese and salami in one loaf and cheddar cheese and roast beef in the other.

3. Wrap each loaf tightly in foil; place on grill rack. Grill, covered, over indirect medium heat for 8-10 minutes or until cheese is melted. Using a serrated knife, separate sandwiches.

Fireside Cheese Spread

When our family and friends get together for holidays or other occasions, I serve this appetizer. If you prefer, try a Swiss cheese spread instead of the cheddar. And if you enjoy garlic, substitute a small clove of minced garlic for the garlic powder.

—DEBBIE TERENZINI-WILKERSON
LUSBY, MD

PREP: 10 MIN. + CHILLING
MAKES: ABOUT 3½ CUPS

- 1 container (16 ounces) cheddar cheese spread, softened
- 2 packages (one 8 ounces, one 3 ounces) cream cheese, softened
- 3 tablespoons butter, softened
- 1 teaspoon Worcestershire sauce
- ½ teaspoon garlic powder
   Paprika
   Snipped fresh parsley
   Assorted crackers

In a medium bowl, combine cheese spread, cream cheese, butter, Worcestershire sauce and garlic powder. Blend thoroughly. Refrigerate at least 3 hours or overnight. Sprinkle with the paprika and parsley. Serve with crackers.

FAST FIX ▶ Sweet and Spicy Peanuts

If watching baseball makes you crave peanuts, try this spiced-up snack. I love how quick and easy it is to put together.
—**BRENDA CAUGHELL** DURHAM, NC

START TO FINISH: 15 MIN.
MAKES: 2 CUPS

- ¼ cup sugar
- 4½ teaspoons water
- ½ teaspoon Cajun seasoning
- ⅛ teaspoon salt
- ⅛ teaspoon cayenne pepper
- ⅛ teaspoon pepper
- 2 cups dry roasted peanuts

In a small saucepan, combine the first six ingredients. Cook and stir over medium heat until mixture comes to a boil. Cook and stir for 2 minutes. Remove from the heat; gradually stir in peanuts. Stir for 1 minute. Pour onto waxed paper; cool. Store in an airtight container.

Appetizer Shrimp Kabobs

Talk about fuss-free! These skewers are simple to assemble, and they grill to perfection in just minutes. My guests enjoy them with a spicy seafood sauce.
—**DIANNA KNIGHT** CLAYTON, NC

PREP: 10 MIN. + STANDING • **GRILL:** 5 MIN.
MAKES: 8 SERVINGS

- 3 tablespoons olive oil
- 3 garlic cloves, crushed
- ½ cup dry bread crumbs
- ½ teaspoon seafood seasoning
- 32 uncooked medium shrimp (about 1 pound), peeled and deveined
  Seafood cocktail sauce

1. In a shallow bowl, mix oil and garlic; let stand for 30 minutes. In another bowl, mix bread crumbs and seafood seasoning. Dip shrimp in oil mixture, then coat with crumb mixture.
2. Thread onto metal or soaked wooden skewers. Grill kabobs, covered, over medium heat for 2-3 minutes or until shrimp turn pink. Serve with seafood sauce.

Red Potato Skewers

As a busy mother of boys, I love to find grilling recipes that my husband can use. A seasoned mayonnaise mixture keeps these quartered potatoes moist and heavenly.
—**DAWN FINCH** PROSSER, WA

PREP: 20 MIN. + MARINATING
GRILL: 10 MIN. • **MAKES:** 6 SERVINGS

- 2 pounds red potatoes (about 6 medium), quartered
- ½ cup water
- ½ cup mayonnaise
- ¼ cup chicken broth
- 2 teaspoons dried oregano
- ½ teaspoon garlic salt
- ½ teaspoon onion powder

1. Place the potatoes and water in an ungreased microwave-safe 2-qt. dish. Cover and microwave on high for 10-12 minutes or until almost tender, stirring once; drain. In a large bowl, combine remaining ingredients; add potatoes. Cover and refrigerate for 1 hour.
2. Drain, reserving mayonnaise mixture. On six metal or soaked wooden skewers, thread potatoes.
3. Grill, uncovered, over medium heat for 4 minutes on each side, brushing occasionally with reserved mayonnaise mixture or until potatoes are tender and golden brown.

NOTE *This recipe was tested in a 1,100-watt microwave.*

Appetizer Shrimp Kabobs

Spicy Peanut Chicken Kabobs

skewers. Moisten a paper towel with cooking oil; using long-handled tongs, rub on grill rack to coat lightly.
3. Grill chicken, covered, over medium heat or broil 4 in. from the heat for 4-5 minutes on each side or until no longer pink. Brush with the reserved sauce before serving.

Picnic Bars

You'll score points with any crowd when you stir together these delicious fudge-like treats. The chocolate chips and walnuts make a pretty topping.
—FRANK BEE EUGENE, OR

PREP: 10 MIN. • **BAKE:** 25 MIN.
MAKES: 3 DOZEN

- 1¾ **cups all-purpose flour**
- 1 **cup sugar**
- ¼ **cup baking cocoa**
- ½ **cup cold butter, cubed**
- 2 **eggs**
- 1 **can (14 ounces) sweetened condensed milk**
- 2 **cups (12 ounces) semisweet chocolate chips, divided**
- 1 **cup chopped walnuts**

1. In a large bowl, combine flour, sugar and cocoa; cut in butter until mixture resembles coarse crumbs. Stir in eggs. Set aside 1½ cups for topping.
2. Press remaining crumb mixture into a greased 13-in. x 9-in. baking pan. Bake at 350° for 6-8 minutes or until set.
3. Meanwhile, in a saucepan, combine milk and 1 cup of chocolate chips; cook and stir over low heat until melted. Carefully spread over crust. Combine reserved crumb mixture with nuts and remaining chips. Sprinkle over the chocolate layer.
4. Bake for 15-20 minutes or until top is set (chips will not look melted). Cool before cutting.

Spicy Peanut Chicken Kabobs

A little sweet, a little sour and a whole lot of flavor! These kabobs make a wonderful snack at any party or get-together.
—NANCY ZIMMERMAN
CAPE MAY COURT HOUSE, NJ

PREP: 20 MIN. + MARINATING
GRILL: 10 MIN. • **MAKES:** 8 APPETIZERS

- ¼ **cup reduced-fat creamy peanut butter**
- 3 **tablespoons reduced-sodium soy sauce**
- 4½ **teaspoons lemon juice**
- 1 **tablespoon brown sugar**
- 1½ **teaspoons ground coriander**
- 1 **teaspoon ground cumin**
- ¾ **teaspoon salt**
- ¼ **teaspoon pepper**
- ¼ **to ½ teaspoon cayenne pepper**
- 1 **garlic clove, minced**
- 1 **large onion, finely chopped**
- 1 **pound boneless skinless chicken breasts, cut into 1-inch cubes**

1. In a small bowl, combine the first 10 ingredients. Set aside 3 tablespoons marinade for sauce. Pour remaining marinade into a large resealable plastic bag; add onion and chicken. Seal bag and turn to coat; refrigerate overnight. Cover and refrigerate sauce.
2. Drain the chicken and discard marinade. Thread chicken onto eight metal or soaked wooden

Happy Hot Dog Relish

This sweet-tart relish combining cranberry sauce and sauerkraut is so good! It's also a nice complement to hamburgers, baked ham and roast pork.
—**ELIZABETH CARLSON** CORVALLIS, OR

START TO FINISH: 25 MIN.
MAKES: 1½ CUPS

- 1 **medium onion, chopped**
- 1 **tablespoon olive oil**
- 1 **cup whole-berry cranberry sauce**
- 1 **tablespoon Dijon mustard**
- 1 **teaspoon sugar**
- ½ **teaspoon garlic powder**
- ¼ **teaspoon hot pepper sauce**
- ½ **cup sauerkraut, rinsed and drained**

In a small saucepan, saute onion in oil until tender. Add the cranberry sauce, mustard, sugar, garlic powder and pepper sauce. Cook and stir for 5-10 minutes or until cranberry sauce is melted. Add sauerkraut; heat through.

FAST FIX ▶
Touchdown Brat Sliders

It's game time when these minis make an appearance! Three things my husband loves—beer, bacon and brats—get jazzed up with crunchy flavored chips.
—**KIRSTEN SHABAZ** LAKEVILLE, MN

START TO FINISH: 30 MIN.
MAKES: 16 SLIDERS

- 5 **thick-sliced bacon strips, chopped**
- 1 **pound uncooked bratwurst links, casings removed**
- 1 **large onion, finely chopped**
- 2 **garlic cloves, minced**
- 1 **package (8 ounces) cream cheese, cubed**
- 1 **cup dark beer or nonalcoholic beer**
- 1 **tablespoon Dijon mustard**
- ¼ **teaspoon pepper**
- 16 **dinner rolls, split and toasted**

- 2 **cups cheddar and sour cream potato chips, crushed**

1. In a large skillet, cook bacon over medium heat until crisp. Remove to paper towels with a slotted spoon; drain, reserving drippings.
2. Cook bratwurst and onion in drippings over medium heat until meat is no longer pink. Add the garlic; cook 1 minute longer. Drain.
3. Stir in the cream cheese, beer, mustard and pepper. Bring to a boil. Reduce heat; simmer, uncovered, for 8-10 minutes or until thickened, stirring occasionally. Stir in bacon. Spoon ¼ cup onto each roll; sprinkle with chips. Replace tops.

Touchdown Brat Sliders

Sparkling Sangria, page 239; Prosciutto-Melon Sliders with Minted Mayo, page 240; Sweet Potato Chips and Cucumber Dip, page 244; Spicy Lamb Kabobs, page 238

Grilled Peach BBQ
Chicken Wings, page 231

IT'S TIME TO BARBECUE...

FOR
Happy Hour!

When the workweek is done, pour some beverages, prepare a few casual bites and fire up the grill! This **bonus chapter** offers everything you need to usher in the weekend with a backyard happy hour that's sure to have friends **cheering TGIF!**

FOR HAPPY HOUR!

FAST FIX ▶ Fresh Lime Margaritas

This basic margarita recipe is easy to modify to your own tastes. Try it frozen or with strawberries.

—TASTE OF HOME TEST KITCHEN

START TO FINISH: 15 MIN.
MAKES: 4 SERVINGS

- 4 lime wedges
- 1 tablespoon kosher salt
- ½ cup tequila
- ¼ cup Triple Sec
- ¼ cup lime juice
- ¼ cup lemon juice
- 2 tablespoons superfine sugar
- 1⅓ cups crushed ice

1. Using lime wedges, moisten rims of four glasses. Holding each glass upside down, dip rim into salt; set aside.

2. In a pitcher, combine the tequila, Triple Sec, lime juice, lemon juice and sugar; stir until sugar is dissolved. Serve in prepared glasses over crushed ice.

FOR FROZEN LIME MARGARITAS
Reduce lemon and lime juices to 2 tablespoons each. Increase the superfine sugar to ¼ cup and the crushed ice to 4 cups. Add ¾ cup limeade concentrate. Prepare glasses as directed. In a blender, combine the tequila, Triple Sec, lime juice, lemon juice, limeade concentrate, superfine sugar and crushed ice; cover and process until smooth. Makes: 5 cups.

FOR FROZEN STRAWBERRY MARGARITAS *Follow directions for Frozen Lime Margaritas, except reduce crushed ice to 2 cups and add 2 cups frozen unsweetened strawberries. Makes: 4 cups.*

Bacon-Wrapped Asparagus

After Hours Ice Cream Sandwiches

Here's an adult version of a traditional ice cream treat.

—TASTE OF HOME TEST KITCHEN

PREP: 10 MIN. + FREEZING
MAKES: 4 SERVINGS

- 8 teaspoons RumChata liqueur
- 4 ladyfingers, split
- ½ cup coffee ice cream, softened
  Baking cocoa

1. Brush liqueur over bottoms of the ladyfinger halves. Spread 2 tablespoons ice cream over the bottom of half of the ladyfingers. Top with the remaining ladyfinger halves.

2. Wrap in plastic wrap. Freeze for at least 1 hour. Just before serving, dust with cocoa.

FAST FIX ▶ Bacon-Wrapped Asparagus

My husband and I cook out almost every night, and I love asparagus for a side dish. I've served these bacon-wrapped spears with grilled meat and sliced fresh tomatoes for many a wonderful meal!

—TRISHA KITTS DICKINSON, TX

START TO FINISH: 30 MIN.
MAKES: 2-3 SERVINGS

- 10 fresh asparagus spears, trimmed
- ⅛ teaspoon pepper
- 5 bacon strips, halved lengthwise

1. Place asparagus on a sheet of waxed paper; coat with cooking spray. Sprinkle with pepper; turn to coat. Wrap a bacon piece around each spear; secure ends with toothpicks.

2. Grill, uncovered, over medium heat for 4-6 minutes on each side or until bacon is crisp. Discard toothpicks.

Grilled Peach BBQ Chicken Wings

These wings come out moist and tender every time. If you like, swap out the fresh peaches for 1 cup of fresh pineapple.
—**SILVANA NARDONE** BROOKLYN, NY

PREP: 20 MIN. + MARINATING
COOK: 30 MIN. • **MAKES:** 4 SERVINGS

- 2 **cups barbecue sauce**
- 2 **cloves garlic, finely chopped, divided**
- 2 **peaches, peeled, pitted and chopped**
  Salt and pepper
- 24 **chicken wings, separated at the joint and tips discarded**
- 1 **cup peach jam, such as Smuckers**
- ¼ **cup apple cider vinegar**
- 2 **tablespoons hot sauce, such as Frank's RedHot, or to taste**
  Scallions, green parts only, thinly sliced, for topping

1. In a food processor, combine the barbecue sauce and half of the garlic. Add the peaches and process until finely chopped; season with about 1½ teaspoons salt and ¼ teaspoon pepper. Reserve ½ cup for basting.
2. In a resealable plastic bag, toss together the chicken wings and remaining peach barbecue sauce; refrigerate for about 30 minutes.
3. Meanwhile, combine peach jam, vinegar, remaining garlic, hot sauce and ½ teaspoon salt in a small saucepan. Cook sauce over medium heat until slightly thickened, about 5 minutes; let cool.
4. Drain and discard marinade from chicken. Moisten a paper towel with cooking oil; using long-handled tongs, rub on grill rack to coat lightly. Grill chicken wings, covered, over medium heat or broil 4 in. from the heat for 12-16 minutes, turning occasionally.
5. Brush with reserved sauce. Grill or broil, uncovered, 8-10 minutes longer or until juices run clear, basting and turning several times. Top with scallions and serve with dipping sauce.

Grilled Peach BBQ Chicken Wings

FAST FIX ▸ Hop, Skip and Go

Pink lemonade gives this pretty drink a touch of sweetness. Make it in the blender for a frothy, fun look...or mix it in a pitcher.
—**TASTE OF HOME TEST KITCHEN**

START TO FINISH: 10 MIN.
MAKES: 4 SERVINGS

- ¾ **cup thawed pink lemonade concentrate**
- 1 **bottle (12 ounces) beer**
- 3 **ounces vodka or rum**
- 1 **cup ice cubes**
GARNISH
  Maraschino cherries

In a blender, combine all ingredients. Cover and process until smooth. Pour into glasses. Garnish as desired.

Mixed Berry Sangria

Ideal for special summer occasions, this light, tasty beverage is wonderful! Serve with spoons so that everyone can enjoy the fresh berries.
—**LINDA CIFUENTES** MAHOMET, IL

PREP: 10 MIN. + CHILLING
MAKES: 10 SERVINGS (¾ CUP EACH)

- 1 **bottle (750 milliliters) sparkling white wine**
- 2½ **cups white cranberry juice**
- ⅔ **cup light or coconut rum**
- ⅓ **cup each fresh blackberries, blueberries and raspberries**
- ⅓ **cup chopped fresh strawberries**
  Ice cubes

In a large pitcher, mix wine, juice and rum; add fruit. Refrigerate for at least 2 hours; serve over ice.

FOR HAPPY HOUR!

Grilled Stuffed
Jalapenos

FAST FIX ▶ **Grilled Stuffed Jalapenos**

These cheese-stuffed jalapenos are always popular whenever my husband and I host a tapas party.

—**MARY J. POTTER**
STERLING HEIGHTS, MI

START TO FINISH: 30 MIN.
MAKES: 10 APPETIZERS

- 4   **ounces cream cheese, softened**
- ½   **cup shredded Monterey Jack cheese**
- ½   **teaspoon garlic powder**
- ½   **teaspoon ground cumin**
- ½   **teaspoon chili powder**
- ¼   **teaspoon salt**
- ¼   **teaspoon smoked paprika or paprika**
- 10 **jalapeno peppers**

1. In a small bowl, combine the first seven ingredients. Cut a lengthwise slit down each pepper, leaving stem intact; remove membranes and seeds. Fill each with 1 tablespoon cheese mixture.

2. Prepare grill for indirect heat. Place peppers in a disposable foil pan. Grill peppers, covered, over indirect medium heat for 8-10 minutes or until the peppers are tender and cheese is melted. Serve warm.

NOTE *Wear disposable gloves when cutting hot peppers; the oils can burn skin. Avoid touching your face.*

Did you know?

All jalapenos are not the same. Their heat level ranges from 2,500 to 8,000 Scoville units. A Scoville is the unit used to measure heat levels in peppers. A sweet green pepper is rated zero.

Sensational Slush

Sensational Slush

Colorful and refreshing, this sweet-tart slush has become a family favorite. I freeze the mix in 2- and 4-cup containers so it can be served in small portions for individuals or for the whole family. I also freeze crushed strawberries to make prep easier.

—**CONNIE FRIESEN** ALTONA, MB

PREP: 25 MIN. + FREEZING
MAKES: 20 SERVINGS

- ½ cup sugar
- 1 package (3 ounces) strawberry gelatin
- 2 cups boiling water
- 1 cup unsweetened pineapple juice
- 2 cups sliced fresh strawberries
- 1 can (12 ounces) frozen lemonade concentrate, thawed
- 1 can (12 ounces) frozen limeade concentrate, thawed
- 2 cups cold water
- 2 liters lemon-lime soda, chilled

1. In a large bowl, dissolve sugar and gelatin in boiling water. In a blender combine the pineapple juice and strawberries; cover and process until blended. Add to gelatin mixture. Stir in concentrates and cold water. Cover and freeze for 8 hours or overnight.
2. Remove from freezer 45 minutes before serving. For each serving, combine ½ cup slush mixture with ½ cup lemon-lime soda; stir well.

Pizza on the Grill

I make pizza at least once a week. The barbecue flavor mingling with the cheese in this version tastes delicious!
—**LISA BOETTCHER** COLUMBUS, WI

PREP: 30 MIN. + RESTING • **GRILL:** 10 MIN.
MAKES: 4 SERVINGS

- 1 package (¼ ounce) active dry yeast
- 1 cup warm water (110° to 115°)
- 2 tablespoons canola oil
- 2 teaspoons sugar
- 1 teaspoon baking soda
- 1 teaspoon salt
- 2¾ to 3 cups all-purpose flour

TOPPINGS
- 2 cups cubed cooked chicken
- ½ to ¾ cup barbecue sauce
- ½ cup julienned green pepper
- 2 cups (8 ounces) shredded Monterey Jack cheese

1. In a large bowl, dissolve yeast in water. Add the oil, sugar, baking soda, salt and 2 cups flour. Stir in enough remaining flour to form a soft dough.
2. Turn dough onto a floured surface; knead until smooth and elastic, about 6-8 minutes. Cover and let rest for 10 minutes. On a floured surface, roll dough into a 13-in. circle. Transfer to a greased 12-in. pizza pan. Build up the edges slightly.
3. Grill, covered, over medium heat for 5 minutes. Remove from grill. Mix the chicken and barbecue sauce; spread over the crust. Sprinkle with green pepper and cheese.
4. Grill, covered, 5-10 minutes longer or until the crust is golden and the cheese is melted.

Pizza on the Grill

**Margarita Chicken
Quesadillas**

Margarita Chicken Quesadillas

Quesadillas have never tasted so good as when they're filled with slightly sweet onions and peppers, then topped with lime butter and salt—the perfect balance of sweet and savory. My recipe is great for a summer party—or a delicious way to bring a little taste of sunshine into the cold winter months!

—**STEPHANIE BRIGHT** SIMPSONVILLE, SC

PREP: 35 MIN. + MARINATING
BAKE: 10 MIN. • **MAKES:** 16 WEDGES

- 4 **boneless skinless chicken breast halves (5 ounces each)**
- ¾ **cup thawed frozen limeade concentrate**
- 1 **large onion, sliced**
- 1 **medium sweet orange pepper, julienned**
- 1 **medium sweet yellow pepper, julienned**
- 2 **tablespoons canola oil**
- ¼ **teaspoon salt**
- ¼ **teaspoon pepper**
- 4 **flour tortillas (10 inches)**
- 1 **cup (4 ounces) shredded Monterey Jack cheese**
- 1 **cup (4 ounces) shredded cheddar cheese**
- 2 **tablespoons butter, melted**
- 1 **tablespoon lime juice**
- 1 **tablespoon chopped fresh cilantro**
  Lime wedges, optional

1. Place chicken in a large resealable plastic bag; add limeade concentrate. Seal bag and turn to coat. Refrigerate for 6 hours or overnight.
2. In a large skillet, saute the onion and sweet peppers in oil until tender; season with salt and pepper. Set aside.
3. Moisten a paper towel with cooking oil; using long-handled tongs, rub on grill rack to coat lightly. Drain and discard marinade. Grill chicken, covered, over medium heat or broil 4 in. from heat for 5-8 minutes on each side or until a thermometer reads 165°. Cut chicken into ¼-in. strips; set aside.
4. On one half of each tortilla, layer Monterey Jack cheese, chicken, pepper mixture and cheddar cheese; fold over. Place quesadillas on a baking sheet. Combine butter and lime juice; brush over tortillas. Bake at 350° for 8-10 minutes or until cheese is melted.
5. Cut each quesadilla into 4 wedges. Sprinkle with cilantro; serve with lime wedges if desired.

Chicken Little Sliders

Fruity salsa dresses up these tiny chicken burgers, ideal for feeding a crowd. The fun name reminds everyone of the childhood story and makes them eager to try one.

—**LAURA MCALLISTER** MORGANTON, NC

PREP: 30 MIN. • **GRILL:** 10 MIN.
MAKES: 1½ DOZEN

SALSA
- 3 **plum tomatoes, seeded and chopped**
- ¼ **cup minced fresh basil or 1 tablespoon dried basil**
- ¼ **cup canned crushed pineapple**
- ¼ **cup chopped red onion**
- 1 **jalapeno pepper, seeded and finely chopped**
- 2 **tablespoons lemon juice**
- 1 **teaspoon grated lemon peel**
- ⅛ **teaspoon salt**
- ⅛ **teaspoon pepper**

MAYO
- ⅓ **cup reduced-fat mayonnaise**
- 2 **tablespoons chopped roasted sweet red pepper**
- ½ **teaspoon grated lemon peel**
  Dash salt

BURGERS
- 1 **egg, beaten**
- ½ **cup finely chopped roasted sweet red peppers**
- 2 **tablespoons plus 2 teaspoons fat-free milk**
- 1½ **teaspoons Dijon mustard**
- 1⅓ **cups soft bread crumbs**
- ¾ **teaspoon salt**
- ¼ **teaspoon pepper**
- 1½ **pounds ground chicken**

SERVING
- ½ **cup crumbled feta cheese**
- 18 **heat-and-serve rolls, split**
- 18 **small lettuce leaves**

1. In two small bowls, mix salsa and mayo ingredients; chill until serving.
2. In a bowl, combine the egg, peppers, milk, mustard, bread crumbs, salt and pepper. Crumble chicken over mixture and mix well. Shape into 18 patties.
3. If grilling burgers, moisten a paper towel with cooking oil; using long-handled tongs, rub on grill rack to coat lightly. Grill burgers, covered, over medium heat or broil 4 in. from the heat for 3-4 minutes on each side or until a thermometer reads 165° and juices run clear.
4. Stir cheese into salsa. Spread rolls with mayo; top each with a lettuce leaf, burger and 2 tablespoons salsa mixture.

NOTE *Wear disposable gloves when cutting hot peppers; the oils can burn skin. Avoid touching your face.*

Chicken Little Sliders

FOR HAPPY HOUR!

FAST FIX ▶ Creamy Mudslide Parfaits

If you like to drink Mudslides, you'll love this dreamy dessert! Use some or all of the garnishes to make it look more appealing.

—TAMMY REX NEW TRIPOLI, PA

START TO FINISH: 15 MIN.
MAKES: 4 SERVINGS

- 1 package (8 ounces) cream cheese, softened
- ¼ cup confectioners' sugar
- 2 tablespoons coffee liqueur
- 1½ cups whipped topping
- 10 Oreo cookies, crushed
  Optional toppings: additional whipped topping, chocolate syrup, maraschino cherries and Oreo cookies

1. In a small bowl, beat cream cheese and confectioners' sugar. Add liqueur; mix well. Fold in whipped topping.

2. Spoon half of cookie crumbs into four parfait glasses. Top with half the cream cheese mixture. Repeat layers. Refrigerate until serving. Serve with toppings of your choice.

Grilled Veggie Tortillas

Creamy Mudslide Parfaits

FAST FIX ▶ Grilled Veggie Tortillas

Your garden's bounty will be put to good use in this delightful entree that looks like a pizza. When I find a recipe as appealing and popular as this one, I make a copy, put it in a protective sleeve and store it in a binder so I can make it again!

—SHARON DELANEY-CHRONIS
SOUTH MILWAUKEE, WI

START TO FINISH: 25 MIN.
MAKES: 4 SERVINGS

- 1 medium zucchini, cut lengthwise into ½-inch slices
- 1 yellow summer squash, cut lengthwise into ½-inch slices
- 1 small sweet red pepper, cut in half
- 2 tablespoons olive oil, divided
- ½ teaspoon salt
- 1 large tomato, chopped
- ¼ cup reduced-fat mayonnaise
- 2 tablespoons prepared pesto
- 1 tablespoon minced fresh basil
- 1 tablespoon minced fresh oregano
- 4 whole wheat tortillas (8 inches)
- 1 cup (4 ounces) shredded part-skim mozzarella cheese

1. Brush the zucchini, summer squash and red pepper with 1 tablespoon oil. Sprinkle with salt. Grill vegetables over medium heat for 4-5 minutes on each side or until tender. Cut into ½-in. cubes and place in a small bowl; stir in the tomato.

2. Combine the mayonnaise, pesto, basil and oregano; set aside. Brush both sides of tortillas with remaining oil. Grill, uncovered, over medium heat for 2-3 minutes or until puffed.

3. Remove from grill. Spread grilled sides with sauce; top with the vegetable mixture. Sprinkle with cheese. Grill, covered, for 2-3 minutes or until the cheese is melted.

Chicken Gyros

These yummy Greek specialties are a cinch to prepare at home! Just start with chicken strips, coat in a creamy cucumber-yogurt sauce, then tuck into pita pockets. Some folks like lettuce and diced tomato on top.

—TASTE OF HOME TEST KITCHEN

PREP: 20 MIN. + MARINATING
COOK: 10 MIN. • **MAKES:** 2 SERVINGS

- ¼ cup lemon juice
- 2 tablespoons olive oil
- ¾ teaspoon minced garlic, divided
- ½ teaspoon ground mustard
- ½ teaspoon dried oregano
- ½ pound boneless skinless chicken breasts, cut into ½-inch strips
- ½ cup chopped peeled cucumber
- ⅓ cup plain yogurt
- ¼ teaspoon dill weed
- 2 whole pita breads
- ½ small red onion, thinly sliced

1. In a large resealable plastic bag, combine lemon juice, oil, ½ teaspoon garlic, mustard and oregano; add chicken. Seal bag and turn to coat; refrigerate for at least 1 hour. In a small bowl, combine the cucumber, yogurt, dill and remaining garlic; cover and refrigerate until serving.

2. Drain and discard marinade. In a large nonstick skillet, cook and stir the chicken for 7-8 minutes or until no longer pink. Spoon onto pita breads. Top with the yogurt mixture and onion; fold in half.

The Elvis Ice Cream Sandwich

Swing back to the days of the King of Rock and Roll with this creamy concoction that combines peanut butter, bananas and bacon. It's heavenly!

—TASTE OF HOME TEST KITCHEN

PREP: 20 MIN. + FREEZING
MAKES: 4 SERVINGS

- ½ cup peanut butter chips
- 2 teaspoons shortening
- 2 cups peanut butter ice cream with peanut butter cup pieces, softened
- 8 slices banana bread
- 4 strips ready-to-serve fully cooked bacon, halved
- 1 tablespoon honey

1. In a microwave, melt the peanut butter chips and shortening; stir until smooth. Cool slightly.

2. Spread ice cream over half of the bread slices. Top with bacon; drizzle with melted chips and honey. Top with remaining bread.

3. Wrap in plastic wrap. Freeze for at least 1 hour.

Chicken Gyros

Spicy Lamb Kabobs

This hearty meal is spicy, sweet and savory—all at the same time. The combination of grilled lamb, crisp salad and honey pita wedges is wonderful!

—MELINDA WINNER JOFFRE, PA

PREP: 40 MIN. + MARINATING
GRILL: 10 MIN. • **MAKES:** 8 SERVINGS

- 1 large cucumber
- 2 cups (8 ounces) sour cream or plain yogurt
- 2 teaspoons lemon juice
- ½ teaspoon salt
- ⅛ teaspoon garlic powder
- ⅛ teaspoon dill weed
- ⅛ teaspoon pepper

KABOBS

- 2 cups buttermilk
- 2 teaspoons ground turmeric
- 2 teaspoons curry powder
- 1 teaspoon coarsely ground pepper
- 1 teaspoon chili powder
- 1 teaspoon minced fresh sage
- ½ teaspoon salt
- 2½ pounds lean boneless lamb, cut into 1-inch cubes
- 16 cubes fresh pineapple (1 inch)
- 16 cherry tomatoes

SALAD

- 8 cups torn leaf lettuce
- 2 cups torn romaine
- 2 cups torn Bibb or Boston lettuce
- ½ large sweet onion, sliced
- ½ medium red onion, finely chopped
- 1 medium tomato, chopped
- ½ cup bean sprouts
- ½ cup green grapes, quartered
- ½ cup chopped walnuts
- ½ cup crumbled feta cheese
- ¼ cup butter, softened
- 2 tablespoons honey
- 4 pita breads (6 inches), halved and warmed

1. Peel cucumber and remove seeds. Place cucumber in a food processor; cover and process until finely chopped. Remove half of cucumber; set aside. Process remaining cucumber until pureed. Combine pureed cucumber and reserved cucumber; stir in the sour cream, lemon juice and seasonings. Refrigerate for at least 1 hour.

2. In a small bowl, combine the first seven kabob ingredients. Pour 1½ cups marinade into a large resealable plastic bag; add the lamb. Seal bag and turn to coat; refrigerate for at least 1 hour. Cover and refrigerate remaining marinade for basting.

3. Drain and discard marinade from lamb. On eight metal or soaked wooden skewers, alternately thread lamb, pineapple and tomatoes.

4. In a bowl, combine the lettuces, onions, tomato, sprouts, grapes and walnuts; sprinkle with cheese. Set aside.

5. Grill kabobs, covered, over medium heat for 5-6 minutes on each side or until lamb reaches desired doneness (for medium-rare, a thermometer should read 145°; medium, 160°; well-done, 170°), basting frequently with reserved marinade.

6. Beat butter and honey until blended; brush over pitas. Serve with kabobs, salad and sauce.

Spicy Lamb Kabobs

Jalapeno Popper Spread

Sparkling Sangria

It took me several attempts to re-create a favorite sangria, but here it is!
—**PAM MELE** FRANKLIN, NJ

PREP: 30 MIN. + CHILLING
MAKES: 32 SERVINGS (6 QUARTS)

- ¾ cup sugar
- ¾ cup water
- ½ vanilla bean, split

SANGRIA

- 1 package (12 ounces) frozen unsweetened strawberries
- 2 medium peaches, peeled and sliced
- 2 medium kiwifruit, peeled and sliced
- 1 can (11 ounces) mandarin oranges, undrained
- 1 jar (10 ounces) maraschino cherries, undrained
- 1 can (8 ounces) unsweetened pineapple chunks, undrained
- 1 medium orange, thinly sliced
- 1 medium lime, thinly sliced
- 1 medium lemon, thinly sliced
- 2 bottles (750 milliliters each) dry red wine
- 2 cups orange juice
- ⅔ cup orange liqueur
- ⅔ cup Cognac or brandy
- ¼ cup lemon juice
- 3 tablespoons lime juice
- 1 bottle (1 liter) carbonated water, chilled

Jalapeno Popper Spread

I've been told by my party guests that this recipe tastes exactly like a jalapeno popper. I love the easiness of making it!
—**ARIANE MCALPINE** PENTICTON, BC

PREP: 10 MIN. • **BAKE:** 25 MIN.
MAKES: 16 SERVINGS

- 2 packages (8 ounces each) cream cheese, softened
- 1 cup mayonnaise
- ½ cup shredded Monterey Jack cheese
- ¼ cup canned chopped green chilies
- ¼ cup canned diced jalapeno peppers
- 1 cup shredded Parmesan cheese
- ½ cup panko (Japanese) bread crumbs
  Sweet red and yellow pepper pieces and corn chips

In a large bowl, beat the first five ingredients until blended; spread into an ungreased 9-in. pie plate. Sprinkle with the Parmesan cheese; top with bread crumbs. Bake at 400° for 25-30 minutes or until lightly browned. Serve with the peppers and chips.

1. In a saucepan, mix the sugar, water and vanilla bean. Bring to a boil over medium heat. Reduce heat; simmer, uncovered, for 3-5 minutes or until sugar is dissolved, stirring occasionally. Remove from the heat; cool to room temperature. Discard vanilla bean.

2. Divide the fruits between two large pitchers. Add the wine, orange juice, liqueur, Cognac, lemon juice, lime juice and vanilla mixture. Refrigerate for at least 4 hours. Just before serving, stir in carbonated water.

FOR HAPPY HOUR!

Grilled Portobello Burgers

Prosciutto-Melon Sliders with Minted Mayo

A classic appetizer—prosciutto-wrapped melon—inspired me to make these bite-size burgers topped with cantaloupe salsa and minty mayonnaise.
—**VERONICA CALLAGHAN**
GLASTONBURY, CT

PREP: 30 MIN. • **GRILL:** 10 MIN.
MAKES: 20 SLIDERS

- ¾ cup mayonnaise
- 2 tablespoons minced fresh mint
- 1½ cups finely chopped cantaloupe
- ½ cup finely chopped red onion
- 2 teaspoons minced fresh parsley
- 2 teaspoons white wine vinegar
- ½ pound thinly sliced prosciutto or deli ham
- 2 teaspoons minced fresh thyme
- ½ teaspoon salt
- 2½ pounds ground beef
- 1 cup shaved Parmesan cheese
- 20 dinner rolls, split
- 20 Bibb or Boston lettuce leaves

1. In a small bowl, combine the mayonnaise and mint. In another bowl, combine the cantaloupe, onion, parsley and vinegar; set aside.
2. In a large bowl, combine the prosciutto, thyme and salt. Crumble beef over mixture and mix well. Shape into 20 patties.
3. Grill burgers, covered, over medium heat for 3-5 minutes on each side or until no longer pink. Top with cheese; cover and grill 1-2 minutes longer or until cheese is melted.
4. Spread each roll bottom with 2 teaspoons mayonnaise mixture; layer with lettuce, burgers and cantaloupe mixture. Replace tops.

FAST FIX ▶ Grilled Portobello Burgers

Tastes like a bistro-style grilled cheese, but eats like a hearty burger—meet the new cheese-bello!
—**MARY HAAS** HEWITT, NJ

START TO FINISH: 25 MIN.
MAKES: 4 SERVINGS

- 4 large portobello mushrooms (4 to 4½ inches), stems removed
- 6 tablespoons reduced-fat balsamic vinaigrette, divided
- 4 slices red onion
- 1 cup roasted sweet red peppers, drained
- 4 slices fresh mozzarella cheese
- 4 kaiser rolls, split
- ¼ cup fat-free mayonnaise

1. Brush the mushrooms with 4 tablespoons vinaigrette. Grill the mushrooms and onion, covered, over medium heat for 3-4 minutes on each side or until tender. Top mushrooms with red peppers, onion and cheese. Grill, covered, 2-3 minutes longer or until cheese is melted. Grill the rolls, uncovered, for 1-2 minutes or until rolls are toasted.
2. Spread the roll bottoms with the mayonnaise and drizzle with the remaining vinaigrette. Top with the mushrooms; replace roll tops.

Grilled Peaches with Brandy Sauce

Grilling fresh peaches on a maple plank gives them a delicate flavor. But the brandy sauce makes this dessert extra-special!

—TASTE OF HOME TEST KITCHEN

PREP: 25 MIN. • **GRILL:** 20 MIN.
MAKES: 6 SERVINGS

Maple grilling plank
- ¼ **cup butter**
- ½ **cup packed brown sugar**
- 2 **tablespoons brandy**
- 3 **medium peaches, peeled and halved**
- 1 **pint vanilla ice cream**

1. Soak the grilling plank in water for 1 hour.

2. In a small heavy saucepan, melt the butter. Stir in the brown sugar until dissolved; remove from the heat. Stir in brandy; set aside.

3. Place the plank on grill over direct medium heat. Cover and heat for 3 minutes or until light to medium smoke comes from the plank and the wood begins to crackle. (This indicates the plank is ready.)

4. Place peaches on plank. Grill, covered, over medium heat for 20-23 minutes or until peaches are tender, brushing occasionally with brandy sauce. To serve, top each peach half with a scoop of ice cream; drizzle with remaining brandy sauce.

Did you know?

The flavor a grilling plank imparts depends on the wood. Maple gives gives a mild smoky and sweet flavor.

Grilled Peaches with Brandy Sauce

So Easy Gazpacho

Pina Colada Fruit Salad

Pour over the fruit; toss to coat. Chill until serving.

FAST FIX ▶ Luau Refresher

Looking to liven up Happy Hour? Try this Polynesian delight. For the most fizz, stir in the soda just before serving.
—**TASTE OF HOME TEST KITCHEN**

START TO FINISH: 10 MIN.
MAKES: 9 SERVINGS

- 4½ cups sweet white wine, chilled
- 3 cups refrigerated passion fruit juice blend
- 3 tablespoons lemon juice
- 3 tablespoons lime juice
- 1½ cups grapefruit soda or citrus soda, chilled
  Ice cubes, optional

In a 3-qt. pitcher or punch bowl, combine the wine and juices. Stir in soda. Serve over ice if desired.

Luau Refresher

So Easy Gazpacho

My daughter got this recipe from a friend and shared it with me. Now I serve it often as an appetizer. My guests like it so much that it often becomes the talk of the party!
—**LORNA SIRTOLI** CORTLAND, NY

PREP: 10 MIN. + CHILLING
MAKES: 5 SERVINGS

- 2 cups tomato juice
- 4 medium tomatoes, peeled and finely chopped
- ½ cup chopped seeded peeled cucumber
- ⅓ cup finely chopped onion
- ¼ cup olive oil
- ¼ cup cider vinegar
- 1 teaspoon sugar
- 1 garlic clove, minced
- ¼ teaspoon salt
- ¼ teaspoon pepper

In a large bowl, mix all the ingredients. Cover and refrigerate at least 4 hours or until chilled.

FAST FIX ▶ Pina Colada Fruit Salad

Give friends a taste of the tropics on warm summer nights with this refreshing fruit blend. For a little extra punch, you could add a splash of coconut rum.
—**CAROL FARNSWORTH** GREENWOOD, IN

START TO FINISH: 15 MIN.
MAKES: 9 SERVINGS

- 1½ cups green grapes
- 1½ cups seedless red grapes
- 1½ cups fresh blueberries
- 1½ cups halved fresh strawberries
- 1 can (8 ounces) pineapple chunks, drained
- ½ cup fresh raspberries
- 1 can (10 ounces) frozen non-alcoholic pina colada mix, thawed
- ½ cup sugar
- ½ cup pineapple-orange juice
- ⅛ teaspoon almond extract
- ⅛ teaspoon coconut extract

In a serving bowl, combine the first six ingredients. In a small bowl, whisk pina colada mix, sugar, juice and extracts until sugar is dissolved.

Sweet Potato Chips and Cucumber Dip

Simple seasoned salt fabulously flavors crisp sweet potato chips. The creamy cucumber sauce is a nice accompaniment.

—**MELINDA WINNER** JOFFRE, PA

PREP: 15 MIN. + CHILLING
COOK: 5 MIN./BATCH
MAKES: 10 CUPS CHIPS (2 CUPS DIP)

- 2 **cups (16 ounces) sour cream or plain yogurt**
- 2 **teaspoons lemon juice**
- ½ **teaspoon salt**
- ⅛ **teaspoon garlic powder**
- ⅛ **teaspoon dill weed**
- ⅛ **teaspoon pepper**
- 1 **large cucumber**
- 3 **large sweet potatoes**
  Oil for deep-fat frying
- 2 **teaspoons seasoned salt**

1. In a small bowl, combine the first six ingredients. Peel cucumber and remove seeds. Place cucumber in a food processor; cover and process until finely chopped. Remove half of cucumber; set aside. Process remaining cucumber until pureed; add chopped and pureed cucumber to sour cream mixture. Refrigerate for at least 1 hour.

2. Cut sweet potatoes into thin slices ¹⁄₁₆ in. thick. Place in a large bowl; cover with cold water. Soak for about 30 minutes.

3. Drain; pat dry with paper towels. In an electric skillet or deep fryer, heat oil to 375°. Fry potatoes in batches for 2-3 minutes or until golden brown, stirring frequently. Remove with a slotted spoon; drain on paper towels.

4. Immediately sprinkle with the seasoned salt; serve with dip. Store leftover chips in airtight containers.

Grilled Sweet Potato Wedges

FAST FIX ▸ Grilled Sweet Potato Wedges

These tasty fries are precooked for a few minutes in boiling water, then finished on the grill for added flavor and texture.

—**NATALIE KNOWLTON** KAMAS, UT

START TO FINISH: 30 MIN.
MAKES: 8 SERVINGS

- 4 **large sweet potatoes, peeled and cut into ½-inch wedges**
- ½ **teaspoon garlic salt**
- ¼ **teaspoon pepper**

DIPPING SAUCE

- ½ **cup reduced-fat mayonnaise**
- ½ **cup fat-free plain yogurt**
- 1 **teaspoon ground cumin**
- ½ **teaspoon seasoned salt**
- ½ **teaspoon paprika**
- ½ **teaspoon chili powder**

1. Place potatoes in a large saucepan and cover with water. Bring to a boil. Reduce heat; cover and simmer for 4-5 minutes or until crisp-tender. Drain; pat dry with paper towels. Sprinkle the potatoes with garlic salt and pepper.

2. Grill, covered, over medium heat for 10-12 minutes or until tender, turning once. In a small bowl, combine the mayonnaise, yogurt and seasonings. Serve with sweet potatoes.

Veggie-Cheese Mini Pizzas

A zesty mustard-horseradish sauce makes this a tasty change of pace from traditional veggie pizza. Feel free to experiment with whatever vegetables are in season.

—ALLENE BARY-COOPER
WICHITA FALLS, TX

PREP: 30 MIN. • **BROIL:** 5 MIN.
MAKES: 8 SERVINGS

- 16 fresh asparagus spears, cut into 4-inch pieces
- 1 tube (13.8 ounces) refrigerated pizza crust
- 1 tablespoon butter, melted
- ⅓ cup Dijon mustard
- 3 tablespoons prepared horseradish
- 8 slices part-skim mozzarella cheese
- 8 slices tomato
- 8 thin slices sweet onion
- ¼ teaspoon salt
- ⅛ teaspoon pepper
- 16 slices Swiss cheese (¾ ounce each), divided
- 2 medium ripe avocados, peeled and sliced
  Fresh basil leaves, optional

1. Place asparagus in a steamer basket; place in a large saucepan over 1 in. of water. Bring to a boil; cover and steam for 3-5 minutes or until crisp-tender. Place asparagus on paper towels; pat dry and set aside.

2. Cut pizza dough into eight pieces. Roll each into a ball; flatten into a 4-in. circle and place on greased baking sheets. Bake at 400° for 8-10 minutes or until golden brown.

3. Brush each crust with butter. In a small bowl, combine the mustard and horseradish; spread over butter. Layer with mozzarella cheese, tomato and onion slices. Sprinkle with the salt and pepper; top each with one slice of Swiss cheese.

4. Broil 5-6 in. from the heat for 1-2 minutes or until the cheese begins to melt. Top with the avocado slices, 2 asparagus spears and the remaining Swiss cheese. Broil 1-2 minutes longer or until the cheese is melted. Garnish with basil if desired.

Savory Stuffed Figs

I turn to this three-ingredient recipe whenever I want a sweet-and-savory appetizer that's simple to make. It can be made ahead for convenience and is nice for both elegant or casual parties.

—TECKLA MISAELIDIS ANCHORAGE, AK

PREP: 30 MIN. • **GRILL:** 5 MIN.
MAKES: 2 DOZEN

- 12 bacon strips
- 24 dried figs
- 24 pecan halves

1. Cut bacon strips in half widthwise. In a large skillet, cook the bacon over medium heat until partially cooked but not crisp. Remove to paper towels to drain; keep warm.

2. Cut a lengthwise slit down the center of each fig; fill with a pecan half. Wrap each with a piece of bacon.

3. Grill, covered, over medium heat or broil 4 in. from the heat for 5-8 minutes or until the bacon is crisp, turning once.

Veggie-Cheese Mini Pizzas

FAST FIX ▶ Blackberry Beer Cocktail

This refreshing hard lemonade has a mild alcohol flavor; the beer adds just enough fizz to dance on your tongue as you sip.

—GINGER SULLIVAN CUTLER BAY, FL

START TO FINISH: 10 MIN.
MAKES: 10 SERVINGS

- 4 bottles (12 ounces each) beer, chilled
- 1 can (12 ounces) frozen raspberry lemonade concentrate, thawed
- ¾ cup fresh or frozen blackberries, thawed
- ½ cup vodka
  Ice cubes
  Lemon slices

In a large pitcher combine the beer, lemonade concentrate, blackberries and vodka. Serve over ice and garnish with lemon slices and berries.

Smoked Salmon Rolls

Even though I've been making these rich roll-ups for more than 30 years, they're always the first appetizers to disappear at parties! The treasured recipe came from my grandmother.

—RADELLE KNAPPENBERGER
OVIEDO, FL

PREP: 40 MIN. • **BAKE:** 15 MIN.
MAKES: 32 APPETIZERS

- 2 cups all-purpose flour
- 1 package (8 ounces) reduced-fat cream cheese
- ½ cup cold butter
- 2 to 3 tablespoons cold water
- 3 packages (3 ounces each) smoked salmon or lox, chopped
- ½ cup finely chopped red onion
- 1 egg, beaten

1. Place flour in a large bowl; cut in cream cheese and butter until crumbly. Gradually add water, tossing with a fork until dough forms a ball.

2. Divide dough in half. Between two sheets of waxed paper, roll each portion into a 9-in. circle. Chill for 10 minutes or until firm. Sprinkle salmon and onion to within ½ in. of edges. Cut each circle into 16 wedges. Roll up wedges from the wide ends and place point side down 2 in. apart on greased baking sheets. Brush with egg.

3. Bake at 425° for 15-18 minutes or until golden brown. Serve warm.

FAST FIX ▶ Salty Dog

You wouldn't even know this is a mixed drink because it's the tangy taste of the grapefruit that really comes through.

—TASTE OF HOME TEST KITCHEN

START TO FINISH: 5 MIN.
MAKES: 1 SERVING

- 1 lime wedge
  Kosher salt
  Ice cubes
- 2 ounces gin or vodka
- ½ cup white grapefruit juice

1. Rub lime wedge around the rim of a highball glass; dip rim in salt. Set aside.

2. Fill a mixing glass or tumbler three-fourths full with ice. Add gin and grapefruit juice; stir until condensation forms on outside of glass. Pour into prepared glass, straining ice if desired.

Blackberry Beer Cocktail

Did you know?

The Salty Dog derived from the drink called the Greyhound. The difference between them is the ring of salt on the glass rim of the Salty Dog, which cuts the bitterness of the grapefruit.

White Bean Salad

Great northern beans and a classic oil-and-vinegar dressing put an updated spin on traditional bean salad. The vibrant color and fantastic flavor will make it a hit at your summer parties.

—JANE ROSSEN BINGHAMTON, NY

PREP: 25 MIN. + SOAKING
MAKES: 10 SERVINGS

- 2 cups dried great northern beans
- 1 medium cucumber, chopped
- 1 large onion, finely chopped
- 1 can (2¼ ounces) sliced ripe olives, drained
- ¼ cup minced fresh parsley
- 6 tablespoons olive oil
- 6 tablespoons cider vinegar
- 1 teaspoon salt
- ½ teaspoon pepper

1. Sort the beans and rinse with cold water. Place beans in a Dutch oven; add water to cover by 2 in. Bring to a boil; boil for 2 minutes. Remove from the heat; cover and let stand for 1 to 4 hours or until beans are softened. Drain and rinse beans, discarding liquid.

2. In a large bowl, combine the beans, cucumber, onion, olives and parsley. In a small bowl, whisk oil, vinegar, salt and pepper. Pour over bean mixture; toss to coat. Cover and chill until serving.

FAST FIX ▶ Ginger Chicken Burgers with Sesame Slaw

Ginger and garlic give this chicken burger a zippy Asian-flavor twist. It's topped off with a fabulous coleslaw. If you like, serve the coleslaw as a side for other grilled items, like chicken breasts, fish fillets or chops.

—DEBORAH BIGGS OMAHA, NE

START TO FINISH: 25 MIN.
MAKES: 2 SERVINGS

- 1 teaspoon minced fresh gingerroot
- ¾ teaspoon minced garlic
- ½ teaspoon kosher salt
- ½ pound ground chicken
- 1¼ cups coleslaw mix
- 2 tablespoons thinly sliced green onion
- 2 tablespoons Asian toasted sesame salad dressing
- 1 tablespoon mayonnaise
- 1¼ teaspoons black sesame seeds or sesame seeds
- 2 sesame seed hamburger buns, split

1. In a small bowl, combine the ginger, garlic and salt. Crumble chicken over mixture and mix well. Shape into two patties. Broil 4-6 in. from the heat for 4-6 minutes on each side or until a thermometer reads 165° and the juices run clear.

2. In a large bowl, combine coleslaw mix, onion, salad dressing, mayonnaise and sesame seeds. Serve burgers on buns with coleslaw.

Ginger Chicken Burgers with Sesame Slaw

FOR HAPPY HOUR!

Thai Turkey Burgers

When we're tired of everyday burgers, I make these turkey patties for a taste of Thailand. The slaw is a fun switch from the traditional burger garnishes.
—**SHELBY GODDARD** BATON ROUGE, LA

PREP: 25 MIN. • **GRILL:** 15 MIN.
MAKES: 4 SERVINGS

SPICY PEANUT SLAW

- 1 tablespoon rice vinegar
- 1 tablespoon Thai chili sauce
- 1 tablespoon peanut butter
- 1 tablespoon Thai red chili paste
- 1 cup shredded cabbage
- 1 small carrot, shredded
- 1 radish, finely chopped
- 1 green onion, finely chopped
- 3 tablespoons dry roasted peanuts, chopped
- 1½ teaspoons minced fresh mint or ½ teaspoon dried mint

BURGERS

- 1 small onion, finely chopped
- 2 tablespoons minced fresh cilantro
- 2 garlic cloves, minced
- 2 to 3 teaspoons Thai red chili paste
- 1 pound ground turkey
- 4 hamburger buns, split and toasted

1. In a small bowl, combine vinegar, chili sauce, peanut butter and chili paste. Add remaining slaw ingredients; toss to coat. Set aside.
2. In a large bowl, combine the onion, cilantro, garlic and chili paste. Crumble turkey over mixture and mix well. Shape into four patties.
3. Moisten a paper towel with cooking oil; using long-handled tongs, rub on grill rack to coat lightly. Grill burgers, covered, over medium heat or broil 4 in. from the heat for 5-7 minutes on each side or until a thermometer reads 165° and juices run clear. Serve on buns with slaw.

Spinach Dip Pull-Aparts

Spinach Dip Pull-Aparts

Getting guys to eat spinach or any other vegetable can be a struggle. But even manly-man guys go for these tasty bites!
—**KELLY WILLIAMS** FORKED RIVER, NJ

PREP: 35 MIN. • **BAKE:** 45 MIN. + COOLING
MAKES: 15 SERVINGS

- 1 package (8 ounces) cream cheese, softened
- 2 garlic cloves, minced
- ¼ teaspoon pepper
- 1 package (10 ounces) frozen chopped spinach, thawed and squeezed dry
- ½ cup shredded part-skim mozzarella cheese
- ¼ cup grated Parmesan cheese
- ¼ cup mayonnaise
- 2 tubes (one 6 ounces, one 12 ounces) refrigerated buttermilk biscuits
  Marinara sauce, warmed, optional

1. Preheat oven to 350°. In a small bowl, beat cream cheese, garlic and pepper until blended. Stir in spinach, cheeses and mayonnaise.
2. Separate biscuit dough. Using a serrated knife, cut each biscuit horizontally in half. Wrap each half around 1 tablespoon spinach mixture, pinching to seal and forming a ball.
3. Layer in a greased 10-in. fluted tube pan. Bake 45 to 50 minutes or until golden brown. Cool in pan 10 minutes before inverting onto a serving plate. Serve warm with marinara sauce.

Bacon & Cheese Meatball Sliders

Sliders are a fun and popular snack at many Happy Hours these days. These mini burgers will please everyone at your party!

—TASTE OF HOME TEST KITCHEN

PREP: 50 MIN. + STANDING
GRILL: 10 MIN. • **MAKES:** 6 SERVINGS

- 12 frozen bread dough dinner rolls
- 1 egg
- 1 teaspoon water
- 1 tablespoon sesame seeds

KABOBS
- ¾ cup seasoned bread crumbs
- 6 bacon strips, cooked and crumbled
- 2 eggs, lightly beaten
- 1½ teaspoons Worcestershire sauce
- ½ teaspoon garlic salt
- 1½ pounds ground sirloin
- 1 medium sweet red pepper or green pepper, cut into 1-inch pieces
- 1 small red onion, cut into 1-inch pieces
- 6 slices process American cheese, cut into quarters

1. Thaw dough according to package directions. Cut each roll in half; reshape portions into balls. Place 2 in. apart on lightly greased baking sheets. Cover with clean kitchen towels; let rise in a warm place until almost doubled, about 30 minutes.

2. Uncover dough; gently press to flatten slightly. Whisk egg and water; brush over tops. Sprinkle with sesame seeds. Bake at 400° for 8-10 minutes or until rolls are golden brown. Remove to wire racks.

3. In a large bowl, combine the first five kabob ingredients. Crumble beef over mixture and mix well. Shape into 24 patties. On 24 metal or soaked wooden skewers, alternately thread the patties, red pepper and onion, inserting patties sideways.

4. Moisten a paper towel with cooking oil; using long-handled tongs, rub on grill rack to coat lightly. Grill the kabobs, covered, over medium-high heat for 4-5 minutes on each side or until the patties are no longer pink. Remove from the grill; immediately top patties with cheese. Cut buns in half; assemble sliders.

FAST FIX ▶ Grilled Potato Skins

The creamy topping on these potato skins is so delicious. They make an excellent summertime treat alongside your favorite grilled meats.

—STEPHANIE MOON BOISE, ID

START TO FINISH: 30 MIN.
MAKES: 4 SERVINGS

- 2 medium potatoes
- 1½ teaspoons butter, melted
- 2 tablespoons picante sauce
- ¼ cup shredded cheddar cheese
- 1 tablespoon real bacon bits
- ¼ cup chopped tomato
- 2 tablespoons chopped green onion

TOPPING
- 3 tablespoons mayonnaise
- 2 tablespoons sour cream
- 1 tablespoon prepared ranch salad dressing
- 1½ teaspoons real bacon bits
- ¼ teaspoon garlic powder

1. Cut each potato lengthwise into four wedges. Cut away the white portion, leaving ¼ in. on the potato skins. Place skins on a microwave-safe plate.

2. Microwave, uncovered, on high for 8-10 minutes or until tender. Brush butter over shells; top with picante sauce, cheese and bacon bits.

3. Grill potatoes, skin side down, uncovered, over medium heat for 4-6 minutes or until lightly browned. Cover and grill 2-3 minutes longer or until cheese is melted. Sprinkle with tomato and onion. In a small bowl, combine topping ingredients. Serve with potato skins.

NOTE *This recipe was tested in a 1,100-watt microwave.*

Bacon & Cheese Meatball Sliders

Greek-Style Chicken Burgers page 31

IN THE BACKYARD

Bourbon Brat Skewers page 217

AT THE GAME